MTEL 07

ENGLISH

Teacher Certification Exam

By Jessica Egan, M.S.

XAMonline
Boston

To obtain permission(s) to use the material from this work for any purpose including workshops or seminars, please submit a written request to:

XAMonline, Inc.
21 Orient Avenue
Melrose, MA 02176
Toll Free: 1-800-509-4128
Email: info@xamonline.com
Web: www.xamonline.com
Fax: 1-617-583-5552

Library of Congress Cataloging-in-Publication Data
Wynne, Sharon A.

English 07: Teacher Certification / Sharon A. Wynne
2nd Ed. ISBN 978-1-60787-467-6

1. English 07 2. Study Guides 3. MTEL
4. Teachers' Certification & Licensure 5. Careers

Disclaimer:
The opinions expressed in this publication are the sole works of XAMonline and were created independently from the National Education Association, Educational Testing Service, or any State Department of Education, National Evaluation Systems, or other testing affiliates.

Between the time of publication and printing, state specific standards as well as testing formats and website information may change that is not included in part or in whole within this product. Sample test questions are developed by XAMonline and reflect similar content as on real tests; however, they are not former tests. XAMonline assembles content that aligns with state standards but makes no claims nor guarantees teacher candidates a passing score. Numerical scores are determined by testing companies such as NES or ETS and then are compared with individual state standards. A passing score varies from state to state.

Printed in the United States of America
MTEL: English 07
ISBN: 978-1-60787-467-6

Certification Requirements

Educators seeking a first Massachusetts Pre K–12 license must achieve a passing score on the Communication and Literacy Skills test AND any relevant Pre K–12 subject matter test(s). Currently, the Massachusetts Tests for Educator Licensure (MTEL) are the only tests aligned with Massachusetts educator licensure regulations that satisfy the communication and literacy skills and subject matter test requirements for a Massachusetts Pre-Kindergarten to Grade 12 license.

Further Information

Further information about MTEL registration and test administration procedures is available in the current version of the Massachusetts Tests for Educator Licensure Registration Bulletin. Readers may view the registration bulletin via the Internet at **www.mtel.nesinc.com** or **www.doe.mass.edu/mtel** or obtain copies of the registration bulletin from schools of education at Massachusetts's colleges and universities, the Massachusetts Department of Education, or from the Massachusetts Tests for Educator Licensure program.

About the MTEL English Exam

The English 07 exam is a Computer-Based Test (CBT) administered year-round by appointment Monday-Saturday. You will be allotted 4 hours to complete this exam, and an additional 15 minutes is provided for reviewing tutorials and nondisclosure agreements.

Performance is evaluated against an establish standard rather than in comparison to other candidates' performances. To provide consistency in reporting scores across tests, the scores are converted to a common scale. The converted scores are called scaled scores. The scaled score is a conversion of the number of points achieved on the test, with a scaled score of 240 representing the qualifying, or passing, score. Candidates who do not achieve the passing score on a test may retake it at any of the subsequent test administrations at which that test is offered.

There are four subareas covered on the exam:

- Literature and Language
  - 51% of the test weight (objectives 01-09)
- Rhetoric and Composition
  - 17% of the test weight (objectives 10-12)
- Reading Theory, Research, and Instruction
  - 12% of the test weight (objectives 13-14)
- Integration of Knowledge and Understanding
  - 20% of the test weight (objective 15)

**Please note: open-response items may include topics from any of the subareas listed above.*

The first three domains are composed of 100 multiple-choice questions (80% of the points available). The allocation of questions corresponds to the weight of that particular section. For example, the Rhetoric and Composition section, which carries 17% of the test weight, will have 17% of the multiple-choice questions. There is no penalty for guessing.

The question breakdown by subarea is as follows:

- Subarea I: 63–65 multiple-choice questions
- Subarea II: 20–22 multiple-choice questions
- Subarea III: 14–16 multiple-choice questions
- Subarea IV: 2 open-response items

The Integration of Knowledge and Understanding section consists of two written response answers, approximately 150 to 300 words each. Each prompt will generally include contextual or background information that presents the subject of the written response question, as well as one or more specific directions or assignments that inform you of what you are expected to provide in your response. Each response takes an estimated 30 minutes to complete.

Your response to each assignment will be evaluated based on the following criteria:

- **PURPOSE:** the extent to which the response achieves the purpose of the assignment
- **SUBJECT KNOWLEDGE:** appropriateness and accuracy in the application of subject knowledge
- **SUPPORT:** quality and relevance of supporting evidence
- **RATIONALE:** soundness of argument and degree of understanding of the subject area

Table of Contents

Subarea I: Literature And Language

Shakespeare, John Donne, John Milton, Samuel Johnson, Alexander Pope, Jonathan Swift, William Blake, William Wordsworth, Samuel Taylor Coleridge, Jane Austen, Percy Bysshe Shelley, Mary Wollstonecraft Shelley, Lord Byron, John Keats) and their significance in the development of the literature of Great Britain from the Anglo-Saxon period through the Romantic period.

OBJECTIVE 0004 **UNDERSTAND THE LITERATURE OF GREAT BRITAIN FROM THE VICTORIAN PERIOD TO THE PRESENT. 17**

For example: the characteristics of significant literary works of Great Britain from the Victorian period to the present; the historical, social, and cultural contexts of Victorian, modern, and contemporary literature of Great Britain; significant genres and themes in Victorian, modern, and contemporary literature of Great Britain; and a range of authors of Great Britain (e.g., Charles Dickens, Emily Brontë, Charlotte Brontë, Matthew Arnold, William Butler Yeats, James Joyce, George Bernard Shaw, Virginia Woolf, Dylan Thomas, Doris Lessing, Seamus Heaney), their representative works, and their significance in the development of the literature of Great Britain from the Victorian period to the present.

OBJECTIVE 0005 **UNDERSTAND LITERATURE FROM THE ANCIENT WORLD TO THE FIFTEENTH CENTURY. 19**

For example: the characteristics of major literary forms, works, and writers associated with literature of the ancient world (e.g., African, Asian, European, and Greek and Roman literature; the Bible; world myths and folk tales); the historical, social, and cultural contexts from which ancient world literature emerged; significant genres and themes in ancient world literature; a range of authors and works (e.g., the Gilgamesh epic, the Vedas, the Old and New Testaments, the Qur'an, Homer, Lao-Tzu, Sappho, Sophocles, Aristophanes, Virgil, Li Po, Murasaki Shikibu, Omar Khayyám, Rumi, Dante Alighieri) and their significance in the development of ancient world literature; historical, social, and cultural aspects of ancient world literature (e.g., the expression of regional, ethnic, and historical values, archetypes, and ideas through literature; ways in which literary works and movements both reflected and shaped culture and history); and characteristics and significance of world mythology and folk literature.

OBJECTIVE 0006 **UNDERSTAND WORLD LITERATURE FROM THE FIFTEENTH CENTURY TO THE PRESENT. 21**

For example: the characteristics of major literary forms, works, and writers associated with world literature (e.g., African, Asian, European, Latin American) from the fifteenth century to the present; the historical, social, and cultural contexts of world literature from the fifteenth century to the present; significant genres and themes in world literature from the fifteenth century to the present; a range of authors (e.g., Michel de Montaigne, Miguel de Cervantes Saavedra, Molière, Jean-Jacques Rousseau, Johann Wolfgang von Goethe, Leo Tolstoy, Anton Chekhov, Franz Kafka, Isak Dinesen, Jorge Luis Borges, Primo Levi, Yehuda Amichai, Nadine Gordimer, Pablo Neruda, Czeslaw Milosz, Wole Soyinka, R. K. Narayan, Margaret Atwood, Derek Walcott, Naguib Mahfouz, Ōe Kenzaburō, V. S. Naipaul), their representative works, and their significance in world literature from the fifteenth century to the present; and social and cultural aspects of world literature from the fifteenth century to the present (e.g., the expression of regional, ethnic, and historical values; ways in which literary works and movements both reflect and shape culture and history).

OBJECTIVE 0007 **UNDERSTAND THE CHARACTERISTICS OF VARIOUS GENRES AND TYPES OF LITERATURE. 26**

For example: characteristics of the major literary genres (e.g., fiction, nonfiction, poetry, drama); elements of fiction (e.g., plot, character, setting, theme); characteristic elements of fiction genres (e.g., novels, short stories); types of fictional narratives (e.g., folk legend, fantasy, mystery, realistic novel) and their characteristics; genres of nonfiction (e.g., biography, autobiography, letters, essays, reports) and their characteristic elements and structures; genres of drama (e.g., serious drama and tragedy, comic drama, melodrama, farce) and their characteristic elements and structures; genres of poetry (e.g., lyric, concrete, dramatic, narrative, epic) and their characteristic elements and structures; types of patterned lyric poetry (e.g., sonnet, ballad, limerick, haiku); criteria for evaluating prose, dramatic, and poetic works of various types; and literary devices (e.g., figurative language, imagery, irony, symbolism, ambiguity, rhythm, rhyme, sensory detail) and ways in which they contribute to meaning and style.

OBJECTIVE 0008 **UNDERSTAND LITERARY THEORY AND CRITICISM........ 43**

For example: various critical approaches to literature (e.g., New Criticism, structuralism, deconstructionism, New Historicism, Marxist criticism, feminism, reader response); the role of major works in classical literary criticism and the theories associated with them; characteristics of neoclassic and Romantic literary theory as developed in major writings associated with each movement; and the use of various critical perspectives to analyze given literary passages.

OBJECTIVE 0009 **UNDERSTAND THE STRUCTURE AND DEVELOPMENT OF THE ENGLISH LANGUAGE. 49**

For example: structural features of languages (e.g., phonological, morphological, syntactic, semantic); historical, social, cultural, and technological influences shaping English language structure and use; significant historical events influencing the development of the English language (e.g., Anglo-Saxon migrations; the Norman Conquest); and additions to the lexicon of the English language throughout its development (e.g., words from Latin and French, regional and social dialects in the United States, words derived from technology).

Subarea II: Rhetoric And Composition

OBJECTIVE 0010 **UNDERSTAND PRINCIPLES OF RHETORIC AS THEY APPLY TO VARIOUS FORMS AND PURPOSES OF ORAL AND WRITTEN COMMUNICATION. 51**

For example: the development of rhetoric from a classical art of persuasive oratory to a modern discipline concerned with the analysis and interpretation of spoken, written, and media communications; modern and contemporary theories of rhetoric; application of modern rhetorical principles (e.g., unity, coherence, emphasis) to produce a desired result in an audience; consideration of subject, subject knowledge, purpose, and audience in producing a communication; use of appropriate arrangement and organization (e.g., logical ordering of ideas), style and tone (e.g., lexical choices, word order, cadence), and form of delivery; similarities and differences between language structures in spoken and written English; how to interpret and apply English grammar and language conventions in oral and written contexts; the role of cultural factors in oral and written communication; strategies for evaluating the content and effectiveness of written and spoken messages; principles of effective speaking and listening for various purposes (e.g., for information and understanding, literary response and expression, critical analysis and persuasion, debate); and techniques for interpreting and analyzing media messages.

OBJECTIVE 0011 **UNDERSTAND THE COMPOSITION PROCESS................ 56**

For example: strategies for writing effectively in a variety of forms and for a variety of audiences, purposes, and contexts; processes for generating and developing written texts (e.g., prewriting, drafting, revising, editing, publishing); techniques for revising written texts to achieve clarity and economy of expression; revision of sentences to eliminate wordiness, ambiguity, and redundancy; development of a thesis; development of an effective introduction and conclusion; effective use of topic sentences; the role of voice and style in writing; effective use of figurative language; identification of logical fallacies; techniques for improving text organization; effective use of transitions to enhance the clarity of an argument; selection of appropriate details to support an argument or opinion; applications of technology in all phases of the writing process; and the distinguishing features of various forms of writing (e.g., reflective essay, autobiographical narrative, editorial, memorandum, summary/abstract, argument, résumé, play, short story, poem, newspaper or journalistic article).

OBJECTIVE 0012 **UNDERSTAND WRITTEN LANGUAGE CONVENTIONS. .. 61**

For example: accurate use and effective application of written language conventions (e.g., sentence and paragraph construction, spelling, punctuation, usage, grammatical expression); techniques for editing written texts to achieve conformity with conventions of standard English usage (e.g., revising sentences and passages to maintain parallel form; revising sentences to eliminate misplaced modifiers; editing written texts to eliminate errors in spelling and punctuation); and strategies for effective proofreading.

Subarea III: Reading Theory, Research, And Instruction

OBJECTIVE 0013 **UNDERSTAND LANGUAGE ACQUISITION, READING PROCESSES, AND RESEARCH-BASED THEORIES RELATING TO READING.. 69**

For example: basic processes of first- and second-language acquisition and use; strategies to research word origins and analyze word formation to understand meanings, derivations, and spellings; relationships among words (e.g., homonyms, synonyms, antonyms) and issues related to word choice (e.g., denotative and connotative meanings, multiple-meaning words); research-based theories relating to the reading process; word analysis skills and strategies (e.g., phonics, syllabication, structural analysis); use of semantic and syntactic cues to verify word meanings; the role of vocabulary skills and strategies in the development of reading proficiency; application of literal, inferential, and evaluative comprehension skills; the use of metacognitive techniques to monitor reading comprehension; the application of strategies before, during, and after reading to promote comprehension of expository texts (e.g., previewing and predicting, self-questioning, writing and discussing); the role of oral reading fluency in facilitating comprehension of texts; and ways in which text characteristics and purposes for reading determine the selection of reading strategies.

OBJECTIVE 0014: UNDERSTAND EFFECTIVE, RESEARCH-BASED READING INSTRUCTION AND THE ROLE OF CHILDREN'S LITERATURE AND YOUNG ADULT LITERATURE IN PROMOTING READING PROFICIENCY. 72

For example: research-based theories and practices relating to reading instruction; methods for planning, managing, and differentiating reading instruction to support students' reading development; the role of children's literature and young adult literature in promoting reading proficiency and motivating students to read independently; instructional strategies to promote development of particular reading skills (e.g., word analysis, vocabulary, comprehension); the adjustment of reading instruction based on ongoing assessment; strategies to promote independent reading; strategies for selecting and using meaningful reading materials at appropriate levels of difficulty for all students; and uses of instructional technologies to promote students' reading development.

Subarea IV: Integration Of Knowledge And Understanding

OBJECTIVE 0015: PREPARE AN ORGANIZED, DEVELOPED ANALYSIS ON A TOPIC RELATED TO ONE OR MORE OF THE FOLLOWING: LITERATURE AND LANGUAGE; RHETORIC AND COMPOSITION; READING THEORY, RESEARCH, AND INSTRUCTION...77

For example: research-based theories and practices relating to reading instruction; methods for planning, managing, and differentiating reading instruction to support students' reading development; the role of children's literature and young adult literature in promoting reading proficiency and motivating students to read independently; instructional strategies to promote development of particular reading skills (e.g., word analysis, vocabulary, comprehension); the adjustment of reading instruction based on ongoing assessment; strategies to promote independent reading; strategies for selecting and using meaningful reading materials at appropriate levels of difficulty for all students; and uses of instructional technologies to promote students' reading development.

Subarea V: Sample Tests 81

- Sample Test One (includes two essay questions) 82
- Sample Test One, Answer Key 119
- Sample Test One Answers with Rationales 120
- Sample Test Two (includes two essay questions) 167

Meet the Authors

Heather M. Hilliard

Earning her bachelor's degree in New Orleans and her two masters degrees from the University of Pittsburgh, Heather M. Hilliard serves as an Adjunct Professor for her undergraduate alma mater, Tulane University. From teaching – both at the collegiate level as well as special courses at a leading independent high school – to her corporate endeavors, she has consciously focused aspects of her career and volunteerism on education. She has received several commendations for her achievements, has been inducted into the national honor society for public health and is one of fewer than 1,000 internationally Certified Emergency Managers in the world. She has published on a variety of topics and edited textbooks as well as other fiction and non-fiction work and focuses on strategic communications and improvements for clients – including writing and editing for XAMonline preparation content and tests including Advanced Placement exams, CLEP materials, and the SAT.

Jessica Egan

With a Master's Degree in English Education from Florida State University, Jessica Egan has expertise in the areas of literature, linguistics, and educational psychology. Jessica has worked as an instructional technologist and has experience in teaching secondary English, English as a Second Language (ESL), college-level composition and Adult Basic Education (ABE). She has authored lesson plans, teacher certification materials, and test preparation texts.

John Keefe

John Keefe is an author and editor from Chicago, Illinois. A graduate of Columbia College Chicago, John Keefe has written fiction and non-fiction for publications such as Chicago Literati, Hair Trigger Magazine, and websites like Cracked.com. He is also an actor and playwright.

Subarea 1: Literature and Language

Throughout history, the politics of each culture are reflected in its literature. Developments in technology, philosophy, and language can be charted through familiarity with each culture's body of work. The MTEL English test has a focus on English language literature, specifically that of the United States and the British Isles, but an understanding of major developments in world literature is also essential. By knowing the major works, authors, and themes of each literary period, you can demonstrate a fuller understanding of the literary canon that shaped the world we live in today.

This subarea can act as a refresher to each literary period throughout world literature, but it's also important to do more in-depth research of specific literary works as you study for the MTEL. An understanding of the historical context of these works is also important.

OBJECTIVE 0001 UNDERSTAND AMERICAN LITERATURE FROM THE COLONIAL PERIOD THROUGH THE END OF THE NINETEENTH CENTURY.

For example: the significance of writers, works, and movements in the development of American literature from the colonial period through the end of the nineteenth century; changes in literary form and style in American literature; the characteristics of major literary periods in American literature (e.g., colonial, Revolutionary, Romantic, Renaissance, realism, Civil War, post–Civil War); the historical, social, and cultural contexts of American literature from the colonial period through the end of the nineteenth century; significant genres and themes in American literature from the colonial period through the end of the nineteenth century; and a range of American authors (e.g., John Winthrop, Anne Bradstreet, Jonathan Edwards, Phillis Wheatley, James Fenimore Cooper, Frederick Douglass, Thomas Jefferson, Edgar Allan Poe, Abraham Lincoln, Nathaniel Hawthorne, Ralph Waldo Emerson, Henry David Thoreau, Walt Whitman, Herman Melville, Emily Dickinson, Mark Twain, Stephen Crane, Harriet Beecher Stowe, Kate Chopin, Henry James), their representative works and themes, and their significance in the development of American literature from the colonial period through the end of the nineteenth century.

AUTHOR	TIME PERIOD	CONTRIBUTIONS & SIGNIFICANT WORKS
John Winthrop	16th Century	English Puritan lawyer; leading contributor and first governor of the Massachusetts Bay colony A Model of Christian Charity The History of New England
Anne Bradstreet	17th Century	American Puritan; first woman recognized as an accomplished New World Poet; first female writer in North America to be published Another Another II The Prologue To My Dear and Loving Husband
John Edwards	18th Century	Protestant preacher; influential theologian and philosopher "Sinners in the Hands of an Angry God" (sermon) The End for Which God Created the World The Life of David Brainerd Religious Affections
Phillis Wheatley	18th Century	First published African American poet; native to West Africa Poems on Various Subjects, Religious and Moral

AUTHOR	TIME PERIOD	CONTRIBUTIONS & SIGNIFICANT WORKS
James Fenimore Cooper	19th Century	Writing influenced by experience working in the US Navy; many of his works referenced life at sea The Spy Leatherstocking Tales
Frederick Douglass	19th Century	African-American social reformer; escaped slave; leader of abolitionist movement Narrative of the Life of Frederick Douglass, An American Slave My Bondage and My Freedom
Thomas Jefferson	19th Century	Founding father; former president of the United States; principal author of the Declaration of Independence
Edgar Allen Poe	19th Century	Poet; short story author; Boston native "The Raven" "A Dream Within a Dream"
Abraham Lincoln	19th Century	Former President of the United States; abolished slavery; assassinated Emancipation Proclamation
Nathaniel Hawthorne	19th Century	Dark romance short story author; Salem, MA native The Scarlet Letter Twice-Told Tales The House of Seven Gables

AUTHOR	TIME PERIOD	CONTRIBUTIONS & SIGNIFICANT WORKS
Ralph Waldo Emerson	19th Century	Leader of the transcendentalist movement; poet; essayist; highly influential to the American romantic movement Essays: First Series Essays: Second Series "Nature" "Uriel" "The Snow-Storm"
Henry David Thoreau	19th Century	Leader of the transcendentalist movement; poet and essayist known for writing about nature and natural history Walden "Civil Disobedience"
Walt Whitman	19th Century	Leader in creation of free verse; poet; essayist; journalist; displayed views from transcendentalism and realism; self-published Leaves of Grass Franklin Evans
Herman Melville	19th Century	Renaissance poet, short story writer, and novelist; spent years at sea before becoming a writer Typee Moby Dick

AUTHOR	TIME PERIOD	CONTRIBUTIONS & SIGNIFICANT WORKS
Emily Dickinson	19th Century	Prolific Romantic poet; thousands of poems found hidden in her room upon her death The Complete Poems of Emily Dickinson
Mark Twain	19th Century	Novelist; known for writing about southern culture The Adventures of Tom Sawyer Adventures of Huckleberry Finn
Stephen Crane	19th Century	Protestant Methodist poet, short story writer, and novelist; demonstrated realism, naturalism, and impressionism in his works The Red Badge of Courage War is Kind
Harriet Beecher Stowe	19th Century	Author of over 30 books; abolitionist; fought for women's rights Uncle Tom's Cabin
Kate Chopin	19th Century	Short story and novel writer; known for fiction; accepted to many prestigious magazines The Awakening
Henry James	19th Century	Realist; known for narrative fiction The Portrait of a Lady

The earliest literature to come out of North America was produced by the various indigenous tribes that inhabited the continent before European settlers appeared. These stories were almost always oral tellings, passed down from generation to generation, dealing with themes such as the interconnectedness of nature and a reverence for family and tradition. After European colonization began, Native American stories took on somber tone as they lamented the destruction of their people and culture.

The **Colonial Period** of American literature, by contrast, was written down instead of told orally, and was deeply Christian and neoclassical in style. In the 1630s, the first printing presses were built by colonists in the New World, and they created writings that borrowed heavily from British literary canon. Colonists were often taught proper English grammar and spelling, and their works depicted the struggles of early colonial life, always with an emphasis on order, family, and religion. William Bradford's Mayflower Compact recounted the daily hardships of colonization during the harsh winter in Massachusetts, whereas Anne Bradstreet explored colonial daily life through poetry. Captain John Smith is sometimes considered the first author of the New World due to his journals recalling his earliest days on the new continent.

Values at this time were distinctly Puritan, emphasizing the church as the center of all daily life. Indeed, much of the writing produced at this time was intended simply to be read aloud during sermons. It wasn't until the **Revolutionary Period** in the mid-1700s that works of a more political nature began to appear.

In 1775, Thomas Paine, a philosopher and agitator, wrote a pamphlet that would go on to become the top-selling piece of American literature of all time. *Common Sense* was an incendiary piece of writing, detailing in clear, simple prose the need for rebellion against British rule. The pamphlet's fierce rhetoric stirred the hearts of the colonial upper class, and its concise style meant it could be read aloud in taverns and town squares so that even the illiterate could hear Paine's words. John Adams would later say, "Without the pen of the author of *Common Sense*, the sword of Washington would have been raised in vain." *Common Sense* epitomized this period of American literature, emphasizing freedom from Britain and the need to forge a new identity as Americans.

Among the educated elite, Enlightenment was the watchword of the day. Enlightenment thinkers criticized the religious and political dogma they had been raised with, insisting a new social order based on reason was necessary to modernize the human race. Some Enlightenment thinkers, like Benjamin Franklin, explored new concepts of morality outside of Puritanism – Franklin's *Poor Richard's Almanack* was a collection of wit and wisdom that detailed Franklin's concepts of common virtue in an entertaining style. Many of Franklin's aphorisms from this book ("A penny saved is a penny earned") survive to this day.

The Revolutionary Period also produced stirring oration – Patrick Henry's "Speech to the Virginia House of Burgesses" produced the timeless quotation "Give me liberty or give me death!" This directness was a necessary component of Revolutionary writing, as it needed to be accessible to even the uneducated and illiterate citizens the upper class wished to recruit.

Even the *Declaration of Independence* exhibits characteristics of good Revolutionary literature. Written by Thomas Jefferson, it offers neoclassical style, direct prose, and plenty of irresistible quotations that deliver a unified political message.

The 1800s saw the rise of the **Romantic Period** in American literature. Romanticism was considered very liberal and radical for its time, a reaction to the Industrial Revolution and the increasing scientific rationalization of nature. Romanticism focused on intense emotions, such as awe, horror, love, lust, and depression, and found artistic beauty in the wonders of nature. American Romanticists also lionized their own exploits – the trials against the Indians, Manifest Destiny, and the triumphs of Revolutionary heroes like George Washington. Later critics would characterize Romanticism as naïve, but the influence of the movement on world literature was indelible.

Washington Irving was an early American Romantic, creating folk tales like "The Legend of Sleepy Hollow" and "Rip Van Winkle", which largely rejected British influence in favor of a new American consciousness. The Romantic period also saw a rise in poetry intended to be read as cozy fireside entertainment. "Fireside Poets" such as James Russell Lowell, Oliver Wendell Holmes, and John Greenleaf Whittier wrote of scenarios familiar to Americans at the time, such as the harshness and beauty of New England winters. Henry Wadsworth Longfellow wrote longer poetic epics like *The Song of Hiawatha* and *The Courtship of Miles Standish* which could thrill as well as educate.

Another prominent American Romantic author is Edgar Allan Poe. Among the first authors to make his living solely by writing, Poe's influence has been felt around the world. With short stories like "Murders in the Rue Morgue", Poe invented the genre of detective fiction, and works like "The Cask of Amontillado" pioneered in the genre of horror. His works explored topics of depression and family strife, drawing heavily upon his own struggles. He had a major influence on other genres like science fiction and mystery, and he's considered one of the all-time masters of the short story, helping to establish it as a major literary form.

Meanwhile, Nathaniel Hawthorne offered some of the first true criticisms of the Puritan lifestyle that had been so prominent in Colonial times. *The Scarlet Letter* is considered his masterwork, depicting the public shaming and ostracization of Hester Prynne, a Puritan woman accused of adultery. Though a fundamentally Romantic book, it eschews much of the wide-eyed naiveté common to the movement, focusing more on the grim realities of human nature.

This political bend in Romantic literature was pushed further by the "Transcendentalists" – Henry David Thoreau and Ralph Waldo Emerson created this subgenre of Romanticism which sought beauty in the simplicity of nature and freedom from the struggles of society. Both authors were intensely political and anti-government, this being reflected in the works *Walden* and the anti-authoritarian screed "On the Duty of Civil Disobedience". In *Walden*, Thoreau painted an attractive portrait of his time living simply in the bounty of nature. The book mixes social commentary, satire, and observations of the natural world to great effect.

But perhaps the single most prominent work of American Romantic literature is Herman Melville's *Moby Dick*. The timeless story pits mad Captain Ahab against the whale that took his leg, casting their struggle as a battle between man and nature, or perhaps man against the very universe itself. Melville explores a heightened dialect in the book, harkening back to the works of Shakespeare or the ancient Greeks, which rejects realism in favor of operatic emotion. Though unappreciated in its time, the story is now considered among the best novels ever produced by an American.

As the Romantic Period faded in the 1850s with the American Civil War, a new **Realist Period** began to take hold. Americans felt Romantic writings no longer reflected the grim realities of life during wartime, and so began producing simpler, more grounded literature, replete with imagery and often expressing cynicism and dissatisfaction.

Walt Whitman was among the early Realist pioneers. His poetry made use of simple images, and was very prose-like. He's considered the "Father of Free Verse" for his influential style, which shirked much of the established rules of poetry for the time. Emily Dickinson is also sometimes considered a Realist. A reclusive woman, Dickinson's body of work is deeply introspective, focusing on intense sensory input and attention to detail which reflects her apprehension of the outside world.

But no one captured the sentiment of post-Civil War America quite like Mark Twain. The pen name of Samuel Longhorn Clemens, Twain is considered by many to be America's first great humorist, penning works of staggering wit that oozed nostalgia, appealing to both young readers and old. His works explore the American South during the Reconstruction period, drawing on his own childhood and adventures as a river boat worker for inspiration. His works, like *The Adventures of Huckleberry Finn*, also explore racial themes and are considered controversial to this day.

Other authors of note include Stephen Crane, whose book, *The Red Badge of Courage*, offered a realistic depiction of a soldier's life during the Civil War. He also wrote *Maggie: A Girl of the Streets*, a cynical tale of a poor woman who turns to prostitution. Upton Sinclair's work is similarly unromantic, with books like *The Jungle* exposing the deplorable working conditions of Chicago meat packers. Sinclair was considered a major agitator in his time. He also wrote *Oil!*, which criticized the greed of American oilmen and proved extremely controversial due to its depiction of a sexual encounter in a motel.

OBJECTIVE 0002 UNDERSTAND AMERICAN LITERATURE FROM THE TWENTIETH CENTURY TO THE PRESENT.

For example: the characteristics of diverse works of American fiction, nonfiction, poetry, and drama from the early twentieth century to the present; the historical, social, and cultural contexts from which modern and contemporary American literature emerged; significant genres and themes in modern and contemporary American literature; and a range of American authors (e.g., Charlotte Perkins Gilman, Gertrude Stein, Edith Wharton, Willa Cather, T. S. Eliot, Countee Cullen, William Faulkner, Langston Hughes, Eugene O'Neill, Gwendolyn Brooks, Ernest Hemingway, Saul Bellow, Arthur Miller, Lillian Hellman, James

Baldwin, Vladimir Nabokov, N. Scott Momaday, Toni Morrison, Maya Angelou, Rita Dove, Leslie Marmon Silko, Louise Erdrich, Rudolfo Anaya, Amy Tan), their representative works and themes, and their significance in the development of American literature in the twentieth and twenty-first centuries.

AUTHOR	TIME PERIOD	CONTRIBUTIONS & SIGNIFICANT WORKS
Charlotte Perkins Gilman	19th Century	Novelist; short story writer; poet; feminist; lecturer for social reform "The Yellow Wallpaper"
Gertrude Stein	20th Century	Writer and poet; contributor to the modernist era Three Lives How to Write
Edith Wharton	20th Century	Novelist; short story writer; Pulitzer Prize winner; known for writing depictions of an affluent lifestyle The Age of Innocence
T.S. Eliot	20th Century	Poet; social critic; leader of the Modernist era; Nobel prize winner "The Love Song of J. Alfred Prufrock" Four Quartets

AUTHOR	TIME PERIOD	CONTRIBUTIONS & SIGNIFICANT WORKS
William Faulkner	20th Century	Author of novels, short stories, essays, plays, and poetry; Nobel Prize winner; known for incorporating stories about southern culture As I Lay Dying The Sound and the Fury
Langston Hughes	20th Century	Harlem Renaissance leader; athor of poems and novels; social activist Let America be America Again The Ways of White Folks
Eugene O'Neill	20th Century	Nobel prize winner; playwright; plays were known for incorporating elements of realism Beyond the Horizon Anna Christie Strange Interlude
Gwendolyn Brooks	20th Century	First African American woman to win the Pulitzer Prize for poetry; Teacher; Poet Negro Hero Annie Allen
Ernest Hemingway	20th Century	Writer of novels and short stories; Pulitzer Prize winner; Nobel Prize winner A Farewell to Arms The Sun Also Rises For Whom the Bell Tolls

AUTHOR	TIME PERIOD	CONTRIBUTIONS & SIGNIFICANT WORKS
James Baldwin	20th Century	Author of novels, poems, and plays; social justice activist; Notes of a Native Son
Toni Morrison	21st Century	Novelist; feminist; Nobel Prize Winner; Pulitzer Prize winner; known for speaking out against racism and sexism Beloved
Maya Angelou	21st Century	Poet, Civil Rights Activist I Know Why the Caged Bird Sings
Louise Erdrich	21st Century	Novelist; poet; children's book author; known for inclusion of Native American culture The Plague of Doves

20th Century literature is very diverse due to the rise of mass media, and can be divided into the realms of fiction, poetry, and drama. Among the greatest American dramatists is Eugene O'Neill, who won an unprecedented four Pulitzer Prizes for Drama for his works. Deeply personal, O'Neill's works reflect his own struggles with depression, alcoholism, and family dysfunction that bordered on abuse. His masterpiece is *Long Day's Journey Into Night*, a semi-autobiographical tale of a family being slowly torn apart by substance abuse and their own incompatible egos. Tennessee Williams is another giant of American drama, penning classics like *Cat On a Hot Tin Roof* and *A Streetcar Named Desire*, which deal with issues of sexuality, gender, and mental illness. Both dramatists evoked the Realist style from decades earlier, creating terse and sometimes pessimistic deconstructions of modern American life through the lenses of volatile families and failed careers.

Of poetry, the 20th century masters include: Maya Angelou, Langston Hughes, and Robert Frost. Angelou was a Civil Rights activist who wrote stunning poems and memoirs on themes of racism and gender, with the autobiographical *I Know Why the Caged Bird Sings* detailing her growth from an insecure and abused young woman into an independent firebrand. Hughes, likewise, wrote detailed accounts of the African-American experience. He was a leading figure in the Harlem Renaissance, a movement in the 1920s that gave a voice to black writers in New York City, many of whom would go on to become massively influential. Meanwhile, Frost's poems are more traditional, detailing the beauty of the natural world he experienced growing up in rural New England and the joys of simple living. His work "The Road Less Traveled" is among the most well-known and acclaimed poems of all time.

Prose fiction has always had the largest reach and biggest influence, and many 20th century American authors have penned works that continue to change the world. In 1925, F. Scott Fitzgerald published *The Great Gatsby*, considered by many to be perhaps the greatest American novel. The book follows wealthy socialite Jay Gatsby as viewed through the eyes of his friend and confidante Nick Carraway, as Gatsby tries in vain to leverage his vast wealth and influence towards winning back the woman of his dreams. The book is considered the ultimate satire on the American Dream, exploring the vacuity of wealth and material gains that so many Americans strive for.

Meanwhile, the works of Ernest Hemingway and John Steinbeck explored the struggles of the lower classes. Steinbeck's *The Grapes of Wrath* follows the doomed Joad family during the Great Depression as they try time and again to carve out a better future for themselves, being stopped at every turn by greedy opportunists and exploitative businessmen. Steinbeck wrote in a very colloquial dialect that made his works extremely popular, but Hemingway took it even farther, pioneering a new style involving simple words and short declarative sentences that emphasized action and image rather than introspection. He wrote philosophical tales of fate like *The Old Man and the Sea* and also wartime narratives like *A Farewell to Arms* and *The Sun Also Rises*, which were inspired by his own experiences in WWI.

And lastly, William Faulkner pioneered in the Southern Gothic genre, exploring grotesque scenarios involving poverty, mysticism, or outcast characters in the American South. Faulkner's work described the lingering effects of slavery and the erosion of traditional Southern institutions in an absurdist and experimental style. *As I Lay Dying* and *The Sound and the Fury* are considered his masterpieces.

Since the beginning, American literature has focused largely on issues of class, race, religion, and the struggle for independence, be it from oppressive institutions, economic inequality, or bigotry. The so-called "pioneer spirit" can still be found in contemporary American iconography, the cowboys and superheroes that Americans enjoy reflect a fierce belief in the power of the individual and the need to struggle against life's unfairness. Much world literature focuses on groups, on collectives or movements, but it is not uncommon for American stories to focus on one character only and tell a more universal tale through their experiences. From the earliest pioneer tales to modern stories of the empty promises of the American Dream, the United States has proved itself a powerhouse in the world of literature.

OBJECTIVE 0003 UNDERSTAND THE LITERATURE OF GREAT BRITAIN FROM THE ANGLO-SAXON PERIOD THROUGH THE ROMANTIC PERIOD.

For example: the significance of writers, works, and movements in the development of the literature of Great Britain through the Romantic period; the characteristics of major literary periods in the development of the literature of Great Britain (e.g., Anglo-Saxon, Middle Ages, Renaissance, Restoration and eighteenth-century, Romantic); the historical, social, and cultural contexts of the literature of Great Britain through the Romantic period; significant genres and themes in the literature of Great Britain from the Anglo-Saxon period through the Romantic period; and a range of authors and works from Great Britain (e.g., Beowulf, the Gawain poet, Geoffrey Chaucer, Sir Thomas Malory, Christopher Marlowe, William Shakespeare, John Donne, John Milton, Samuel Johnson, Alexander Pope, Jonathan Swift, Robert Burns, William Blake, William Wordsworth, Samuel Taylor Coleridge, Jane Austen, Percy Bysshe Shelley, Mary Wollstonecraft Shelley, Lord Byron, John Keats) and their significance in the development of the literature of Great Britain from the Anglo-Saxon period through the Romantic period.

AUTHOR	TIME PERIOD	CONTRIBUTIONS & SIGNIFICANT WORKS
Unknown	~700-1000 AD	Old English epic poem from the Anglo-Saxon period; the exact date is unknown, and the author is also a mystery; arguably the oldest poem ever written in Old English "Beowulf"
The Gawain poet / Unknown	14th Century	Poems written in Middle English; author unknown; Pearl Sir Gawain and the Green Knight

AUTHOR	TIME PERIOD	CONTRIBUTIONS & SIGNIFICANT WORKS
Geoffrey Chaucer	15th Century	Poet; known as the "Father of English literature"; arguably the best poet of the Middle Ages The Canterbury Tales

The most significant direct influence on American literature comes from our neighbors across the Atlantic in the British Isles. During the Anglo-Saxon period between the 8th and 11th centuries, the English language was still coming into its own as a unique dialect separate from Latin or German. Among the earliest works in the English language is *Beowulf*, an epic poem describing the exploits of its titular hero as he attempts to slay the monstrous creature, Grendel. *Beowulf*'s author is not known, and the story likely originated as an oral telling that distorted real historical events into the realm of fairy tale.

The medieval period lasted until the 15th century and introduced many other stories that have become an essential part of British consciousness. Thomas Malory's *La Morte D'Arthur* is one of the first Arthurian legends, describing the exploits of King Arthur, Guinevere, Sir Lancelot, and the rest of the Knights of the Round Table which have made an indelible mark on world literature. But Geoffrey Chaucer's *Canterbury Tales* is the true apex of Medieval British literature. The book, which follows a group of pilgrims engaged in a storytelling contest as they travel to a famous shrine, featured an unprecedented mastery of common language and a massive cast of characters from all walks of life who painted an ironic and critical view of English life. Chaucer introduced many new words and phrases into the English language with *Canterbury*, and his view of English life as seen through the eyes of worldly lower class laborers has proven invaluable to historians ever since.

Of course, no mention of British literature is complete without Shakespeare and his contemporaries who worked during the **Renaissance Era** of the 14th through 17th centuries. Considered by many to be the greatest writer in the English language, William Shakespeare produced thirty-nine plays and over one hundred sonnets, ranging from broad comedies to heartfelt tragedies and bloody historical tellings. Shakespeare was a master of iambic pentameter, a poetical meter with each line having five iambs or "feet", each containing a stressed and unstressed syllable. This style of verse was said to mimic the beating of the human heart, and it leant Shakespeare's prose much lively energy that has proved attractive to actors and readers for centuries. Shakespeare was also a great wit and an incredible craftsmen of language. No other author has contributed more words to the English language than Shakespeare. His contemporaries, such as Christopher Marlowe and John Webster, also experimented wildly with new forms of vernacular storytelling, often repackaging ancient Greek tales for popular consumption.

In the 17th century, British literature largely focused on religious concerns. John Milton, a staunch Puritan, gave *Paradise Lost* to the world. The epic poem details the fall of the archangel Lucifer from heaven and his subsequent rebellion against God. The work proved so influential that it is sometimes mistaken for Biblical canon. John Bunyan's *The Pilgrim's Progress* is also staunchly religious, telling of a man's journey towards heaven after death. For many years, the book was second only to the Bible in terms of sales. John Donne's poetry, meanwhile, was more personal and satirical. Common turns of phrase like "for whom the bell tolls" and "no man is an island" come from his works.

18th century British literature became even more intensely political following the revival of the monarchy under Charles II. **Neoclassical** writing was the rule at this time, as British citizens sought to elevate and reconnect with their past. Notable authors include Alexander Pope, a poet who dabbled in a variety of neoclassical forms, and Robert Burns, a Scotsman who explored common Scottish brogue in his poems such as "To A Mouse". But William Blake came to be viewed as the eminent voice of this generation – a notably progressive thinker with decidedly anti-church politics, Blake's work fought for the dissolution of gender roles and more critical views towards religion. He was a friend and contemporary of Thomas Paine, and the two shared many views popular amongst Enlightenment figures at this time.

The works of Blake help usher in an era of **Romanticism** in British literature in the 1800s. The "First Generation" of Romantics included William Wordsworth and Samuel Taylor Coleridge, who collaborated *Lyrical Ballads*, a collection of experimental poems like "Rime of the Ancient Mariner" which epitomized the Romantic style and essayed Wordsworth's philosophical belief that men are inherently good but often become corrupted by society. The Second Generation of Romantics include John Keats, Lord Byron, and Percy Bysshe Shelley, who churned out sonnets, epics, and narrative poems featuring gorgeous prose and keen wit. Byron's *Don John* is a masterpiece of British satire, and his autobiographical *Childe Harold's Pilgrimage* is exceedingly self-deprecating. Shelley's works feature remarkable sensory detail – his poem "Ozymandias" describes a traveler who discovers a monument to some forgotten king whose grand empire has crumbled to dust. Keats' works display maturity far beyond his years, as the poet died at the tender age of 25.

OBJECTIVE 0004 UNDERSTAND THE LITERATURE OF GREAT BRITAIN FROM THE VICTORIAN PERIOD TO THE PRESENT.

For example: the characteristics of significant literary works of Great Britain from the Victorian period to the present; the historical, social, and cultural contexts of Victorian, modern, and contemporary literature of Great Britain; significant genres and themes in Victorian, modern, and contemporary literature of Great Britain; and a range of authors of Great Britain (e.g., Charles Dickens, Emily Brontë, Charlotte Brontë, Matthew Arnold, Gerard Manley Hopkins, Thomas Hardy, William Butler Yeats, James Joyce, George Bernard Shaw, D. H.

Lawrence, Virginia Woolf, W. H. Auden, Dylan Thomas, Doris Lessing, Seamus Heaney), their representative works, and their significance in the development of the literature of Great Britain from the Victorian period to the present.

The Romantic and **Victorian** eras produced some of the first prominent female authors in British history, creating a feminist perspective that was often missing from literature until that point. Jane Austen is the most popular author from this time, and her works, such as *Pride & Prejudice* and *Mansfield Park*, provided realistic characters and cutting social commentary that have endured in popularity to the present day. Charlotte and Emily Bronte were sisters and professional rivals, who wrote *Jane Eyre* and *Wuthering Heights* respectively, two novels focusing on duplicity and unrequited love amongst the landed gentry of England. These authors struggled against societal expectations of women during this period, and many critics were less than generous with their reviews, leading another prominent author, Mary Ann Evans, to write under the alias of George Eliot to get a fairer appraisal of her work.

The rise of printed media in the 1800s created a diverse range of literature in Britain, ranging from the sharply **satirical** to the proudly **adventurous**. Great satirists like Oscar Wilde skewered the manners and customs of the upper class, earning scorn from censors and traditionalists while keeping readers enraptured. It was also a great time for young adult literature – Robert Louis Stevenson's *Treasure Island* and *20,000 Leagues Under the Sea* wove action-packed tales of high adventure that appealed to young readers. Still other authors focused their attentions on social commentary, such as Rudyard Kipling, who crafted many fables and parables that taught valuable lessons in *The Jungle Book*. Charles Dickens's works were more critical, deconstructing Victorian values of greed and decadence, focusing his attentions on the downtrodden orphans and lower-class laborers who suffered during the Industrial Revolution. He also wrote immensely popular potboilers, such as *A Christmas Carol*, which helped re-popularize the Christmas holiday and has never once been out of publication since its first printing.

This experimentation and variety has continued in the 20th century, establishing the British Isles as a major force in world literature. Irish authors James Joyce and Samuel Beckett pioneered **Modernist** literature, which remixed and recontextualized existing dramatic forms in absurd, experimental new ways. Beckett's *Waiting for Godot* is among the most influential plays ever written, examining the tragedy and comedy of the human condition via two clownish vagabonds contemplating their own inability to take control of their lives. The play is a landmark work of Absurdist and Post-Modern theater, two experimental styles that pushed the limits of what audiences could expect from the stage.

Joyce's *Ulysses* is considered by many critics to be among the greatest English language novels – it experiments and invents in nearly every literary style, using a dreamlike stream-of-consciousness narrative to tell the story of a man's madcap journey through Dublin on a single day. The works of George Orwell are more political. A former police officer in English-occupied Burma, Orwell's works are fiercely anti-fascist, providing grave warnings about the dangers of totalitarianism. His science-fiction/dystopian novel *1984* is considered his masterpiece, telling the tale of a common man's struggle against his brutally conformist society ruled over by the mysterious dictator, "Big Brother".

British literature has flitted between proud lionization of their own accomplishments and self-deprecating laughter at their failings. Traditions of satire and wordplay run deep in English writings, from the comedies of Gilbert and Sullivan with their puns and double entendres, to the biting, controversial ironies of Oscar Wilde. Still other authors have sought to elevate institutions of British life, such as religion or the monarchy. British writings owe a strong debt to the works of the ancient Greeks, whose tragedies and philosophical writings inspired countless English-language works. The body of work produced by these small island nations continues to grow and evolve, further cementing their place as a force to be reckoned with in the literary world.

OBJECTIVE 0005 UNDERSTAND LITERATURE FROM THE ANCIENT WORLD TO THE FIFTEENTH CENTURY.

For example: the characteristics of major literary forms, works, and writers associated with literature of the ancient world (e.g., African, Asian, European, and Greek and Roman literature; the Bible; world myths and folk tales); the historical, social, and cultural contexts from which ancient world literature emerged; significant genres and themes in ancient world literature; a range of authors and works (e.g., the Gilgamesh epic, the Vedas, the Old and New Testaments, the Qur'an, Homer, Lao-Tzu, Sappho, Sophocles, Aristophanes, Virgil, Li Po, Murasaki Shikibu, Omar Khayyám, Rumi, Dante Alighieri) and their significance in the development of ancient world literature; historical, social, and cultural aspects of ancient world literature (e.g., the expression of regional, ethnic, and historical values, archetypes, and ideas through literature; ways in which literary works and movements both reflected and shaped culture and history); and characteristics and significance of world mythology and folk literature.

Literary allusions are drawn from classical mythology, national folklore, and religious writings with which the reader is assumed to be familiar so he or she can recognize the comparison between the subject of the allusion and the person, place, or event in the current reading. Children and adolescents who have knowledge of proverbs, fables, myths, epics, and the Bible can understand these allusions and thereby appreciate their reading to a greater degree than those who cannot recognize them.

Fables and Folktales

This literary genre of stories and legends was originally transmitted orally to new audiences in order to provide models of exemplary behavior or to celebrate deeds worthy of recognition and homage.

In fables, animals talk, feel, and behave like human beings. The fable always has a moral, and the animal characters allude to specific people or groups without directly identifying them. For example, in Aesop's Fables, the lion is the king and the wolf is the cruel, unfeeling noble class. In the fable of "The Lion and the Mouse," the moral is that

"Little friends may prove to be great friends." In "The Lion's Share," it is "Might makes right." Many British folktales—such as *Robin Hood* or *St. George and the Dragon*—explore the relationship between power and morality.

Classical Mythology

English literature draws many allusions to the mythology of **ancient Greece and Rome**. For millennia, these stories have been translated and disseminated, providing a framework that much of English literature is built on. Some Norse myths are also well known. These stories sought to provide insight into the order and ethics of life. Some tales told of ancient heroes who overcame the terrors of the unknown, while others gave meaning to natural phenomena - thunder and lightning, the changing of the seasons, and the magical creatures of the forests and seas.. There is often a childlike quality in the emotions of these supernatural beings. Many good translations of these myths exist for readers of all levels, but Edith Hamilton's *Mythology* is the definitive work for adolescents.

Ancient Greek philosophers such as Sophocles, Euripedes, and Aeschylus wrote many tragedies that have formed the backbone of much of Western literature. Greek tragedies focus largely on the failings of the main character, on their pride (or "hubris") that causes them to subvert the natural order of things and earn the ire of the gods, which leads to their downfall (a "catharsis" or cleansing). Most plays contain a mythic or religious component, and many end with direct intervention from the gods themselves (termed a "deus ex machina", a sudden ending where a godlike figure appears and re-establishes order). Important Greek tragedies include *Oedipus Rex*, *Medea*, and *Antigone*. The works of Homer are also noteworthy, which include *The Iliad* and *The Odyssey*, two epic poems that described the exploits of brave Greek warriors and their struggles against each other and the gods themselves. Homer is sometimes considered the first great European author, and his influence cannot be overstated.

Fairy Tales

Fairy tales are lively fictional stories involving children or animals that come in contact with supernatural beings through magic. They provide happy solutions to human dilemmas, and are often peopled by fantastic creatures such as trolls, elves, dwarfs, and pixies.

Among the most famous fairy tales are "Beauty and the Beast," "Cinderella," "Hansel and Gretel," "Snow White and the Seven Dwarfs," "Rumpelstiltskin," and "Tom Thumb." In each tale, the protagonist struggles against prejudice, imprisonment, ridicule, or even death itself to receive justice in a cruel world.

Older readers encounter a kind of fairy-tale world in Shakespeare's *The Tempest* and *A Midsummer Night's Dream*, which use pixies and fairies as characters. Adolescent readers today are fascinated by the creations of fantasy realms in the works of Piers Anthony, Ursula K. LeGuin, and Anne McCaffrey. An extension of interest in the supernatural is science fiction, which harnesses fantasy and imagination to predict a possible course for the future.

Angels (or similar spiritual figures, such as fairy godmothers) play a role in some fairy tales, and English author John Milton also used symbolically resonant angels and devils in *Paradise Lost* and *Paradise Regained.*

English literature also alludes frequently to the Bible. The Bible's **parables**, which are moralistic tales like fables but with human characters, include the stories of the Good Samaritan and the Prodigal Son. References to the treachery of Cain and the betrayal of Christ by Judas Iscariot are common in English works.

American Folktales

American folktales are divided into two categories: imaginary tales and real tales.

Imaginary tales, also called **tall tales**, are humorous tales based on nonexistent, fictional characters developed through blatant exaggeration. For example, the story of John Henry is about a two-fisted steel driver who beats a steam drill in a competition, and the tale of Rip Van Winkle features the titular character sleeping for 20 years in the Catskill Mountains, and upon awakening cannot understand why no one recognizes him. In another American tall tale, Paul Bunyan is a giant lumberjack. He owns a great blue ox named Babe and has extraordinary physical strength. He is said to have plowed the Mississippi River, and the impressions of Babe's hoof prints created the Great Lakes.

Real tales, also called **legends**, are based on real persons who accomplished the feats that are attributed to them, even if they are exaggerated somewhat. For example, for more than 40 years, Johnny Appleseed (real name John Chapman) roamed Ohio and Indiana planting apple seeds. Daniel Boone— the scout, adventurer, and pioneer—blazed the Wilderness Trail and made Kentucky safe for settlers. And Paul Revere, a colonial patriot, rode through the New England countryside warning of the approach of British troops.

OBJECTIVE 0006 UNDERSTAND WORLD LITERATURE FROM THE FIFTEENTH CENTURY TO THE PRESENT.

For example: the characteristics of major literary forms, works, and writers associated with world literature (e.g., African, Asian, European, Latin American) from the fifteenth century to the present; the historical, social, and cultural contexts of world literature from the fifteenth century to the present; significant genres and themes in world literature from the fifteenth century to the present; a range of authors (e.g., Michel de Montaigne, Miguel de Cervantes Saavedra, Molière, Jean-Jacques Rousseau, Johann Wolfgang von Goethe, Leo Tolstoy, Feodor Dostoevski, Anton Chekhov, Rabindranath Tagore, Rainer Maria Rilke, Franz Kafka, Federico García Lorca, Isak Dinesen, Albert Camus, Jorge Luis Borges, Primo Levi, Yehuda Amichai, Nadine Gordimer, Aleksandr Solzhenitsyn, Pablo Neruda, Czeslaw Milosz, Wole Soyinka, R. K. Narayan, Margaret Atwood, Derek Walcott, Naguib Mahfouz, Ōe Kenzaburō, V. S. Naipaul), their representative works, and their significance in world literature from the fifteenth century to the present; and social and cultural aspects of world literature from the fifteenth century to the present (e.g., the expression of regional, ethnic, and historical values; ways in which literary works and movements both reflect and shape culture and history).

Genres of World Literature

World folk epics are poems (or sometimes prose works) that are an integral part of a people's culture. In many cases, they were originally oral tellings that became recorded in writing.

Some examples of world folk epics include:

- *Soundiata*, an African epic
- *Tunkashila*, a Native American epic
- *Gilgamesh*, the oldest known epic, from Mesopotamia
- *Aeneid*, a Roman epic
- *Moby-Dick*, which some consider an American folk epic.

A **national myth** is an inspiring narrative or anecdote about a nation's past. These often dramatize true events, omit important historical details, or add details for which there is no evidence for dramatic effect. A national myth can be a fictional story that no one takes to be true, such as *Paul Bunyan*, which was created by French Canadians during the Papineau Rebellion of 1837, when they revolted against the young English Queen. In older nations, national myths may be more spiritually-minded, and refer to the nation's founding by gods or other supernatural beings.

Some national myths:

- The legend of King Arthur in Great Britain
- Sir Francis Drake in England
- The Pilgrims and the Mayflower in the United States
- Pocahontas, who is said to have saved the life of John Smith from her savage father, Powhatan
- The legendary ride of Paul Revere
- The last words of Nathan Hale
- The person of George Washington and apocryphal tales about him, such as his cutting down a cherry tree with a hatchet and then facing up to the truth: "I cannot tell a lie."

Germany

German poet and playwright Friedrich von Schiller is best known for his history plays, *William Tell* and *The Maid of Orleans*. He is a leading literary figure in the "golden age" of German literature. Also from Germany, Rainer Maria Rilke, the great lyric poet, is one of the masters of the stream-of-consciousness style. Germany also has given the world Herman Hesse (*Siddhartha*), Gunter Grass (*The Tin Drum*), and the greatest of all German writers, Goethe.

Scandinavia

Scandinavian literature includes the work of Hans Christian Andersen in Denmark, who advanced the fairy tale genre with such wistful stories as "The Little Mermaid" and "Thumbelina." The social commentary of Henrik Ibsen in Norway startled the world of drama with such issues as feminism (*A Doll's House* and *Hedda Gabler*) and the effects of sexually transmitted diseases (*The Wild Duck* and *Ghosts*). Sweden's Selma Lagerlof is the first woman to ever win the Nobel Prize for literature. Her novels include *Gosta Berling's Saga* and the world-renowned *The Wonderful Adventures of Nils*, a children's work.

Russia

Literary greats from Russia include Leo Tolstoy, who described Napolean's capture of the city of Moscow in *War and Peace*, and Fyodor Dostoyevski, who wrote *The Brothers Karamazov*, a satirical and philosophical depiction of the dissolving relationship between three brothers and their father which eventually culminates in murder. Tolstoy also wrote *Anna Karenina*, a prime example of Realist fiction, following the exploits of its titular heroin as she pursues a doomed affair with a wealthy count.

The 20th century gave Vladimir Nabokov to the world. The controversial author of such works as *Lolita*, which describes the relationship between a literarily-minded pedophile and his stepdaughter, Nabokov's works are replete with sensory detail and are sharply ironic, offering many cutting observations about the American culture that Nabokov gradually assimilated into.

Anton Chekov is considered Russia's prime dramatist, giving the world stories like *Uncle Vanya* and *The Cherry Orchard*, which stretched the limits of actors' abilities and paved new ground for concepts like subtext and psychological realism in theater. Alexander Pushkin is famous for great short stories, and Yevgeny Yevtushenko for poetry (*Babi Yar*). Boris Pasternak won the Nobel Prize (*Dr. Zhivago*). Aleksandr Solzhenitsyn (*The Gulag Archipelago*) was exiled from Russia for his writings on the gulag system. Ilya Varshavsky, who creates dystopian fictional societies, represents the genre of science fiction.

France

France has a multifaceted canon of great literature that is universal in scope, almost always championing some social cause: the poignant short stories of Guy de Maupassant; the fantastic poetry of Charles Baudelaire (*Fleurs du Mal*); and the groundbreaking lyrical poetry of Rimbaud and Verlaine.

Drama in France is best represented by Rostand's *Cyrano de Bergerac* and the neoclassical dramas of Racine and Corneille (*Le Cid*). The great French novelists include Andre Gide, Honoré de Balzac (*Cousin Bette*), Stendhal (*The Red and the Black*), and the father/son duo of Alexandre Dumas Sr. and Jr. (*The Three Musketeers* and *The Man in the Iron Mask*).

Victor Hugo is the Charles Dickens of French literature, having penned the masterpieces *The Hunchback of Notre Dame* and the French national novel *Les Misérables*. The innovative stream-of-consciousness style of Marcel Proust's *Remembrance of Things Past* and the absurdist theatre of Samuel Beckett and Eugene Ionesco (*Rhinoceros*) attest to the groundbreaking genius of the French writers.

French literature of the twentieth century is defined by the existentialism of Jean-Paul Sartre (*No Exit*, *The Flies*, *Nausea*), Andre Malraux (*The Fall*), and Albert Camus (*The Stranger*, *The Plague*), the recipient of the 1957 Nobel Prize for literature. Feminist writings include those of Sidonie-Gabrielle Colette, known for her short stories and novels, as well as Simone de Beauvoir.

Spain

Spain's great writers include Miguel de Cervantes (*Don Quixote*) and Juan Ramon Jimenez. The anonymous national epic *El Cid* has been translated into many languages.

Italy

Italy's greatest writers include Virgil, who wrote the great epic *The Aeneid*; Giovanni Boccaccio (*The Decameron*); and Dante Alighieri (the *Divine Comedy*).

Far East

The classical age of Japanese literary achievement includes works of father-son duo Kiyotsugu Kanami, and Motokkiyo Zeami, who developed the theatrical experience known as Noh drama to its highest aesthetic degree. Zeami is said to have authored over 200 plays, of which 100 still are extant.

Katai Tayama (*The Quilt*) is touted as the father of the genre known as the Japanese confessional novel. His work is in the genre of naturalism, and is definitely not for the squeamish.

The "slice of life" psychological writings of Ryunosuke Akutagawa gained him acclaim in the Western world. His short stories, especially "Rashomon" and "In a Grove," are greatly praised for style as well as content.

China, too, has contributed to the literary world. Li Po, the T'ang dynasty poet from the Chinese Golden Age, revealed his interest in folklore by preserving the folk songs and mythology of China. Po further allows his reader to explore the Chinese philosophy of Taoism and to know his sentiment against expansionism during the T'ang dynastic rule. During the T'ang dynasty, which was one of great diversity in the arts, the Chinese version of the short story was created with the help of Jiang Fang. His themes often express love between a man and a woman.

Asia has many modern writers whose works are being translated for Western readers. India's Krishan Chandar has authored more than 300 stories. Rabindranath Tagore won the Nobel Prize for literature in 1913 (*Song Offerings*). Narayan, India's most famous writer (*The Guide*) is highly interested in mythology and legends of India. Santha Rama Rau's work, *Gifts of Passage*, is her autobiographical story of life in a British school where she tries to preserve her Indian culture and traditional home.

Revered as Japan's most famous female author, Fumiko Hayashi (*Drifting Clouds*) had written more than 270 literary works at the time of her death.

In 1968, the Nobel Prize for literature was awarded to Yasunari Kawabata (*The Sound of the Mountain*, *The Snow Country*, considered to be his masterpieces). His *Palm-of-the-Hand Stories* take aspects of Haiku poetry and transform them into the short story genre.

Modern feminist and political concerns are written eloquently by Ting Ling, who used the pseudonym Chiang Ping-Chih. Her stories reflect her concerns about social injustice and her commitment to the women's movement.

North America

North American literature is divided among the United States, Canada, and Mexico. Canadian writers of note include feminist Margaret Atwood (*The Handmaid's Tale*); Alice Munro, a remarkable short story writer; and W. P. Kinsella, another short story writer whose two major subjects are Native Americans and baseball. Mexican writers include 1990 Nobel Prize winning poet Octavio Paz (*The Labyrinth of Solitude*) and feminist Rosarian Castellanos (*The Nine Guardians*).

Africa

African literary greats include South Africans Nadine Gordimer (winner of the Nobel Prize for literature) and Peter Abrahams (*Tell Freedom: Memories of Africa*, an autobiography of life in Johannesburg). Chinua Achebe (*Things Fall Apart*) and the poet Wole Soyinka hail from Nigeria. Mark Mathabane's autobiography *Kaffir Boy* is about growing up in South Africa. Egyptian writer Naguib Mahfouz and British writer Doris Lessing, who lived in Zimbabwe, write about race relations in their respective countries. Because of her radical politics, Lessing was banned from her homeland and South Africa, as was Alan Paton, whose simple story, *Cry, the Beloved Country*, brought the plight of black South Africans under apartheid to the rest of the world.

Central America/Caribbean

The Caribbean and Central America encompass a vast area and cultures that reflect oppression and colonialism by England, Spain, Portugal, France, and the Netherlands. Caribbean writers include Samuel Selvon of Trinidad and Armado Valladres of Cuba. Central American authors include dramatist Carlos Solorzano from Guatemala, whose plays include *Dona Beatriz*, *The Hapless*, *The Magician*, and *The Hands of God.*

South America

Chilean Gabriela Mistral was the first Latin American writer to win the Nobel Prize for literature. She is best known for her collections of poetry, including *Desolation.* Chile was also home to Pablo Neruda, who in 1971 also won the Nobel Prize for his poetry. His 29 volumes of poetry have been translated into more than 60 languages, attesting to his universal appeal. *Twenty Love Poems* and *Song of Despair* are justly famous. Isabel Allende is carrying on the Chilean literary standards with her acclaimed novel *The House of the Spirits.* Argentinian Jorge Luis Borges is considered by many literary critics to be the most important writer of his century from South America. His collection of short stories, *Ficciones*, brought him universal recognition.

Also from Argentina, Silvina Ocampo, a collaborator with Borges on a collection of poetry, is famed for her poetry and short story collections, which include *The Fury* and *The Days of the Night.*

Noncontinental Europe

Horacio Quiroga represents Uruguay, and Brazil has Joao Guimaraes Rosa, whose novel, *The Devil to Pay*, is considered first-rate world literature.

Slavic nations

Austrian writer Franz Kafka (*The Metamorphosis*, *The Trial*, and *The Castle*) is considered by many to be the most important literary voice of the first half of the twentieth century. Kafka wrote accounts of depression, anxiety, and isolation that blended the realistic and surreal. He was among the first authors to criticize bureaucratic institutions, with works like *The Trial* and *In the Penal Colony*, which feature characters being tormented by shady government figures for reasons that are never fully explained. He also delved into more fantastical subject matter with works like *The Metamorphosis*, a tale of a traveling salesman who awakens one day to find he has been transformed into a massive bug. The term "Kafkaesque" is common in literary criticism today, describing situations in which a main character is being persecuted for unclear reasons and has no clear method of rectifying their terrible situation. Representing the Czech Republic is the poet Vaclav Havel. Slovakia has dramatist Karel Capek (*R.U.R.*), and Romania is represented by Elie Wiesel (*Night*), a Nobel Prize winner.

OBJECTIVE 0007 UNDERSTAND THE CHARACTERISTICS OF VARIOUS GENRES AND TYPES OF LITERATURE.

For example: characteristics of the major literary genres (e.g., fiction, nonfiction, poetry, drama); elements of fiction (e.g., plot, character, setting, theme); characteristic elements of fiction genres (e.g., novels, short stories); types of fictional narratives (e.g., folk legend, fantasy, mystery, realistic novel) and their characteristics; genres of nonfiction (e.g., biography, autobiography, letters, essays, reports) and their characteristic elements and structures; genres of drama (e.g., serious drama and tragedy, comic drama, melodrama, farce) and their characteristic elements and structures; genres of poetry (e.g., lyric, concrete, dramatic, narrative, epic) and their characteristic elements and structures; types of patterned lyric poetry (e.g., sonnet, ballad, limerick, haiku); criteria for evaluating prose, dramatic, and poetic works of various types; and literary devices (e.g., figurative language, imagery, irony, symbolism, ambiguity, rhythm, rhyme, sensory detail) and ways in which they contribute to meaning and style.

Poetry Versus Prose

Poetry follows a structure with metric or rhyme scheme, while **prose** does not have a standard style of writing. In addition, poetry often leads the reader to read between the lines, while prose has a much more literal approach. There is minimal critical thinking involved when it comes to reading a piece of prose - you are simply reading a story. You do not have to continuously question the author's intention or the intended meaning of the piece.

Poetry	Prose
• Written in verse form	• Written in narrative form
• Contains poetic meter	• Contains paragraphs
• It's up to the reader to determine the author's intention	• Includes a setting, characters, plot, and point of view
• Metaphorical	• Literal

Prose Categories

Fictional prose

The most common example of fictional prose is a novel. Using a narrative form of writing, fictional prose has been used to tell tales of adventure, erotica, and mystery. Other examples include romance and short story.

Nonfiction prose

Nonfiction prose is based on facts, but it may also include fictional elements. It is used to be informative and persuasive, yet it does not include any scientific evidence to support its claims. Examples include: journal entry, biography, and essay.

Heroic prose

Also written in the narrative form, heroic prose has a dramatic style that allows for the works to be recited or performed. The most common form of heroic prose is the legend.

Rhymed prose

The difference between prose and poetry is not always clear. Rhymed prose is written with rhymes that are not metrical and is considered to be an artistic, skilled form of writing across the world. Examples include Rayok in Russian culture, Saj' from Arabic culture, and Fu from Chinese culture.

Prose poetry

Prose poetry can be considered a combination, or fusion, of both poetry and prose. It uses extreme imagery, yet does not include the typical metrical structure or rhyme scheme found in a poem.

Types of Prose

Allegory: A story in verse or prose with characters representing virtues and vices. An allegory has two meanings: symbolic and literal. John Bunyan's The Pilgrim's Progress is the most renowned of this genre.

Epistle: A letter that was not always intended for public distribution, but due to the fame of the sender and/or recipient, becomes widely known. Paul wrote epistles that were later placed in the Bible.

Essay: Typically a relatively short prose work focusing on a topic, propounding a definite point of view and using an authoritative tone. Great essayists include Carlyle, Lamb, DeQuincy, Emerson, and Montaigne, who is credited with defining this genre.

Legend: A traditional narrative or collection of related narratives, popularly regarded as historically factual but actually a mixture of fact and fiction. *The Tales of King Arthur* or *Robin Hood* could be described as legends.

Novel: The longest form of fictional prose containing a variety of characters, settings, local color, and regionalism. Most have complex plots, expanded description, and attention to detail. Some of the great novelists include Austen, the Brontë sisters, Twain, Tolstoy, Hugo, Hardy, Dickens, Hawthorne, Forster, and Flaubert.

Romance: A highly imaginative tale set in a fantastical realm dealing with the conflicts between heroes, villains, and/or monsters. "The Knight's Tale" from Chaucer's *Canterbury Tales*, *Sir Gawain and the Green Knight*, and Keats' "The Eve of St. Agnes" are representatives.

Short story: Typically a terse narrative, with less development and background about characters; may include description, author's point of view, and tone. Poe emphasized that a successful short story should create one focused impact. Some great short story writers are Hemingway, Faulkner, Twain, Joyce, Shirley Jackson, Flannery O'Connor, de Maupassant, Saki, Edgar Allen Poe, and Pushkin.

Analyzing Prose

The analysis of prose, similar to the analysis of poetry, also calls for attention to structural elements so as to discern meaning, purpose, and themes. The author's intentions are gleaned through the elements he or she uses and how they are used. Because your written response questions will most likely include either poetry or prose within the prompt, it's critical to deeply analyze all structural elements (plot, characters, setting, and point of view). This will assist you in supporting your own claims and will give you the best opportunity for a high score on the writing portion.

Plot

The plot is the sequence of events (it may or may not be chronological) that the author chooses to represent the story to be told—both the underlying story and the externals of the occurrences the author relates. An author may use "flashbacks" to tell the back story (or what went before the current events begin). Often, authors begin their stories in media res, or in the middle of things, and, over time, supply the details of what has gone before to provide a clearer picture to the reader of all the relevant events.

Sometimes authors tell parallel stories in order to make their points. For example, in Count Leo Tolstoy's classic *Anna Karenina*, the unhappy extramarital affair of Anna Karenina and Count Vronsky is contrasted with the happy marriage of Lev and Kitty through the use of alternating chapters devoted to each couple. The plot consists of the progress of each couple: Anna and Count Vronsky into deeper neurosis, obsession, and emotional pain, and Lev and Kitty into deeper and more meaningful partnership through growing emotional intimacy, parenthood, and caring for members of their extended family.

In good novels, each part of the plot is necessary and has a purpose. For example, in *Anna Karenina*, a chapter is devoted to a horse race Count Vronsky participates in. This might seem like mere entertainment, but, in fact, Count Vronsky is riding his favorite mare, and, in a moment of carelessness in taking a jump, puts the whole weight of his body on the mare's back, breaking it. The horse must be shot. Vronsky loved and admired the mare, but being overcome by a desire to win, he kills the very thing he loves. Similarly, Anna descends into obsession and jealousy as their affair isolates her from society and separates her from her child, and ultimately kills herself. The chapter symbolizes the destructive that effect Vronsky's love, coupled with inordinate desire, has upon what and whom he loves.

Other authors use repetitious plot lines to reveal the larger story over time. For example, in Joseph Heller's tragic-comedy *Catch-22*, the novel repeatedly returns to a horrific incident in an airplane while flying a combat mission. Each time the protagonist, Yossarian, recalls the incident, more detail is revealed. The reader knows from the beginning that this incident is key to why Yossarian wants to be discharged from the army, but it is not until the full details of the gruesome incidents are revealed late in the book that the reader knows why the incident has driven Yossarian almost mad. Interspersed with comedic and ironic episodes, the book's climax (the full revealing of the incident) remains powerfully with the reader, showing the absurdity, insanity, and inhumanity of war. The comic device of Catch-22, a fictitious army rule from which the title is derived, makes this point in a funny way: Catch-22 states that a soldier cannot be discharged from the army unless he is crazy; yet, if he wants to be discharged from the army, he is not crazy. This rule seems to embody the insanity, absurdity, and inhumanity of war.

Characters

Characters usually represent or embody an idea or ideal acting in the world. For example, in the *Harry Potter* series, Harry Potter's goodness, courage and unselfishness as well as his capacity for friendship and love make him a powerful opponent to Voldemort, whose selfishness, cruelty, and isolation make him the leader of the evil forces in the epic battle of good versus evil. Memorable characters are many-sided: Harry is not only brave, strong, and true, he is vulnerable and sympathetic: orphaned as a child, bespectacled, and often misunderstood by his peers, Harry is not a stereotypical hero.

Charles Dickens's *Oliver Twist* is the principle of goodness, oppressed and unrecognized, unleashed in a troubled world. Oliver encounters a great deal of evil, which he refuses to cooperate with, and also a great deal of good in people who have sympathy for his plight. In contrast to the gentle, kindly, and selfless Maylies who take Oliver in, recognizing his goodness, are the evil Bill Sykes and Fagin—thieves and murderers—who are willing to sell and hurt others for their own gain. When Nancy, a thief in league with Sykes and Fagin, essentially "sells" herself to help Oliver, she represents redemption from evil through sacrifice.

Setting

The setting of a work of fiction adds a great deal to the story. Historical fiction relies firmly on an established time and place: *Johnny Tremain* takes place in revolutionary Boston; the story could not take place anywhere else or at any other time. Ray Bradbury's *The Most Dangerous Game* requires an isolated, uninhabited island for its plot. Settings are sometimes changed in a work to represent different periods of a person's life or to compare and contrast life in the city or life in the country.

Point of View

The point of view is the perspective of the person who is the focus of the work of fiction: a story told in the first person is from the point of view of the narrator. In more modern works, works told in the third person usually concentrate on the point of view of one character or else the changes in point of view are clearly delineated, as in *Cold Mountain* by Charles Frazier, who names each chapter after the person whose point of view is being shown. Sudden, unexplained shifts in point of view—i.e., going into the thoughts of one character after another within a short space of time—are a sign of amateurish writing.

Famous prose works of note include:

- Jane Austen - *Pride & Prejudice* (1813)
- Charlotte Brontë - *Jane Eyre* (1847)
- Emily Brontë - *Wuthering Heights* (1847)
- Robert Louis Stevenson - *Treasure Island* (1883)
- Rudyard Kipling – *The Jungle Book* (1894)
- James Joyce – *Ulysses* (1922)
- F. Scott Fitzgerald - *The Great Gatsby* (1925)
- William Faulkner - *The Sound and the Fury* (1929); *As I Lay Dying* (1930)
- John Steinbeck -*The Grapes of Wrath* (1939)
- Ernest Hemingway - *The Sun Also Rises* (1926); *A Farewell to Arms* (1929); *The Old Man and the Sea* (1952)

Poetry

Poetry is the use of words to convey image and emotion. Poetry is often less explicit than prose, relying on implication and suggestion rather than overt statement of fact. Poetry is not always concerned with "realism", often shirking basic tenets of grammar and syntax for better artistic effect. There are few true "answers" in poetry, as poems are often interpreted in a variety of ways, but certain conclusions can be drawn from a close reading of the text. This is an essential skill for the AP English exam, which focuses largely on poetic forms, styles, movements, and nomenclature.

For the MTEL English exam, you will want to ask yourself the following questions while considering poetry: What was the author trying to accomplish? How did they achieve their goal? What poetic devices did they employ in this pursuit and how effective were they?

Poetic Terminology

- **Rhyme:** Indicates a repeated end sound of lines or words within a poem. Rhymes usually occur at the ends of lines, though they can also be internal.
  - **Example:** "Because I could not stop for Death / He kindly stopped for me / The Carriage held but just Ourselves / And Immortality." – Emily Dickinson, "Because I could not stop for Death". "Me" and "Immortality" rhyme in this poem, lending a sense of finality to the last line and giving it a pleasing rhythm.
- **Rhyme scheme:** The pattern of rhymes in each line of a poem. Rhyme schemes are usually indicated with letters. Some poets follow strict rhyme schemes, some shirk them entirely, but most employ repetitive rhyme schemes when aesthetically appropriate and then subvert them for stronger effect.
  - **Example:** "A wonderful bird is the pelican;
His beak can hold more than his belly-can.
He can hold in his beak
Enough food for a week,
Though I'm damned if I know how the hell-he-can!"
— Dixon Lanier Merritt

    This is an example of a Limerick, a short, humorous poem employing a five line rhyme scheme. Limericks always follow an AABBA rhyme scheme – the first two lines rhyme, the next two shorter lines have a different rhyme, and the fifth line calls back to the original rhyme. Limerick structure is intentionally simplistic, highlighting the absurdity of the subject matter and allowing the poet to focus more on wordplay. The B rhymes of the third and fourth lines build anticipation for the final reveal on the fifth line, where the author can reveal a witty subversion.
- **Slant Rhyme:** A slant rhyme is also known as a "near rhyme", "half rhyme" or "lazy rhyme". Slant rhymes sometimes have the same vowel sounds but different consonants, or the reverse. Slant rhymes are sometimes considered childish or uncreative, but many poets of have made use of them in order to avoid clichés, to create disharmony in a piece, or to draw unusual connections between words.
  - **Example:** "WHEN have I last looked on
The round green eyes and the long wavering bodies
Of the dark leopards of the moon?
All the wild witches, those most noble ladies"
– W. B. Yeats, "Lines Written in Dejection"

"*On*" and "*moon*" are slant rhymes, as are "*bodies*" and "*ladies*". This could be said to suggest the author's discordant, dejected state of mind. Perhaps in a happier poem these rhymes would be clearer and more musical. But not here.

- **Stanza:** A group of lines, offset by punctuation or spacing, forming a metrical unit or verse in a poem.
    - o **Example:** "Do not go gentle into that good night, / Old age should burn and rave at close of day; / Rage, rage against the dying of the light.

      Though wise men at their end know dark is right, / Because their words had forked no lightning they / Do not go gentle into that good night." – Dylan Thomas, "Do not go gentle into that good night".

      Each short stanza contains three lines and ends with either "do not go gentle into that good night" or "rage, rage against the dying of the light". This ending rhyme repeats throughout the entire poem, ensuring that each stanza delivers the essential message in a profound and affecting way.

- **Meter:** The basic rhythmic structure of a poem, the "music" of it. Some poetic forms prescribe their own metrical structure, but other poets invented or modified their own.
    - o **Example:** "Shall I compare thee to a summer's day? / Thou art more lovely and more temperate / Rough winds do shake the darling buds of May, / And summer's lease hath all too short a date." – William Shakespeare, "Sonnet 18".

Almost any poem could be said to have some form of meter, but Shakespeare's "iambic pentameter" is among the most famous styles. This metrical style is divided into "iambs", five of them per line, each containing a stressed and unstressed syllable. The pattern could be described as "ba-BUM, ba-BUM, ba-BUM", not unlike the beating of a heart. This metrical rhythm permeates Shakespeare's work, proving very attractive to actors who appreciate the clear, emphatic delivery.

- **Alliteration:** The use of repeated sounds at the start of words in quick succession. Alliteration is often used to draw attention to specific words or sounds, to lend emphasis to specific aspects of the poem. It can also be used to provide an entertaining and engaging voice to a poem.
    - o **Example:** "One short sleepe past, wee wake eternally, / And death shall be no more; death, thou shalt die." – John Donne, "Death Be Not Proud".

In this poem, the alliterative *W* and *D* sounds draw parallels between their respective words, and creating sort of a vocal punctuation for the line. A *D* sound begins the last line and a *D* sound ends it, creating a sense of urgency, of continuity and finality in the line.

- **Assonance:** Similar to alliteration, except that the repeated sounds are contained *within* certain words.
    - o **Example:** "And miles to go before I sleep, / And miles to go before I sleep." – Robert Frost, "Stopping by Woods on a Snowy Evening".

The repeated *O* sounds create a sense of speed and urgency. The sound carries us through the line, creating contrast with the *E* sound in "sleep", where both the narrator and reader finally rest.

- **Enjambment:** An enjambed line flows into the next without a break. No punctuation divides one line from the next, it simply continues.
    - o **Example:** "April is the cruellest month, breeding
      Lilacs out of the dead land, mixing
      Memory and desire, stirring
      Dull roots with spring rain." – T. S. Eliot, The Waste Land.

      Eliot's use of enjambment in *The Waste Land* creates a sense of suspense in the poem. The action of breeding, mixing, and stirring are lent equal or superior importance to the actual subjects these actions are done to. The enjambment also creates a slant rhyme as well, with each line ending on an "-ing" until we arrive at "rain".

- **Free Verse:** Poetry that avoids an identifiable meter or rhyme scheme could be said to be "free". The style became more popular amongst avant-guarde, modern, and post-modern poets. It was comparatively rare in classical poetry.
    - o **Example:**
      i carry your heart with me(i carry it in
      my heart)i am never without it(anywhere
      i go you go,my dear;and whatever is done
      by only me is your doing,my darling)
      – e e cummings, "i carry your heart with me".

Cummings' style shirked literary conventions, creating poems that challenged traditional assumptions about form and aesthetic appeal through his use of strange capitalization, heavy enjambment, and free verse. Cummings' poems defy clear explanation, but some critics suggest he wrote in this manner to evoke a childish, earnest state of mind.

- **Metaphor:** An indirect comparison between two things, denoting one object or action in place of another to suggest a comparison between them. This is distinct from a **simile**, which directly compares two things using words such as "like" or "as".
    - o **Example:** "I'm a riddle in nine syllables, / An elephant, a ponderous house, / A melon strolling on two tendrils. / O red fruit, ivory, fine timbers!" – Sylvia Plath, "Metaphors".

Appropriately enough, Sylvia Plath's "Metaphors" contains several playful metaphors used to describe her pregnancy. Plath uses herself as a subject, comparing her pregnant state to an elephant, a melon, and in several ways to a shelter for the life growing inside her. At first the metaphors seem self-deprecating and humorous, but later in the poem, where she calls herself a "means, a stage" and mentions how she's "boarded the train there's no getting off", the metaphors take on darker connotation as they reflect her dehumanization and resigned acceptance that she's become merely an incubator for the child she now carries.

- **Sonnet:** A poetic form that originated in Italy, consisting of fourteen lines which follow a clear alternating rhyme scheme. Conventions of sonnets have shifted through the centuries, and the form has proved popular in England, Italy, and France.
    - **Example:**

      Do not stand at my grave and weep:
      I am not there; I do not sleep.
      I am a thousand winds that blow,
      I am the diamond glints on snow,
      I am the sun on ripened grain,
      I am the gentle autumn rain.
      When you awaken in the morning's hush
      I am the swift uplifting rush
      Of quiet birds in circling flight.
      I am the soft starshine at night.
      Do not stand at my grave and cry:
      I am not there; I did not die.
      – Mary Elizabeth Frye, "Do not stand at my grave and weep".

      This sonnet showcases much of what is attractive about the form to poets. The simple rhyme scheme is unpretentious and readable, and the poem's format lends itself well to repetition. The repeated "I am's" creating a soothing rhythm, sort of a lullaby quality. The subject matter is bittersweet, as with many sonnets that have explored romance, mortality, or spirituality. The first and last two lines mirror each other, suggesting change and finality. The poem's subject matter insists we not fear the end, and this is reflected in the sonnet's form.

- **Imagery:** Any sequence of words that refers to a sensory experience can be considered imagery. Rather than merely describing the visual aspect of something, imagery often relies on taste, touch, smell, or sound to draw a fuller portrait of the subject.
    - **Example:**

      "Whirl up, sea—
      Whirl your pointed pines,
      Splash your great pines
      On our rocks,
      Hurl your green over us—
      Cover us with your pools of fir." – Hilda Doolittle, "Oread".

Doolittle's poem neatly encapsulates a style known as Imagism, a short-lived movement in the early 20th century that sought to reduce poetic language to its barest components. Each line, each word in this poem reveals something new – Doolittle likens a forest to a sea (or perhaps a sea to a forest), encouraging us to imagine green trees like torrential waves, evoking sound, color, and texture to maintain this dual metaphor. The poem is unique in that there is no "correct" image. Both the sea and the forest are equally valid interpretations of this poem, drawn together by their shared sensory features.

- **Onomatopoeia:** A "sound effect", a word that imitates that actual sound it describes. "Buzz" or "hiss" both sound like the actions of buzzing or hissing.
  - **Example:** "I chatter over stony ways, / In little sharps and trebles, / I bubble into eddying bays, / I babble on the pebbles." – Alfred, Lord Tennyson, "The Brook".

    The onomatopoeia in Tennyson's "The Brook" evoke the sounds of its subject. The assonant *B* and *T* sounds suggest the burbling of a river.
- **Personification:** When human qualities are applied to a non-human entity, such as an animal, an emotion, an object, or something more esoteric.
  - **Example:** "Let the rain kiss you / Let the rain beat upon your head with silver liquid drops / Let the rain sing you a lullaby" – Langston Hughes, "April Rain Song".

    In this poem, Hughes suggests that the rain has the human ability to kiss and to sing. Rather than merely describing pleasant, "realistic" aspects of rain, he personifies it as a friendly, motherly figure to better describe his feelings towards rain.
- **Couplet:** A pair of rhyming lines with the same meter. A "heroic couplet" is a couplet in iambic pentameter that is "self-contained" and not enjambed. Shakespeare often ended his sonnets with a heroic couplet, allowing the piece to build towards a climactic, self-contained final rhyme that delivered the sonnet's chief message.
  - **Example:** "Sol thro' white Curtains shot a tim'rous Ray, / And op'd those Eyes that must eclipse the Day; / Now Lapdogs give themselves the rowzing Shake, / And sleepless Lovers, just at Twelve, awake:" – Alexander Pope, "Rape of the Lock".

    Pope's "Rape of the Lock" is a satirical narrative poem written entirely in heroic couplets. The subject matter of the piece, regarding a baron's attempts to gain a lock of a woman's hair, is silly and banal. Thus, the constant use of triumphant, heroic couplets renders the whole thing a bizarre parody.
- **Narrative poem:** Appropriately enough, a narrative poem is a poem that tells a story. It can make use of narrators, characters, plot, setting, and other literary devices, though they often contain more poetic features, such as rhyme, meter, and metaphor. An "epic poem" is a type of narrative poem that's usually lengthy and recounts heroic deeds and mythology.
  - **Example:** "By the shore of Gitche Gumee,
By the shining Big-Sea-Water,
At the doorway of his wigwam,
In the pleasant Summer morning,
Hiawatha stood and waited."

– Henry Wadsworth Longfellow, "The Song of Hiawatha".

Longfellow's epic poem, "The Song of Hiawatha", recalls the mythologized exploits of the titular Native American hero. Hiawatha is based on a few historical persons, but as with much epic poetry, his exploits are expanded into something superhuman.

When setting out to interpret a poem, authorial intention is a good starting point. What message was the author intending to convey with the piece? Read it through a few times, and pause to consider words or references you don't understand. Start with the easy solution, not every poem is a labyrinth of mysterious interpretations. Consider the fact that, in an enduring poem, nothing happens by accident. Each line, each word was selected very carefully by the poet for a specific effect. This will allow you to go deeper off of your original assessment of the poem, and to infer the meaning of unclear references and unusual devices.

Example Analysis

The following is one of the most revered poems in the English canon, "Ozymandias" by Percy Bysshe Shelley. Read it through, and see what your initial reactions are. Try reading it out loud as well. Some poems are better understand when heard.

I met a traveller from an antique land

Who said: "Two vast and trunkless legs of stone

Stand in the desert . . . Near them, on the sand,

Half sunk, a shattered visage lies, whose frown,

And wrinkled lip, and sneer of cold command,

Tell that its sculptor well those passions read

Which yet survive, stamped on these lifeless things,

The hand that mocked them, and the heart that fed:

And on the pedestal these words appear:

'My name is Ozymandias, king of kings:

Look on my works, ye Mighty, and despair!'

Nothing beside remains. Round the decay

Of that colossal wreck, boundless and bare

The lone and level sands stretch far away."

First, let's summarize the literal basics. What is the "story" of this poem? What is the "plot", the actual event being described? Our narrator is unnamed, and the story is told by him second hand, a tale he recalls from some traveler from an "antique land". The traveler describes a two pillars of stone he found in the endless desert, and next to them lay a shattered stone face, well-carved but slowly eroding away. Beside the face is a pedestal telling of some "king of kings", Ozymandias, who declares his "works" would cause even the mighty to despair. What "works" this describes is not clear to the traveler, for they seem to have crumbled to dust in the endless centuries, leaving only sand as far as the eye can see.

On a surface level, this is a simple tale of a stranger remembering a statue he found in the desert. Why is this important? Why did Shelley find this necessary to recount?

To answer this, we need to look past what is literally stated to find what is implied. We can infer that the pedestal once referred to some grander structure, a monument perhaps, or maybe a castle or city. The face and pillars, at the very least, likely towered above the desert sometime in the past, depicting their fearsome subject for all to see. Surely this Ozymandias must have been wealthy to erect such a large sculpture, and it is telling that he wished to be depicted with a commanding sneer. The face was carved by some sculptor who either feared or greatly revered his subject. Ozymandias fancied himself a conqueror, one who would inspire awe in all who saw his monument.

But it did not last. The monument is crumbling, the desert around it is bare. Even this traveler from his "antique land" knows nothing of great Ozymandias except what he read on some plinth in the desert. Why did Ozymandias fade from memory? Who can say? Whatever great and terrible things Ozymandias accomplished, it was not enough to save him or his memory from the ravages of time.

The pedestal thus becomes sadly ironic – whereas once the mighty may have despaired upon seeing a fearsome monument that dwarfed them, today they will despair upon seeing that even the "king of kings", Ozymandias, has been forgotten for all time. Shelley is trying to teach us that even the mightiest of conquerors can die and be forgotten. Time waits for no man.

What poetic devices are on display here? The poem is a sonnet, though not a typical one. There is a rhyme scheme but it is far less pronounced than in most sonnets – it makes frequent use of slant rhymes, such as "stone" and "frown" or "fear" and "despair", and the enjambment of the piece alters its flow, preventing "sing-song" rhymes from appearing. It contains no heroic couplet. The poem also features iambic pentameter, though it is less pronounced than in works such as Shakespeare's. Each line contains five iambs of two syllables each, with exactly one exception: line 10, "my name is Ozymandias", breaks the ten syllable pattern, offering eleven syllables instead. Perhaps this is Shelley's way of drawing attention to that line and to Ozymandias himself. Truly, Ozymandias was so great that even sonnet form could not contain him.

The poem also makes sparing using of alliteration, particularly in the last two lines with "boundless and bare" and "lone and level sands stretch". This seems to be Shelley's substitute for the heroic couplet. Rather than offering a two-line rhyme to announce the poem's final thought, he builds more subtly with alliterative turns of phrase that offset the final words "far away". This is the note he leaves us on. There is nothing in the desert but sand, lone and level, boundless and bare. This is what history remembers and this is what he offers as his final word on the subject. It is also worth noting that the poem is told second hand – even the narrator is hearing about this from some nameless traveler from a nameless land. He's simply repeating what he heard. The great Ozymandias has been reduced to a half-remembered plaque in some forgotten desert that our raconteur thinks he remembered a stranger describe.

That's a heavy message for such a short poem, and it is Shelley's mastery of poetic forms that allow him to deliver it so forcefully. An MTEL English exam will likely require you to interpret a poem along a more specific guideline, such as how it might reflect the styles and forms of a specific movement of poetry. But if you can demonstrate a strong core knowledge of poetic style, you will have little trouble passing the exam.

Drama

Drama is the primary expression of narrative in performance. Any type of creative display involving performers and an audience could be said to have its roots in drama. In Greek, the word **drama** means "action", derived from the verb form *draō*, meaning "to do" or "to act". More specifically, "drama" often refers to a composition of verse or prose, delivered to a live audience, involving characters and a conflict of some sort. Thus, things that are not true drama, such as poems, songs, or real-life situations that contain elements of conflict and high emotion are often said to be *dramatic*. Drama is also a unique art form in that is, by necessity, collaborative - an author needs only a pen and paper to write a story, but a drama requires multiple voices, such as actors, authors, and directors of some kind, to deliver the performance, as well as an audience to receive it. Drama is a fundamental understanding of storytelling that stretches back to the earliest creations in the western canon.

Ancient Greek Drama

The first Western dramatists to record their works were the Greeks, and it is from their experiments that much of our modern dramatic structures are derived. It was the understanding of Greek dramatists like Sophocles, Aeschylus, and Euripides, that drama was governed by the laws of comedy and tragedy, represented by the famous grinning and weeping masks. The Greeks saw a clear delineation between comedy and tragedy, deciding that essentially, a comedy could be defined as a drama with a happy ending whereas a tragedy would have a sad one. This terminology continued up through the Renaissance, where even the works of Shakespeare and Marlowe can be clearly separated into comedies and tragedies. Comedies, to the Greeks, were life-affirming romps, often containing satire, clowning, and jokes involving scatological references and innuendo.

Tragedies, on the other hand, were serious business. The "Greek Tragedy" is considered the most enduring gift of the ancient Greeks. The most famous of these is the *Oedipus The King*, Sophocles' magnum opus, describing the rise and fall of the mighty Oedipus, doomed by fate to slay his father and marry his mother. A common trope in Greek tragedy is the prophecy, delivering the will of the gods to the hero via an oracle, which the hero ignores or seeks to defy more often than not. This reveals the hero's ***hamartia***, his fatal flaw that brings about his downfall. For Oedipus, this is ***hubris***, a great pride that sets him above the will of the gods and thus incurs their wrath. In the play, Oedipus was a brilliant man, able to solve the Sphinx's riddle and become king of Thebes, but even his vaunted intellect could not save him from his prophecy. In a fit of blind rage, King Oedipus slays a traveler he meets on the road, later revealed to be his father, Laius. He also unwittingly took his mother, Jocasta, to bride, who bore him four children before their true relationship was uncovered. In true tragic form, the play ends with a ***catharsis***, a cleansing act brought on by extreme emotion: Jocasta hangs herself due to shame, and Oedipus, upon finding the body, takes the pins from her dress and plunges them into his eyes.

These concepts as outlined by the Greeks would go on to define Western drama for millennia, even as drama declined in relevance over the centuries as European languages evolved and borders were drawn. Most performance in Europe up to the Middle Ages was strictly religious in nature: drama amongst the working classes amounted to little more than campfire stories and folk songs, whereas the church dabbled in live re-enactments, feeling they could be a useful imparting Biblical tales to the illiterate masses. High drama for the purposes of entertainment or art was little known. This changed in the 16th century with the rise of vernacular English, or "Middle English", and the flowering of literary giants like Christopher Marlowe, John Webster, and William Shakespeare.

British Dramatists

Considered perhaps the greatest and most influential author in the English language, **William Shakespeare** wrote 39 plays, 154 sonnets, and two long-form poems, displaying a mastery of language that has a larger influence on the Western canon of drama than any other figure. He invented or popularized roughly 1700 words that are in common use to this day (only Geoffrey Chaucer can claim to have created nearly as many), and displayed a stunning deftness with the tropes and forms common in Greek tragedy, immortalizing their styles for centuries to come.

Like the Greeks, Shakespeare divided his works into comedies and tragedies, with a few historical plays belonging to neither category. Shakespeare's tragedies exhibit many Greek forms: in the tragedy of *Macbeth*, for instance, the plot is set in motion by supernatural forces, though Shakespeare substitutes three meddlesome witches for an oracle. Macbeth, our protagonist, possesses the hamartia of ambition – he seeks to become king of Scotland, and is driven to commit many terrible crimes in this pursuit. In the end, this destroys him, as the honorable MacDuff avenges the deaths of his family by beheading Macbeth in single combat, thus bringing peace and order back to the realm, albeit at a terrible cost. The comedies of Shakespeare, likewise, are light-hearted romps involving romance, wordplay, physical comedy, and numerous innuendos.

Shakespeare dabbled in satire and social commentary, but his works are still fundamentally religious and pro-status quo. More often than not, order is restored through royal decree or divine intervention. Conflicts have a tendency to resolve themselves or peter out entirely, as is the case in *Much Ado About Nothing*, where the villainous Don John is captured by unnamed soldiers with no help from the main characters. This kind of abrupt conclusion harkens back to another term coined by the ancient Greeks: the ***deus ex machina***, a sudden conclusion brought on by forces not previously established in the play. In Greek plays, it was not uncommon for the action to be resolved by the appearance of a literal god onstage. Zeus may appear, brandishing thunderbolts, to destroy the wicked, punish the prideful, and restore the natural order of things, before disappearing just as suddenly. Even the Greeks considered the deus ex machina to be a hallmark of lazy writing, Aristotle being one of the trope's most famous critics, but the plot device endured in the works of Shakespeare, sometimes as tongue-in-cheek parody, and other times as an earnest expression of the belief that godly order will naturally assert itself, even in bizarre or dangerous situations.

Stylistically, Shakespeare's works reveal an astounding command of the nascent English language. Though he invented many words and phrases that became common to English speakers, his dialogue was intentionally heightened and unrealistic for dramatic effect. Shakespeare wrote in **blank verse**, a type of poetic style involving regular metrical lines with only occasional rhymes. Each line in blank verse has the same poetic meter, consisting of equal syllables on each line. More specifically, Shakespeare's style of blank verse made use of **iambic pentameter**, a style innovated by Shakespeare's contemporary Christopher Marlowe, which uses ten syllables per line divided into five "feet" consisting of a stressed and unstressed syllable. This creates sort of a galloping or heartbeat cadence for each line, a *buh-BUM buh-BUM buh-BUM* rhythm that has proved attractive to actors for centuries. The limitations imposed by iambic pentameter are numerous, but Shakespeare mastered the form, creating dialogue that was heightened enough to be dramatic yet witty and ribald enough to be understood and enjoyed by the common listener.

The styles of Renaissance artists like Shakespeare and Marlowe, as well as the Greeks who inspired them, provided much inspiration for English and American dramatists in the centuries to come. The first professional theater company to perform in America, the Lewis Hallam troupe, staged Shakespeare's *The Merchant of Venice* in Williamsburg, Virginia in 1752. Their run in the colonies was a mild success, though theater companies struggled to find an audience in more conservative areas where Puritan communities considered theater to be, at best, a frivolous distraction and at worst, blasphemy. It was not until after the Revolutionary War, where the populace had been inspired by the fiery orations of leaders like Patrick Henry ("Give me liberty or give me death!") and the lean, aggressive prose of authors like Thomas Paine, that American drama would find its own identity.

American Dramatists

William Dunlap is considered the father of American theater. A painter, historian, and artist, Dunlap produced over sixty plays in his career, many of them being translations of German or French works displaying a broad knowledge of politics and a fierce loyalty to the newly minted American identity. His most famous works include *Andre*, a tragedy that dramatizes the trial of Major John Andre, a British soldier who was hanged as a spy for his support of Benedict Arnold, and *The Italian Father*, a comedy which borrowed heavily from the works of English dramatist Thomas Dekker.

In the 19th century, American theater was largely melodramatic. American authors mimicked the style of the classical greats who inspired them, creating broad and operatic pieces dealing with issues of class, race, and the American dream. *Uncle Tom's Cabin* was by far the most popular American play of the 1800s. Due to sparsely-enforced copyright laws and the immense popularity of **Harriet Beecher Stowe**'s source novel, many "Tom shows" were performed throughout the United States and England, incorporating elements of heightened soap opera and blackface minstrelsy. Though the novel is staunchly anti-slavery, it resorts heavily to stereotypes, and theaters portrayed these with varying degrees of sensitivity and clownishness. It was not uncommon at this time for white actors to portray black characters, complete with darkened faces and exaggerated African-American dialects, and the various "Tom shows" and minstrel shows this spawned dominated the American theatrical scene for some time. These shows often validated the racist attitudes of Americans instead of challenging them, and they became symbolic of the American South's troubled history with race.

The 20th century saw a flowering of American theater. The Civil War, the Depression, and the rise of mechanization and industry left many Americans nostalgic for simpler times and confused about the modern world they lived in, with its promises of a mythical American Dream. The early quarter of the century was dominated by vaudeville revues featuring circus acts, burlesque, music, and fast-paced comedy. After WWII, American drama would finally discover its own voice in the works of Eugene O'Neill, Tennessee Williams, and Arthur Miller, each of whom would explore distinctly American themes relating to family, individuality, sexuality, and the failings of a capitalist system.

Eugene O'Neill was born into a family with deep ties to the theater. His father, James O'Neill, was considered one of the greatest actors of his generation, at least until he squandered his career playing in a successful production of *The Count of Monte Cristo* for a full six thousand performances, causing many critics to label him a sell-out. The family James built with his wife, Mary Ellen Quinlan, was rife with dysfunction, alcohol abuse, and emotional manipulation. Eugene dropped out of school at a young age and spent several years at sea, struggling with alcoholism and depression. He became a popular fixture in Greenwich village's literary scene before writing his first play, *Beyond the Horizon*, in 1920. The play would win the young author a Pulitzer Prize for Drama. O'Neill would earn three more of the prizes over his vaunted career, an unprecedented accomplishment for any author.

Other great works by O'Neill include *Strange Interlude*, *Anna Christie*, *The Hairy Ape*, and his masterpiece, *Long Day's Journey Into Night*, which depicts in brutal detail the emotional manipulation and substance abuse that turned his childhood into a living hell. O'Neill was among the first authors to explore American vernacular as a legitimate dialect of the theater. His works often dealt with alcoholism and masculinity, and his plays often featured characters who lived on the fringes of society, such as prostitutes, addicts, and homeless people. O'Neill was also the first author to write a major play starring an African-American in a serious role: *The Emperor Jones*, which was influential in the black literary community despite resorting to stereotypes to get its message across. O'Neill died in 1953 after years of declining health, with his final play, *Long Day's Journey*, being considered one of the greatest dramatic achievements of all time.

Like his contemporary, **Tennessee Williams** struggled with various addictions and depression throughout his life, channeling these struggles into his plays. Williams was also a closeted homosexual – this revelation, an open secret during much of Williams' career but not formally acknowledged until after his death, has caused many critics to re-evaluate Williams' works from a new perspective. The machismo and violence of many of his male characters, such as the brutish Stanley Kowalski from *A Streetcar Named Desire*, represents a stern commentary by Williams on the strict gender roles that had caused him to hide his sexuality for much of his life. Williams' was also very close with his sister, Rose, who was diagnosed with schizophrenia at a young age and spent much of her life in institutions. Williams used her as an inspiration for many similar characters, such as the disabled Laura in *The Glass Menagerie* and even in *Streetcar's* Blanche Dubois, who suffers a mental breakdown at the end of the play after being preyed upon by the overly masculine Stanley.

Williams other works deal with the identity of the American South and the notion of the "fading Southern belle", an upper class woman struggling with new realities after her money runs out and her looks begin to go. This trope is explored in some of Williams' best works, such as *Cat on a Hot Tin Roof*, *Orpheus Descending*, and *The Glass Menagerie*, in which the mother, Amanda, wishes to recapture her glamorous youth by living vicarious through Laura, whose illness prevents her from socializing. Williams was also instrumental in advancing the careers of great talents like director Elia Kazan, and actors Kate Hepburn and Marlon Brando, the latter of whom originated the role of Stanley Kowalski, considered by many to be one of the great stage performances of all time.

Arthur Miller's output was largely concerned with the social upheaval of the 1950s. He was forced to testify in front of Senator Joseph McCarthy's House Un-American Activities committee to ascertain his supposed communist sympathies, and he became a controversial voice during the period known as the Red Scare. This formed the basis for his classic play, *The Crucible,* which explores the paranoia of the time by transplanting it back to the Salem Witch Trials. His other great works include *All My Sons*, a tragic play centering around a family business and WWII, and *Death of a Salesman*, which follows fading businessman Willy Loman as he slides into obscurity and purposelessness. Miller's works were harshly critical of the American Dream, prompting Sen. McCarthy's interest in attacking Miller's reputation. Miller's career survived the hearings, though he did out several of his contemporaries as communist sympathizers.

Modern American Drama

In the latter half of the 20th century, American theater became a dominant cultural force, even as the popularity of the art form was long-since eclipsed by film. The Civil Rights movement of the 1960s spurring many new plays dealing with issues of race, such as Lorraine Hansberry's *A Raisin in the Sun*, which followed the struggles of a black family in Chicago. The play won a Pulitzer Prize, making Hansberry the first African-American to win the award. Her works were heavily influenced by the Harlem Renaissance of the

1920s, a movement amongst black intellectuals such as Langston Hughes and Zora Neale Hurston to forge a new African-American identity in the United States through artistic and political action in the Harlem neighborhood of New York.

In recent years, American drama has proven to be experimental and uncompromising, displaying a facility with both naturalistic and heightened dialogue as well as finding strong humanity in characters from all walks of life. Dominant theatrical voices since the 1950s include David Mamet (*Glengarry Glen Ross*, *Speed-The-Plow*), Neil Simon (*Lost in Yonkers*, *The Odd Couple*), Henry David Hwang (*M. Butterfly*), and Tony Kushner (*Angels in America*). American drama continues to explore themes of sexuality, race, class, and gender as they affect all walks of life. The forms and styles owe a heavy debt to Renaissance artists like Shakespeare and the Greek forerunners that inspired them, but the soul is distinctly American.

OBJECTIVE 0008 UNDERSTAND LITERARY THEORY AND CRITICISM.

For example: various critical approaches to literature (e.g., New Criticism, structuralism, deconstructionism, New Historicism, Marxist criticism, feminism, reader response); the role of major works in classical literary criticism and the theories associated with them; characteristics of neoclassic and Romantic literary theory as developed in major writings associated with each movement; and the use of various critical perspectives to analyze given literary passages.

Originating hundreds of years ago, **literary theory** has given readers the opportunity to analyze texts from a variety of angles. These angles, also known as lenses, invite the reader to question different elements of a story to gain a better understanding of the meaning behind the text. Biographical, sociological, economic, and stylistic influences can produce different meanings for the same text. One might consider: the author's background, the era in which they were raised, their religious outlook, their sexual orientation, their financial stability, and their views on government. Intentional stylistic patterns, well-crafted literary devices, and a persuasive point of view also have an impact on meaning and interpretation.

Here is a broad timeline of literary theory, from BC to present day:

~360 BC-present	Moral Criticism, Dramatic Construction
1920s-present	Structuralism
1930s-present	New Criticism, Formalism
1930s-present	Psychoanalytic Criticism
1930s-present	Marxist Criticism
1960s-present	Reader-Response Criticism
1960s-present	Deconstruction
1960s-present	Feminist Criticism

New Criticism

New Criticism emphasizes the importance of both structure and semantics when doing an analysis of a text. External factors, such as the identity of the author, the society in which he or she lives, and/or the author's overall intentions for the work are not taken into consideration. Proponents of New Criticism believe the literary text itself is the paramount concern.

When an analysis is performed, a text is evaluated and interpreted through *close reading*. The goal of close reading is to arrive, without biographical or sociological distractions, at an objective understanding and appreciation of a literary work. Close reading emphasizes the relationship between the form in which the text is written and the meaning. Patterns within the text, imagery, point of view, and literary devices all play a role in determining the impact form may have on overall meaning.

Structuralism and Deconstructionism

Like New Criticism, the structural approach does not take external influences into consideration. Structuralism simply examines the structure of a literary work. Following the same guidelines of Formalism, emphasis is placed on the work as a whole and its literary form.

Formulated by Jacques Derrida in the 1960s, Deconstructionism takes an extremely detailed analytical approach. The text is broken down (deconstructed) and questioned piece by piece. A reader becomes more critical and skeptical when analyzing the intended meaning within the writing. The author's background and the context in which the text was written has no impact on the meaning, according to this theory.

Marxist Criticism

Based on the ideas of Karl Marx, Marxism can be viewed as taking the opposite approach when compared to New Criticism, Deconstructionism, and Structuralism. This lens focuses specifically on dialectic, environmental, and socioeconomic influence. For example, politics (particularly the Capitalist system) and religion are easily identifiable when views are reflected within literature.

Some of the key components of this critical theory include:

- General conflicts within class systems.
- Capitalist or bourgeoisie (those who possess and control economic capital) exploitation and oppression of the proletariat (the working classes) for economic and political gains.
- Overthrowing capitalists and their socio-economic system, resulting in a "dictatorship of the proletariat."
- Creating a classless society in which most private property is abolished in favor of collective ownership.
- A "workers' paradise," created by a unitary, worldwide socialist society free of class conflict.
- The inevitable triumph of capitalism.

- The Marxist doctrine's validation by its' scientific and materialist approach to history.
- Social injustice and the abuse of power.

A few works of interest to Marxist scholars include:

- *The Jungle* by Upton Sinclair;
- Stephen Crane's *Maggie, a Girl of the Streets*;
- Theodore Dreiser's *Sister Carrie* and *An American Tragedy*;
- John Steinbeck's *Grapes of Wrath*;
- Virginia Woolf's *A Room of One's Own*; and
- Fyodor Dostoevsky's *Crime and Punishment* and *The Brothers Karamazov*.

When viewing a text with a Marxist lens, questions that may guide your analysis include:

- What is the social class of the main character(s)?
- What is the political view of the author?
- What time period was this written (keeping a focus on political activities)?
- What is the social class of the author?
- What is the religion of the author?
- Does the social class or religion of the author differ from what is being represented within the text?
- Was the goal of this text to be informative or persuasive?
- Who will benefit from reading this text?

Feminist Criticism

Feminist critics emphasize the ways that literary works are informed and inspired by an author's gender, their opinions about gender and gender roles, and societal norms in which the author has been immersed in. Of prime concern to the feminist critical enterprise is the advocacy of women as intellectual, social, and artistic equals to men. Some feminists emphasize class, others race, still others sexual orientation, when critiquing texts or social norms and conditions affecting women's lives. Feminist criticism is not limited to works by women, nor is it hostile or opposed to male writers or males in general. It simply promotes a level playing field.

When introducing feminist writing and criticism to high school students, teachers should consider giving a comprehensive summary of what feminism is, along with historical details that explain when, where, and why it arose. While more modern topics might include equal rights in the workplace, maternity leave, abortion rights, and equal pay, it is important to note that feminism has existed for over 200 years. To educate students beyond the 1960s feminist movement, teachers can explore works by these eighteenth or nineteenth-century authors with their classes:

- Mary Wollstonecraft
- Margaret Fuller
- Sojourner Truth

- Susan B. Anthony
- Elizabeth Cady Stanton
- Frederick Douglass
- Virginia Woolf
- Charlotte Perkins Gillman

Some popular twentieth-century works relevant to feminist thought and suitable for high school students are listed below:

- *A Room of One's Own* by Virginia Woolf (nonfiction)
- *The Yellow Wallpaper* by Charlotte Perkins Gilman (novella)
- *The Color Purple* by Alice Walker (novel)
- *Beloved* by Toni Morrison (novel)
- *Good Woman* by Lucille Clifton (poems)
- *She Had Some Horses* by Joy Harjo (poems)
- *The Joy Luck Club* by Amy Tan (novel)
- *The Secret Life of Bees* by Sue Monk Kidd (novel)

There are numerous up-to-date anthologies of women's literature and feminist criticism available through major publishers. The groundbreaking anthology, *The New Feminist Criticism*, edited by Elaine Showalter, offers an excellent variety of feminist essays on Western literature. Although some of these essays are dated, the collection gives an overview of key concerns that animated "second wave" feminism in the 1960s and 70s.

A few suggestions for writing prompts to fit in a unit on feminism include:

- Should men and women have equality in today's society?
- How has life in America been affected by women's campaigns for equal rights?
- What are your thoughts about gender-based roles, norms, and social expectations in today's America?
- When do you think women will gain access to equal pay?
- What control should the government have over a woman's reproductive rights?
- What do you believe the standard maternity leave should be in our country?

Using a feminist lens, these prompts allow students to compare and contrast their personal beliefs, while incorporating the views of those expressed in a literary work or works listed above.

Psychoanalytic, or Freudian, criticism

Based initially on the works of Sigmund Freud in the late 1800s, this theory has been expanded to include the ideas of other psychoanalysts.

Freudian psychoanalysis holds that the human mind is a tripartite structure (divided into three parts) composed of:

- *id*, which generates and seeks to satisfy all of a person's urges and desires;
- the *superego*, which "polices" and counters the id;
- and the *ego*, which is the psychic result of the id/superego conflict. The ego is characterized by a person's thoughts and behaviors.

The formation of human character—including sexual behavior—begins at birth. The infant is said to pass through various stages—the oral stage, the anal stage, and so on—as its needs and urges arise and are either satisfied or frustrated; and as it learns (or doesn't learn) to master human relationships and bodily functions.

All humans are said to have inexorable conflicts between drives such as Eros (the sex drive) and Thanatos (the death wish), which are also played out in the contests between id and superego.

Neurotic behavior results from fixations on one of the above physical factors, or from an imbalance in the powers of the id and superego, or from deeply embedded (unconscious) memories of pleasant or unpleasant experiences, or from a combination of these. Neurosis is usually rooted in infancy or early childhood.

To discover the nature of a person's mind, the psychoanalyst looks for recurrent thoughts, images, speech patterns, and behaviors evident in the person being analyzed. By carefully observing and listening to a patient, the psychoanalyst uncovers previously unknown truths about the how's and why's of the patient's predicament.

The psychoanalytic literary critic applies Freudian theories to writings and authors in order to better understand the psychological underpinnings of literary works, writers, and, sometimes, society itself. Topics that will assist in analyzing a text from a Freudian perspective might include:

- The author's mental state
- Strange patterns of obsession or fascination (for example, death)
- The author's intention for provoking certain feelings in the reader
- Hidden meanings
- Evidence of writing in the subconscious

Writers that have garnered much attention from Freudian critics include Edgar Allen Poe, the Marquis de Sade, Moses, Madame de Stahl, and William S. Burroughs. Not surprisingly, sex and violence feature prominently in these writers' works. Representative examples of psychoanalytic criticism include "Moses and Monotheism" by Sigmund Freud, and *Edgar Allen Poe* by Marie Bonaparte.

Stories and poems by Poe that directly relate to one or another facet of Freudian thought include:

"The Tell-Tale Heart,"

"The Black Cat,"

"The Fall of the House of Usher,"

"The Premature Burial,"

"The Cask of Amontillado," and

"The Raven," and "Annabelle Lee. "

Reader-Response

In this critical theory, readers create meaning through individual understandings and responses. Some critics focus solely on the readers' experiences. Others experiment with defined groups to determine reader response. The author, context, and style of the text are all second to the reader's personal connection to the writing.

A pioneer in reader response theory, Louise Rosenblatt paved the way on the concept of treating the relationship between the reader and the text as a transaction. Her famous text, *Literature as Exploration*, explains and facilitates the interaction one might have with a piece of writing.

Neoclassic and Romantic

The Neoclassic Period (1660-1798) is associated with such authors as John Dryden and Alexander Pope. Because this period followed the Renaissance, many of the stylistic patterns used by the Romans and Greeks can be found in the literature of this era. The Neoclassic Period is known as the time of the "quarrel with the Ancients and the Moderns." The Neoclassicists argued that the classics were not the last word in literature, only a foundation upon which to develop an even higher art form.

The Neoclassic Period can be broken into three parts:

- The Restoration Period (1660-1700)
    - John Milton - *Paradise Lost*
- The Augustan Period (1700-1750)
    - Daniel Defoe - *Robinson Crusoe*
- The Age of Johnson (1750-1798)
    - Samuel Johnson - *The Dictionary of the English Language*

The classical ideals of proportion, common sense, and reason were still preferred over raw emotion and imagination, yet the purpose of prose and poetry was not to extol these ideals but to use them to instruct and teach. Prose often came in the form of an essay, whereas the ode dominated poetry.. These writers were critics of their age and employed wit and satire to expose the foibles and of human nature. They paid a great deal of attention to where they stood in a larger social context.

Few did this better than Pope, who in his "Essay on Man" finds that, although capable of reason, the sentient human being does not always employ it. Not using this gift gives rise to a form of evil, which Pope identifies as coming from humankind's failure to live up to its divine potential, making humanity "The glory, jest, and riddle of the world."

The Romantic Movement (1798-1870) is perhaps best defined by what poet Matthew Arnold referred to as an "intellectual and spiritual passion for beauty." During this period of literature, a great emphasis was placed on feelings, emotions, and passions. Art, music, and appreciation for nature were essential components of this literary style.

While the writers of the Neoclassic Period still honored the classical ideals of reason and common sense, the Romantics believed the emotions held the key to a higher perception of reality. The most notable work from this time period is *Lyrical Ballads*, a collection of poems by William Wordsworth and Samuel Taylor Coleridge. This collection is said to have been the start of the Romantic period. John Keats, another prominent Romantic poet, spoke of the importance of an artist's sense of self. Some of his major works include "Hyperion" and "Ode on a Grecian Urn."

Another extremely influential Romantic, William Blake, viewed the rationalism of the preceding period as cold, analytical, and essentially inhumane. Believing that the imagination was the sole route to reviving a world that had been lost to reason, Blake argued for the supremacy of the emotions and imagination—to the point of mysticism. Some of his major works include "Songs of Innocence," "Songs of Experience," and "Mock on, Mock on, Voltaire, Rousseau."

OBJECTIVE 0009 UNDERSTAND THE STRUCTURE AND DEVELOPMENT OF THE ENGLISH LANGUAGE.

For example: structural features of languages (e.g., phonological, morphological, syntactic, semantic); historical, social, cultural, and technological influences shaping English language structure and use; significant historical events influencing the development of the English language (e.g., Anglo-Saxon migrations; the Norman Conquest); and additions to the lexicon of the English language throughout its development (e.g., words from Latin and French, regional and social dialects in the United States, words derived from technology).

Known as the smallest unit of language, a **morpheme** is used to develop words. Morphemes, unlike words, do not always have the ability to stand alone. Their meaning is most significant when combined to create a word. They can be broken down into three categories: prefixes, suffixes, and root words. The prefix and suffix are simply added to a root word to create meaning.

For example:

Un- (Prefix)	-deny- (Root)	-able (Suffix)
Un- (Prefix)	-believe- (Root)	-able (Suffix)
Socio- (Prefix)	-path- (Root)	
Arachno-	-phobia-	

(Prefix)	(Root)	
	-pharmac- (Root)	-ist (Suffix)
	-tract- (Root)	-or (Suffix)

While it would be near impossible to include every morpheme, here are a few examples of prefixes and suffixes:

Prefixes	Suffixes
Anti-	-able
De-	-ary
Dis-	-er
Ex-	-full
Pre-	-ian
Post-	-ism
Sub-	-ist
Un-	-ly

Morphology identifies meaning in words built from morphemes, and **phonology** focuses on the sounds. There is a systematic combination of sounds included in each and every word. When broken down, **phonemes** are the smallest unit of sound in a word. They are often composed of a single letter.

While linguistic texts do not all agree on the exact number, there are approximately 44 units of sound in the English language:

Phoneme	Options for spelling	Examples
/b/	b, bb	Bag, babble
/d/	d, dd, ed	Sad, mad
/f/	f, ff, ph, gh, lf, ft	Phone, four, graph
/g/	g, gg, gh,gu,gue	Goose, ghost
/h/	h, wh	Hope, hop
/j/	j, ge, g, dge, di, gg	Juice, hedge
/k/	k, c, ch, cc, lk, qu ,q(u), ck, x	Cream, bouquet
/l/	l, ll	Leave, sullen
/m/	m, mm, mb, mn, lm	Men, summer, solemn
/n/	n, nn, kn, gn, pn	Now, sunny
/p/	p, pp	Pen, sippy cup
/r/	r, rr, wr, rh	Red, carrot
/s/	s, ss, c, sc, ps, st, ce, se	Set, psychiatrist
/t/	t, tt, th, ed	Ten, stutter
/v/	v, f, ph, ve	Veronica, seven
/w/	w, wh, u, o	Where, why
/y/	y, i, j	Yam
/z/	z, zz, s, ss, x, ze, se	Zoo, Susan
/a/	a, ai, au	Mat, pat

Subarea II: Rhetoric and Composition

OBJECTIVE 0010 UNDERSTAND PRINCIPLES OF RHETORIC AS THEY APPLY TO VARIOUS FORMS AND PURPOSES OF ORAL AND WRITTEN COMMUNICATION.

For example: the development of rhetoric from a classical art of persuasive oratory to a modern discipline concerned with the analysis and interpretation of spoken, written, and media communications; modern and contemporary theories of rhetoric; application of modern rhetorical principles (e.g., unity, coherence, emphasis) to produce a desired result in an audience; consideration of subject, subject knowledge, purpose, and audience in producing a communication; use of appropriate arrangement and organization (e.g., logical ordering of ideas), style and tone (e.g., lexical choices, word order, cadence), and form of delivery; similarities and differences between language structures in spoken and written English; how to interpret and apply English grammar and language conventions in oral and written contexts; the role of cultural factors in oral and written communication; strategies for evaluating the content and effectiveness of written and spoken messages; principles of effective speaking and listening for various purposes (e.g., for information and understanding, literary response and expression, critical analysis and persuasion, debate); and techniques for interpreting and analyzing media messages.

Rhetoric is a way to describe a manner of speaking or writing that is meant to generate a substantial effect on its audience. Some people say a person uses rhetoric well when they claim "she has a way with words" or perhaps state "he makes a good argument." The word may also refer to the study of the way someone speaks or presents words. But for this exam, rhetoric refers to the way an image is created through word choice, emphasis, and the intent to influence beliefs. These things count when you are reading passages in the multiple choice section as well as passages for your essay prompts. Be cautious, as rhetoric is not just a philosophy being presented, a means of persuasion, or merely speaking well. Rather, it is the intention behind the statements and selection of the words used — not just what's said.

What Are Rhetorical Techniques?

The techniques used in rhetoric are the same things students have been told for years that good essays will answer — who, what, how — as well as the way information is delivered, the actual content, and the method used to convey the message. Two main rhetorical techniques, also known as devices, are **tropes** and **schemes**.

Tropes are figures of speech that provide an unexpected twist in the meaning of words, and are used when there is a change in words that embellishes or energizes a phrase. The four most frequently used tropes (and the most essential ones) are metaphor, metonymy, synecdoche, and irony. We define these for you below, so you will have a quick reference list. Schemes are the pattern and format of words. A trope is also sometimes called a "figure of thought" whereas when the pattern changes for schemes, it may be called "figure of speech."

How is Rhetoric Created or Used?

There are different ways that people use words to get a point across, to persuade listeners to believe in what they are saying. These ways include the pace or speed of their delivery, the tone of voice of the speaker (or author) and the interaction with body language as the words are spoken. You can see that rhetoric likely does not work very well on the phone (where other distractions can pull a listener away from a speaker's delivery and there is no way to see the body language); similarly, to be understood well in writing, the author must be very accomplished indeed.

The way to achieve good writing and speaking is through a rhetorical device. It's how the speaker persuades the listener to understand and convert to a different perspective. The primary purpose is for the listener to believe in the argument, though side effects (of emotional response or reaction) are likely to occur depending on the method used by the speaker.

Some Important Philosophers Who Used Rhetoric

Since this is an English exam and not one in philosophy, these particular individuals won't likely be asked about on the MTEL, but you will possibly understand English devices better when you understand their views. The great ancient orators employed rhetoric successfully to speak on any topic, persuading listeners even when the speaker was not extraordinarily informed on a particular subject. Frequently rhetoric was used in politics. It is important to remember that rhetoric is important for communication in any field; These four orators were rhetorical geniuses:

Confucius

A Chinese philosopher who focused on eloquence of speech and economy of words, Confucius was a very sophisticated user of rhetoric. Though his is one of the earliest examples of a recognizable historical name, some think that rhetoric dates back even further to ancient Mesopotamia and Egypt — several thousand years before Confucius.

Plato

Plato used criticism against the "art" of rhetoric to show its usefulness in expanding deceit rather than expounding and exposing truths. Plato considered rhetoric as lowly flattery and flowery language, not as an educated and sophisticated debate tactic. He considered Sophists (wandering lecturers) to use rhetoric in their efforts to attract followers — in a non-positive light.

Aristotle

Although a student of Plato, Aristotle believed in the positive attributes of rhetoric and explained there were three genres available for people to use as the best method to persuade listeners in any given situation. However, he also firmly believed that rhetoric was the domain of politicians and not "just anyone" could use it to their own ends (another "opposite" of his teacher's ideas).

Aristotelian analysis consists of genres as well as methods. According to the philosopher, there are three genres, or paths, rhetoric takes in speaking or writing:

deliberative (debating about future options and which decision to make);

forensic (as television lingo the truth of evidence presented);

and **epideictic** (the emotional appeal to an audience).

Quick tip: depending on your essay prompts, you may use one or all three of these on your exam answer in the essay section. Aristotle also defined the three methods by which rhetoric could be used: **pathos** (presenting using emotions to persuade following through to a conclusion), **ethos** (believability of a speaker based on what could be described as points of ethics), and **logos** (the "l" stood for logic, such as inductive or deductive reasoning, to prove a point). Another quick tip: you should concentration on using logic for your essay replies.

Cicero

A Roman, Cicero is considered one of the greatest orators in history. He was able not only to utilize rhetoric in his speeches but also in his letters and documents. He used nearly all rhetorical devices and all of the rhetorical canons as he developed speeches to persuade his audiences. More information on the canons comes later in this chapter. The conflict between Plato and Aristotle — everyone can employ rhetoric versus only politicians can use rhetoric — has led to a contemporary divergence of thought and analysis. Neo-sophistic views align with Plato, that anyone can use rhetoric to make a point (whereas "original" Sophists were those learned men who went from town to town educating the townspeople by lecturing in large assemblies). Conversely, Neo-Aristotelians believe only political purposes and those in that sphere can truly use rhetoric.

In very modern times, debate clubs are a way to try to train college students (and now high school students as well) in the "art" of rhetoric — and speaking groups also were opportunities for group discussion and cultured interactions between learned people. While there are additional recent philosophies and leaders of thought on "who can use rhetoric," the only ones with which you likely need to be familiar are the ancient Greeks. Names of other historical yet more modern rhetorical experts include Francis Bacon, Thomas Hobbes, and John Quincy Adams among many others.

What Are Examples of Rhetorical Devices?

Devices or different "mechanisms" are used to convey ideas, and they are very important in successful rhetoric. Here is a partial list of rhetorical devices in alphabetical order, including the most common (the most likely to be used or asked in definitions on the MTEL). You need to know the definitions as well as be able to identify/create examples and to help you on the multiple choice section. If you understand these — and don't just memorize them — you will be able to consider the provided answers faster in context with the reading selection, ruling out one if not two answers immediately, then you will be able to select the most appropriate answer from the ones remaining. Some of these are called "sonic" because they depend on sound and they are marked by (s) to help you distinguish them. Others classified as "imagery" because they conjure visions and they are marked by (i) for ease in identification.

Adynaton — a ridiculous over-exaggeration, much more than "just" hyperbole; "when donkey's fly" was a quote from an old television show when a waitress didn't believe something would happen

Alliteration (s) — repetitive initial consonant sounds, usually with an overtone of humor or nonsense; she sells sea shells by the sea shore. *Assonance* (s) would be the same, though with vowel sounds.

Allusion — a reference to an event, literary work or person; "he's as fast as The Flash"
Antanagoge — places a criticism and compliment together.

Antonomasia — using an epithet or nickname instead of a person's true name; "The Lionheart"

Epithet (i) — using an adjective or adjective phrase to describe. This can be metaphorical or transferred (adjective modifying something it normally doesn't); "lazy road" and "blind mouths", respectively.

Euphemism — replacing a harsh plain phrase with a less offensive one; "her elevator doesn't go to the top"

Hypocatastasis (i) — labeling far beyond metaphor or simile; "that snake"

Irony — saying something contrary to make a point — but in rhetoric, it's most often used a device of humor to reduce an option for a course of action; Abraham Lincoln said about an adversary that he "died down deeper into the sea of knowledge and came up drier than any other man he knew. "

Metaphor (i) — compares two things without "as" or "like"; "she is a lion"

Metonymy — when a similar word is substituted for the actual or typical word or when you describe something or a person by describing what's around the item being depicted; like "redneck" to describe someone who lives in a rural area (in a negative way)

Onomatopoeia (s) — words that sound like what they describe; "bang"

Oxymoron — a two word paradox; "near miss"

Simile (i) — compares one object to another with "like" or "as" "strong as the sun"

Synecdoche — when parts are used to name a whole (can be a subvariant of metonymy; "a new set of wheels" to describe a new car

When Are Rhetorical Canons Used?

Cicero (mentioned above) was very effective in persuading listeners to accept his point of view by using various rhetorical canons. These styles, or categories, provide a template of the author's argument.

- Invention — a derivative of Aristotle's logos, this is when the author finds (or "invents") something to say and bases the point on logic. It may include an "if... then" technique to explain cause and effect or compare different aspects to reach the desired conclusion. This is generally a brainstorming phase, where the author must consider the audience, the facts are available to use in the presentation, the best Aristotelian method to present those facts, and the time he has to deliver the argument.
- Arrangement — in this process, Cicero uses all of the tools from Aristotle, beginning with an introduction using ethos; the next sections of facts, divisions, proofs, refutations, and pathos.
- Style — the style in which something is said. Style is very intentional in rhetoric and one should remember that the style used gives clues to the author's meaning. Style includes grammar, consideration of audience, address of appeal, decorum (appropriateness and "situation"), and ornamental language. Style is more than pathos — it incorporates ethos as well, or persuasion effect.
- Memory — Cicero often had to improvise and interact with his audience, and thus this style was intended to continue the direction of the speech but give sensitivity to "input" (verbal or other visual cues) from an audience. This is a psychological component of the rhetoric in addition to the formality of a speech, especially since the most effective speeches in ancient times were totally memorized. (In fact, ancient orators were scorned if they used notes; memorization was a must.)
- Delivery — Very important, though frequently not considered as important as word choice, is how something was said. This is what Cicero termed delivery. As you may have experienced yourself, the way a teacher presents a topic can get you engaged . . . or not. Delivery can significantly alter the way something is interpreted, thus pathos is integral to successful delivery. Today, people are very skeptical of someone who has a speech memorized and polished — they almost prefer a little authenticity and "humanness" in a composition, though if it is too rough the speaker will get criticized for that, too!

OBJECTIVE 0011 **UNDERSTAND THE COMPOSITION PROCESS.**

For example: strategies for writing effectively in a variety of forms and for a variety of audiences, purposes, and contexts; processes for generating and developing written texts (e.g., prewriting, drafting, revising, editing, publishing); techniques for revising written texts to achieve clarity and economy of expression; revision of sentences to eliminate wordiness, ambiguity, and redundancy; development of a thesis; development of an effective introduction and conclusion; effective use of topic sentences; the role of voice and style in writing; effective use of figurative language; identification of logical fallacies; techniques for improving text organization; effective use of transitions to enhance the clarity of an argument; selection of appropriate details to support an argument or opinion; applications of technology in all phases of the writing process; and the distinguishing features of various forms of writing (e.g., reflective essay, autobiographical narrative, editorial, memorandum, summary/abstract, argument, résumé, play, short story, poem, newspaper or journalistic article).

Organization in Your Essays

To organize your essay, you might consider one of the following patterns.

1. Examine individual elements such as **plot, setting, theme, character, point of view, tone, mood,** or **style**.

SINGLE ELEMENT OUTLINE

- Intro: Main idea statement
- Main point 1 with at least two supporting details
- Main point 2 with at least two supporting details
- Main point 3 with at least two supporting details
- Conclusion (restates main ideas and summary of main points)

2. **Compare and contrast two elements.**

POINT-BY-POINT	BLOCK
Introduction Statement of main idea about A and B	Introduction Statement of main idea about A and B
Main Point 1 Discussion of A Discussion of B	Discussion of A Main Point 1 Main Point 2 Main Point 3
Main Point 2 Discussion of A Discussion of B	Discussion of B Main Point 1 Main Point 2 Main Point 3
Main Point 3 Discussion of A Discussion of B	Conclusion Restatement of main idea
Conclusion Restatement or summary of main idea	

Practice

Prewrite ideas for analyzing another poem or identifying how the author develops a character or theme in a novel. (When creating a prewriting graphic organizer for students, match the organizer with the task.)

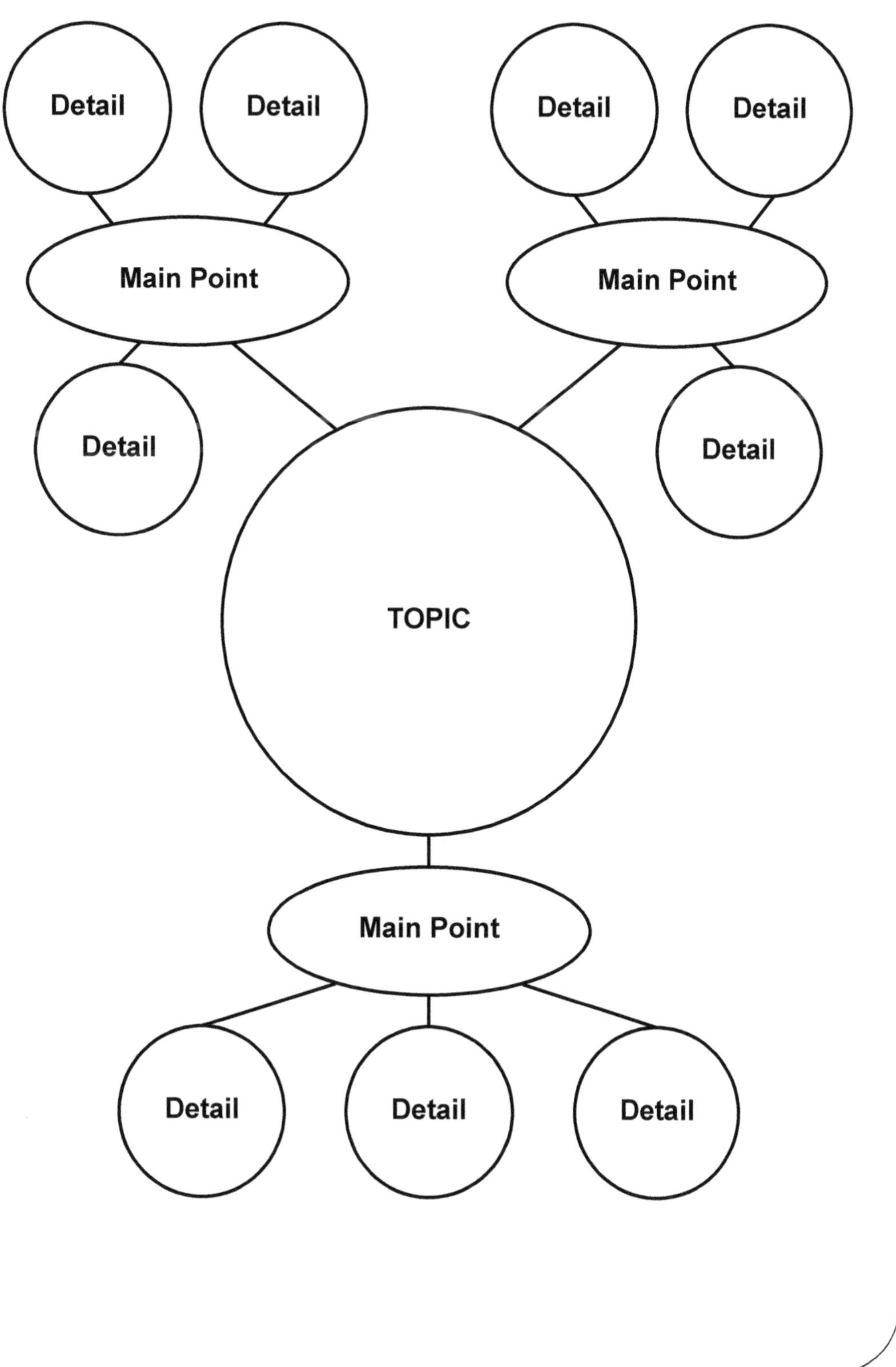

STUDENTS AND THE WRITING PROCESS

Expository and Persuasive Essays

When teaching students to write an expository or persuasive essay, audience and purpose must be determined. A preliminary review of literature is helpful. For example, if the topic is immigration, a cursory review of the various points of view in the debate going on in the country will help the writer decide what this particular written piece will try to accomplish. The purpose could be to review the various points of view, which would be an *informative purpose*. On the other hand, the writer might want to take a point of view and provide proof and support with the purpose of changing the reader's mind. The writer might even want the reader to take some action as a result of reading. Another possible purpose might be simply to write a description of a family of immigrants.

Once a cursory review has been completed, it is time to begin research in earnest and to prepare to take notes. If the thesis has been clearly defined and some thought has been given to what will be used to prove or support this thesis, a tentative outline can be developed. A thesis plus three points is typical. However, less importance is now given to this "formulaic" five-paragraph structure in an essay. Instead, writing that is organized and possesses a strong voice is what really matters.

Decisions about introduction and conclusion should be deferred until the body of the paper is written. Note-taking is much more effective if the notes are being taken to provide information for an outline. With this purpose in mind it is less likely that the writer will go off on time-consuming tangents when taking notes.

Formal outlines inhibit effective writing. However, a loosely constructed outline can be an effective device for note-taking that will yield the information for a worthwhile statement about a topic. Sentence outlines are better than topic outlines because they require the writer to do some thinking about the direction a subtopic will take.

Once this preliminary note-taking phase is over, the first draft can be developed. The writing at this stage is likely to be highly individualistic. However, successful writers tend to just write, keeping in mind the purpose of the paper, the point that is going to be made, and the information that has been turned up in the research. Student writers need to understand that this first draft is just that—the first one. It takes more than one draft to write a worthwhile statement about a topic. This is what successful writers do. It can be helpful to have students read the various drafts of a story by a well-known writer.

When the draft is on paper, a stage that is sometimes called **revision** occurs. Revision is rereading objectively, testing the effectiveness on a reader of the arrangement and the line of reasoning. The kinds of changes that will need to be made are rearranging the parts, changing words, adding information that is missing but necessary, and deleting information that doesn't fit or contribute to the accomplishment of the purpose.

Once the body of the paper has been shaped to the writer's satisfaction, the introduction and conclusion should be fashioned. An introduction should grab the reader's interest and perhaps announce the purpose and thesis of the paper unless the reasoning is inductive. In this case purpose and thesis may come later in the paper. The conclusion must reaffirm the purpose in some way. Finally, the paper should be edited for correct grammar and mechanics.

Tips for Revising an Essay

Enhancing interest:

- Start out with an attention-grabbing introduction. This sets an engaging tone for the entire piece and will be more likely to engage the reader.
- Use dynamic vocabulary and varied sentence beginnings and sentence structures. Keep the readers on their toes. If they can predict what you are going to say next, switch it up.
- Avoid using clichés (as cold as ice, the best thing since sliced bread, nip it in the bud). These are easy shortcuts but they are not interesting, memorable, or convincing.

Ensuring understanding:

- Avoid using words like "clearly," "obviously," and "undoubtedly." Often things that are clear or obvious to the author are not as apparent to the reader. Instead of using these words, make your point so strongly that it is clear on its own.
- Use the word that best fits the meaning you intend, even if it is longer or a little less common. Try to find a balance and choose a familiar yet precise word.
- When in doubt, explain further.

Techniques to maintain focus:

- **Focus on a main point.** The point should be clear to readers and all sentences in the paragraph should relate to it.
- **Start the paragraph with a topic sentence.** This should be a general, one-sentence summary of the paragraph's main point, relating both back toward the thesis and toward the content of the paragraph. A topic sentence is sometimes unnecessary if the paragraph continues a developing idea clearly introduced in a preceding paragraph or if the paragraph appears in a narrative of events where generalizations might interrupt the flow of the story.
- **Stick to the point.** Eliminate sentences that do not support the topic sentence.
- **Be flexible.** If there is not enough evidence to support the claim your topic sentence is making do not fall into the trap of wandering or introducing new ideas within the paragraph. Either find more evidence or adjust the topic sentence to collaborate with the evidence that is available.

Narrative Writing

It seems simplistic, yet it's true: The first and most important measure of a story is the story itself. *The story's the thing.* However, a good story must have certain elements and characteristics.

Plot is the series of events, involving conflict, that make up the story. Without conflict there is no story, so determining what the conflicts are should be a priority for the writer. Once the conflicts are determined, the outcome of the story must be decided. Who wins? Who loses? What factors go into making one side of the equation win out over the other? The pattern of the plot is also an important consideration. Where is the climax going to occur? Is denouement necessary? Does the reader need to see the unwinding of all the strands? Many stories fail because a denouement is needed but not supplied.

Characterization, the choice the writer makes about the devices he or she will use to reveal character, requires an understanding of human nature and the artistic skill to convey a personality to the reader. This is usually accomplished subtly through dialogue, interior monologue, description, and the character's actions and behavior. In some successful stories, the writer comes right out and tells the reader what this character is like. However, sometimes there will be discrepancies between what the narrator tells the reader about the character and what is revealed about the character, in which case the narrator is unreliable, and that unreliability of the voice on which the reader must depend becomes an important and significant device for understanding the story.

Point of view is essentially the eyes through which the reader sees the action. It is a powerful tool not only for the writer but also for the enjoyment and understanding of the reader. The writer must choose among several possibilities: first-person narrator objective, first-person narrator omniscient, third-person objective, third-person omniscient, and third-person limited omniscient.

The most common point of view is the third-person objective. If the story is seen from this point of view, the reader watches the action, hears the dialogue, and reads descriptions and must deduce characterization from all of these. In third-person objective, an unseen narrator tells the reader what is happening, using the third-person pronouns: *he, she, it, they*. The effect of this point of view is usually a feeling of distance from the plot.

More responsibility is on the reader to make judgments than in other points of view. However, the author may intrude and evaluate or comment on the characters or the action.

The first-person narrator is also a common point of view. The reader sees the action through the eyes of a character in the story who is also telling the story. In writing about a story that uses this voice, the writer must analyze the narrator as a character. What sort of person is he or she? What is this character's position in the story—observer, commentator, or actor? Can the narrator be believed, or is he or she biased? The value of this voice is that, while the reader is able to follow the narrator around and see what is happening through that character's eyes, the reader is also able to feel what the narrator feels. For this reason the writer can involve the reader more intensely in the story itself and move the reader by invoking feelings—pity, sorrow, anger, hate, confusion, disgust, etc. Many of the most memorable novels are written in this point of view.

Another narrative voice often used may best be titled "omniscient" because the reader is able to get into the mind of more than one character or sometimes all the characters.

This point of view can also bring greater involvement of the reader in the story. By knowing what a character is thinking and feeling the reader is able to empathize when a character feels great pain and sorrow, which tends to make a work memorable. On the other hand, knowing what a character is thinking makes it possible to get into the mind of a pathological murderer and may elicit horror or disgust.

Style, the unique way a writer uses language, is often the writer's signature. The reader does not need to be told that William Faulkner wrote a story to know this because his style is so distinctive that his work is immediately recognizable.

The writer must be cognizant of his or her own strengths and weaknesses and continually work to hone the way sentences are written, words are chosen, and descriptions are crafted until they are razor sharp. The best advice to the aspiring writer is to read the works of successful writers. If a writer wants to write a best-seller, then the writer needs to be reading best-sellers.

OBJECTIVE 0012 UNDERSTAND WRITTEN LANGUAGE CONVENTIONS.

For example: accurate use and effective application of written language conventions (e.g., sentence and paragraph construction, spelling, punctuation, usage, grammatical expression); techniques for editing written texts to achieve conformity with conventions of standard English usage (e.g., revising sentences and passages to maintain parallel form; revising sentences to eliminate misplaced modifiers; editing written texts to eliminate errors in spelling and punctuation); and strategies for effective proofreading.

Grammar is the proper usage of words and phrases. For a tests such as MTEL Enlgish, it is critical to demonstrate proper use of grammar to avoid errors in usage, spelling, diction, and rhetoric.

Multiple choice questions will test your knowledge of a variety of English grammar rules, such as: parts of speech, syntax, sentence types, sentence structure, sentence combining, phrases and clauses, modifiers, and capitalization. Writing prompts will give you an opportunity to showcase your knowledge of these rules. Patterns of error in the written sections will immediately result in a lower grade. You will want to be sure to avoid fragments and run-on sentences. Recognition of sentence elements necessary to make a complete thought, proper use of independent and dependent clauses, and proper punctuation will correct such errors. Reviewing the following grammar points will assist in higher scores for both multiple choice and essay questions.

Parts of Speech

There are eight parts of speech: nouns, verbs, adjectives, adverbs, pronouns, conjunctions, prepositions, and interjections.

Noun	A person, place or thing. (*student, school, textbook*)
Verb	An action word. (*study, read, run*)

Adjective	Describes a verb or noun. (*smart, beautiful, colorful*)
Adverb	Describes a verb. (*quickly, fast, intelligently*)
Pronoun	Substitution for a noun. (*he, she, it*)
Conjunction	Joins two phrases. (*because, but, so*)
Preposition	Used before nouns to provide additional details. (*before, after, on*)
Interjection	Express emotion. (*Ha!, Hello!, Stop!*)

Syntax

Although widely different in many aspects, written and spoken English share a common basic structure or syntax (subject, verb, and object) and the common purpose of fulfilling the need to communicate—but there, the similarities end.

Spoken English follows the basic word order mentioned above (subject, verb object) as does written English. We would write as we would speak: "I sang a song." It is usually only in poetry or music that that word order or syntax is altered: "Sang I a song."

Types of Sentences

Sentence variety is a great way to demonstrate your knowledge of the various sentence types in the writing portions for the AP English exam.

Sentence Types

Declarative	Makes a statement. *I bought a new textbook.*
Interrogative	Asks a question. *Where did you buy the textbook?*
Exclamatory	Expresses strong emotion. *I can't believe it's your birthday today!*
Imperative	Gives a command. *Put the birthday cake on the table.*

Clauses are connected word groups that are composed of at least one subject and one verb. (A subject is the doer of an action or the element that is being joined. A verb conveys either the action or the link.)

Students are waiting for the start of the assembly.
subject verb

At the end of the play, students waited for the curtain to come down.
subject verb

Clauses can be independent or dependent. **Independent clauses** can stand alone or can be joined to other clauses, either independent or dependent. Words that can be used to join clauses include the following:

- for
- and
- nor
- but
- or
- yet
- so

Dependent clauses, by definition, contain at least one subject and one verb. However, they cannot stand alone as a complete sentence. They are structurally dependent on an independent clause (the main clause of the sentence). There are two types of dependent clauses: (1) those with a subordinating conjunction and (2) those with a relative pronoun

Coordinating conjunctions include the following:

- although
- when
- if
- unless
- because

Example: Unless a cure is discovered, many more people will die of the disease. (dependent clause with coordinating conjunction [unless] + independent clause)

Relative pronouns include the following:

- who
- whom
- which
- that

Example: The White House has an official website, which contains press releases, news updates, and biographies of the president and vice president.
(independent clause + relative pronoun [which] + relative dependent clause)

Sentence Structure

Recognize simple, compound, complex, and compound-complex sentences. Use dependent (subordinate) and independent clauses correctly to create these sentence structures.

Simple	Joyce wrote a letter.
Compound	Joyce wrote a letter and Dot drew a picture.
Complex	While Joyce wrote a letter, Dot drew a picture.
Compound/complex	When Mother asked the girls to demonstrate their newfound skills, Joyce wrote a letter and Dot drew a picture.

**Note: Do not confuse compound sentence elements with compound sentences.*

Simple sentence with compound subject:

Joyce and Dot wrote letters.
The girl in row three and the boy next to her were passing notes across the aisle.

Simple sentence with compound predicate:

Joyce wrote letters and drew pictures.
The captain of the high school debate team graduated with honors and studied broadcast journalism in college.

Simple sentence with compound object of preposition:

Coleen graded the students' essays for style and mechanical accuracy.

Parallelism

Recognize parallel structures using phrases (prepositional, gerund, participial, and infinitive) and omissions from sentences that create the lack of parallelism.

Prepositional phrase/single modifier:
Incorrect: Coleen ate the ice cream with enthusiasm and hurriedly.
Correct: Coleen ate the ice cream with enthusiasm and in a hurry.
Correct: Coleen ate the ice cream enthusiastically and hurriedly.

Participial phrase/infinitive phrase:
Incorrect: After hiking for hours and to sweat profusely, Joe sat down to rest and drinking water.
Correct: After hiking for hours and sweating profusely, Joe sat down to rest and drink water.

Recognition of Misplaced and Dangling Modifiers

Dangling phrases are attached to sentence parts in such a way that they create ambiguity and incorrectness of meaning.

Participial phrase:
Incorrect: Hanging from her skirt, Dot tugged at a loose thread.
Correct: Dot tugged at a loose thread hanging from her skirt.

Infinitive phrase:
Incorrect: To improve his behavior, the dean warned Fred.
Correct: The dean warned Fred to improve his behavior.

Prepositional phrase:
Incorrect: On the floor, Father saw the dog eating table scraps.
Correct: Father saw the dog eating table scraps on the floor.

Particular phrases that are not placed near the word they modify often result in misplaced modifiers. Particular phrases that do not relate to the subject being modified result in dangling modifiers.

Error: Weighing the options carefully, a decision was made regarding the punishment of the convicted murderer.

Problem: Who is weighing the options? No one capable of weighing is named in the sentence. Thus, the participle phrase "weighing the options carefully" dangles. This problem can be corrected by adding a subject of the sentence who is capable of doing the action.

Correction: Weighing the options carefully, the judge made a decision regarding the punishment of the convicted murderer.

Error: Returning to my favorite watering hole brought back many fond memories.

Problem: The person who returned is never indicated, and the participle phrase dangles. This problem can be corrected by creating a dependent clause from the modifying phrase.

Correction: When I returned to my favorite watering hole, many fond memories came back to me.

Recognition of Syntactical Redundancy or Omission

These errors occur when superfluous words have been added to a sentence or key words have been omitted from a sentence.

Redundancy

Incorrect: Joyce made sure that when her plane arrived that she retrieved all of her luggage.

Correct: Joyce made sure that when her plane arrived she retrieved all of her luggage.

Incorrect: He was a mere skeleton of his former self.

Correct: He was a skeleton of his former self.

Omission

Incorrect: Dot opened her book, recited her textbook, and answered the teacher's subsequent question.

Correct: Dot opened her book, recited from the textbook, and answered the teacher's subsequent question.

Avoidance of Double Negatives

This error occurs from positioning two negatives that cancel each other out (create a positive statement).

Incorrect: Dot didn't have no double negatives in her paper.

Correct: Dot didn't have any double negatives in her paper.

Spelling

Spelling rules are extremely complex, based as they are on rules of phonics and letter doubling, and replete with exceptions. Even adults who have a good command of written English benefit from using a dictionary. Adolescent students will also benefit from learning how to use a dictionary and thesaurus.

Most plurals of nouns that end in hard consonants or hard consonant sounds followed by a silent *e* are made by adding *s*. Some nouns ending in vowels only add *s*.

fingers, numerals, banks, bugs, riots, homes, gates, radios, bananas

Nouns that end in the soft consonant sounds *s*, *j*, *x*, *z*, *ch*, and *sh* add *es*. Some nouns ending in *o* add *es*.

dresses, waxes, churches, brushes, tomatoes, potatoes

Nouns ending in *y* preceded by a vowel just add *s*.

boys, alleys

Nouns ending in *y* preceded by a consonant change the *y* to *i* and add *es*.

babies, corollaries, frugalities, poppies

Some noun plurals are formed irregularly or are the same as the singular.

sheep, deer, children, leaves, oxen

Some nouns derived from foreign words, especially Latin, may make their plurals in two different ways, one of them anglicized. Sometimes, the meanings are the same; other times, the two plurals are used in slightly different contexts. It is always wise to consult the dictionary.

appendices, appendixes
criterion, criteria
indexes, indices
crisis, crises

Make the plurals of closed (solid) compound words in the usual way except for words ending in -ful, which make their plurals on the root word.

timelines, hairpins, cupsful

Make the plurals of open or hyphenated compounds by adding the change in inflection to the word that changes in number.

fathers-in-law, courts-martial, masters of art, doctors of medicine

Make the plurals of letters, numbers, and abbreviations by adding s.

fives and tens, IBMs, 1990s, ps and qs (Note that letters are italicized.)

Capitalization

Capitalize all proper names of persons (including specific organizations or agencies of government); places (countries, states, cities, parks, and specific geographical areas); things (political parties, structures, historical and cultural terms, and calendar and time designations); and religious terms (any deity, revered person or group, or sacred writing).

> Percy Bysshe Shelley, Argentina, Mount Rainier National Park,
> Grand Canyon, League of Nations, the Sears Tower, Birmingham,
> Lyric Theater, Americans, Midwesterners, Democrats, Renaissance,
> Boy Scouts of America, Easter, God, Bible, Dead Sea Scrolls, Koran

Capitalize proper adjectives and titles used with proper names.

> California Gold Rush, President John Adams, Senator John Glenn

Note: Some words that represent titles and offices are not capitalized unless used with a proper name.

Capitalized	**Not Capitalized**
Congressman McKay	the congressman from Florida
Commander Alger	commander of the Pacific Fleet
Queen Elizabeth	the queen of England
President George Washington	the president

Subarea III: Reading Theory, Research & Instruction

OBJECTIVE 0013 UNDERSTAND LANGUAGE ACQUISITION, READING PROCESSES, AND RESEARCH-BASED THEORIES RELATING TO READING.

For example: basic processes of first- and second-language acquisition and use; strategies to research word origins and analyze word formation to understand meanings, derivations, and spellings; relationships among words (e.g., homonyms, synonyms, antonyms) and issues related to word choice (e.g., denotative and connotative meanings, multiple-meaning words); research-based theories relating to the reading process; word analysis skills and strategies (e.g., phonics, syllabication, structural analysis); use of semantic and syntactic cues to verify word meanings; the role of vocabulary skills and strategies in the development of reading proficiency; application of literal, inferential, and evaluative comprehension skills; the use of metacognitive techniques to monitor reading comprehension; the application of strategies before, during, and after reading to promote comprehension of expository texts (e.g., previewing and predicting, self-questioning, writing and discussing); the role of oral reading fluency in facilitating comprehension of texts; and ways in which text characteristics and purposes for reading determine the selection of reading strategies.

Early theories of **language development** were formulated from learning theory research. The assumption was that language development evolved from learning the rules of language structures and applying them through imitation and reinforcement. This approach also assumed that language, cognitive, and social developments were independent of each other. Thus, children were expected to learn language from patterning after adults who spoke and wrote Standard English. No allowance was made for communication through child jargon, idiomatic expressions, or grammatical and mechanical errors resulting from overly strict adherence to the rules of inflection (*childs* instead of *children*) or conjugation (*runned* instead of *ran*). No association was made between physical and operational development and language mastery.

Linguistic Approach

Studies spearheaded by Noam Chomsky in the 1950s formulated the theory that language ability is innate and develops through natural human maturation as environmental stimuli trigger acquisition of syntactical structures appropriate to each exposure level. The assumption of a hierarchy of syntax downplayed the significance of semantics. Because of the complexity of syntax and the relative speed with which children acquire language, linguists attributed language development to biological rather than cognitive or social influences.

Cognitive Approach

Researchers in the 1970s proposed that language knowledge derives from both syntactic and semantic structures. Drawing on the studies of Piaget and other cognitive learning theorists (see Skill 4.7), supporters of the cognitive approach maintained that children acquire knowledge of linguistic structures after they have acquired the cognitive structures necessary to process language. For example, joining words for specific meaning necessitates sensory motor intelligence. The child must be able to coordinate movement and recognize objects before he or she can identify words to name the objects, or word groups to describe the actions performed with those objects.

Adolescents must have developed the mental abilities for *organizing concepts as well as concrete operations, predicting outcomes,* and *theorizing* before they can assimilate and verbalize complex sentence structures, choose vocabulary for particular nuances of meaning, and examine semantic structures for tone and manipulative effect.

Socio-cognitive Approach

Other theorists in the 1970s proposed that language development results from sociolinguistic competence. Language, cognitive, and social knowledge are interactive elements of total human development. Emphasis on verbal communication as the medium for language expression resulted in the inclusion of speech activities in most language arts curricula.

Unlike previous approaches, the socio-cognitive approach believes that determining the appropriateness of language in given situations for specific listeners is as important as understanding semantic and syntactic structures. By engaging in conversation, children at all stages of development have opportunities to test their language skills, receive feedback, and make modifications. As a social activity, conversation is as structured by social order as grammar is structured by the rules of syntax. Conversation satisfies the learner's need to be heard and understood and to influence others. Thus, his choices of vocabulary, tone, and content are dictated by his ability to assess the language knowledge of his listeners. He is constantly applying his cognitive skills to using language in a social interaction. If the capacity to acquire language is inborn, without an environment in which to practice language a child would not pass beyond the grunts and gestures of primitive man.

Of course, the varying degrees of environmental stimuli to which children are exposed at all age levels affects the speed of language development. Some children are prepared to articulate concepts and recognize symbolism by the time they enter fifth grade because they have been exposed to challenging reading and conversations with well-spoken adults at home or in their social groups. Others are still trying to master the sight recognition skills and are not yet ready to combine words in complex patterns.

Concerns for the Teacher

Because teachers must, by virtue of tradition and the dictates of the curriculum, teach grammar, usage, and writing as well as reading and literature, the problem becomes when to teach what to whom. The profusion of approaches to teaching grammar alone are mind-boggling. At a university level we learn about transformational grammar, stratification grammar, sectoral grammar, etc. But in practice, most teachers, supported by presentations in textbooks and by the methods they have learned themselves, keep coming back to the same traditional prescriptive approach (read and imitate) or structural approach (learn the parts of speech, the parts of a sentence, punctuation rules, and sentence patterns). For some educators, the best solution is the worst—not teaching grammar at all.

Problems also occur in teaching usage. One question that is difficult to answer is: Do we require students to communicate strictly in Standard English? Different schools of thought suggest that a study of dialect and idiom and a recognition of various jargons is a vital part of language development. Social pressures to be accepted within their peer groups and to speak the nonstandard language spoken outside the school make adolescents resistant to the corrective, remedial approach. In many communities where the immigrant populations are high, new words are entering English from other languages even as words and expressions that were common when we were children have become rare or obsolete.

Regardless of differences of opinion concerning language development, a language arts teacher will be most effective using the styles and approaches with which she is most comfortable. And, if she subscribes to a student-centered approach, she may find that the students have a lot to teach her and each other. Moffett and Wagner, in the Fourth Edition of *Student-centered Language Arts K–12*, they support a socio-cognitive approach to language development by stressing the three I's: individualization, interaction, and integration. By providing an opportunity for the student to select his own activities and resources, his instruction is individualized. By centering on and teaching each other, students are interactive. Finally, by allowing students to synthesize a variety of knowledge structures, they integrate them. The teacher's role becomes that of a facilitator.

Benefits of the Socio-cognitive Approach

Most basal readers utilize an integrated, cross-curricular approach to successful grammar, language, and usage. Reinforcement becomes an intradepartmental responsibility. Language classes incorporate diction and terminology across the curriculum. Standard usage is encouraged and supported by both the core classroom textbooks and current software for technology. Teachers need to acquaint themselves with the computer capabilities in their school district and at their individual school sites. Advances in new technologies require the teacher to familiarize herself with programs that would serve her students' needs. Students respond enthusiastically to technology. Several highly effective programs are available in various formats to assist students with initial instruction or remediation. Grammar texts, such as the Warriner's series, employ various methods to reach individual learning styles. The school library media center should become a focal point for individual exploration.

OBJECTIVE 0014: UNDERSTAND EFFECTIVE, RESEARCH-BASED READING INSTRUCTION AND THE ROLE OF CHILDREN'S LITERATURE AND YOUNG ADULT LITERATURE IN PROMOTING READING PROFICIENCY.

For example: research-based theories and practices relating to reading instruction; methods for planning, managing, and differentiating reading instruction to support students' reading development; the role of children's literature and young adult literature in promoting reading proficiency and motivating students to read independently; instructional strategies to promote development of particular reading skills (e.g., word analysis, vocabulary, comprehension); the adjustment of reading instruction based on ongoing assessment; strategies to promote independent reading; strategies for selecting and using meaningful reading materials at appropriate levels of difficulty for all students; and uses of instructional technologies to promote students' reading development.

Children's books are a reflection of both **developmental** theories and social changes. Reading provides children with the opportunity to become more aware of societal differences, to measure their behavior against the behavior of realistic fictional characters or the subjects of biographies, to become informed about events of the past and present that will affect their futures, and to acquire a genuine appreciation of literature.

As educators, we have an obligation to guide children in the selection of books that are appropriate to their reading ability and interest levels. Of course, there is a fine line between guidance and censorship. As with discipline, parents learn that to make forbidden is to make more desirable. To publish a list of banned books is to make them suddenly attractive. Most children/adolescents left to their own selections will choose books on topics that interest them and are written in language they can understand.

Social changes since World War II have significantly affected adolescent literature. The civil rights movements, feminism, the protests against the Vietnam War, and issues surrounding homelessness, neglect, teen pregnancy, drugs, and violence all have given rise to contemporary fiction that helps adolescents understand and cope with the world they live in.

Popular books for preadolescents deal more with establishing relationships with members of the opposite sex and learning to cope with their changing bodies, personalities, or life situations, such as in Judy Blume's *Are You There, God? It's Me, Margaret.* Adolescents enjoy the fantasy and science fiction genres, as well as popular juvenile fiction. Middle school students might enjoy reading the *Little House on the Prairie* series and the mysteries of the Hardy Boys and Nancy Drew. Teens value the works of Emily and Charlotte Brontë, Willa Cather, Jack London, William Shakespeare, Mark Twain, and J. R. R. Tolkien as much as those of Piers Anthony, S. E. Hinton, Suzanne Collins, Madeleine L'Engle, Stephen King, J. K. Rowling, and Stephenie Meyer.

Why? Because they're fun to read, whatever their underlying literary worth may be.

Older adolescents enjoy the writers in these genres:

- Fantasy: Piers Anthony, Ursula K. LeGuin, Anne McCaffrey
- Horror: V. C. Andrews, Stephen King
- Juvenile fiction: Judy Blume, Robert Cormier, Rosa Guy, Virginia Hamilton, S. E. Hinton, M. E. Kerr, Harry Mazer, Norma Fox Mazer, Richard Newton Peck, Cynthia Voigt, Paul Zindel
- Science fiction: Isaac Asimov, Ray Bradbury, Arthur C. Clarke, Frank Herbert, Larry Niven, H. G. Wells

These classic and contemporary works combine aspects of multiple theories. Functioning at the concrete operations stage (Piaget), being of the "good person" orientation (Kohlberg), still highly dependent on external rewards (Bandura), and exhibiting all five needs previously discussed from Maslow's hierarchy, eleven to twelve-year-olds should appreciate the following titles, grouped by reading level. These titles are also cited for interest at that grade level and do not reflect high-interest titles for older readers who do not read at grade level.

Reading level 6.0 to 6.9

Barrett, William. *Lilies of the Field*
Cormier, Robert. *Other Bells for Us to Ring*
Dahl, Roald. *Danny, Champion of the World; Charlie and the Chocolate Factory*
Lindgren, Astrid. *Pippi Longstocking*
Lindbergh, Anne. *Three Lives to Live*
Lowry, Lois. *Rabble Starkey*
Naylor, Phyllis. *The Year of the Gopher; Reluctantly Alice*
Peck, Robert Newton. *Arly*
Speare, Elizabeth. *The Witch of Blackbird Pond*
Sleator, William. *The Boy Who Reversed Himself*

For seventh and eighth grades

Most seventh- and eighth-grade students, according to learning theory, are still functioning cognitively, psychologically, and morally as sixth graders. As these are not inflexible standards - there are some twelve- and thirteen-year-olds who are much more mature socially, intellectually, and physically than the younger children who share the same school. They are becoming concerned with establishing individual and peer group identities, and this can present conflicts with authority figures and their rules. Some at this age are still tied firmly to the family and its expectations, while others identify more with those their own age or older.

Enrichment reading for this group must help them cope with life's rapid changes or provide escape and thus must be either realistic or fantastic depending on the child's needs. Adventures and mysteries (the Hardy Boys and Nancy Drew series) are still popular today. Preteens also become more interested in biographies of contemporary figures than those of legendary figures of the past.

Reading level 7.0 to 7.9

Armstrong, William. *Sounder*
Bagnold, Enid. *National Velvet*
Barrie, James. *Peter Pan*
London, Jack. *White Fang; Call of the Wild*
Lowry, Lois. *Taking Care of Terrific*
McCaffrey, Anne. The *Dragonsinger* series
Montgomery, L. M. *Anne of Green Gables* and sequels
Steinbeck, John. *The Pearl*
Tolkien, J. R. R. *The Hobbit*
Zindel, Paul. *The Pigman*

Reading level 8.0 to 8.9

Cormier, Robert. *I Am the Cheese*
McCullers, Carson. *The Member of the Wedding*
North, Sterling. *Rascal*
Twain, Mark. *The Adventures of Tom Sawyer*
Zindel, Paul. *My Darling, My Hamburger*

For ninth grade

Depending upon the school environment, a ninth grader may be top dog in a junior high school or underdog in a high school. Much of ninth graders' social development and thus their reading interests become motivated by their peer associations. Ninth graders are technically adolescents operating at the early stages of formal operations in cognitive development. Their perception of their own identity is becoming well defined, and they are fully aware of the ethics required by society. These students are more receptive to the challenges of classic literature but still enjoy popular teen novels.

Reading level 9.0 to 9.9

Brown, Dee. *Bury My Heart at Wounded Knee*
Defoe, Daniel. *Robinson Crusoe*
Dickens, Charles. *David Copperfield*
Greenberg, Joanne. *I Never Promised You a Rose Garden*
Kipling, Rudyard. *Captains Courageous*
Mathabane, Mark. *Kaffir Boy*
Nordhoff, Charles. *Mutiny on the Bounty*
Shelley, Mary. *Frankenstein*
Washington, Booker T. *Up From Slavery*

For tenth through twelfth grades

All high school sophomores, juniors, and seniors can be expected to handle all but a few of the most difficult titles, like *Moby-Dick* or *Vanity Fair*. However, since many high school students do not progress to the eleventh- or twelfth-grade reading level, they will still have their favorites among authors whose writings they can easily understand.

Many will struggle with assigned novels but still read age-targeted books for pleasure. A few high-interest titles for late adolescents are listed below without reading level designations, though most are 6.0 to 7.9.

Bauer, Joan. *Squashed*
Borland, Hal. *When the Legends Die*
Danzinger, Paula. *Remember Me to Herald Square*
Duncan, Lois. *Stranger with My Face*
Hamilton, Virginia. *The Planet of Junior Brown*
Hinton, S. E. *The Outsiders*
Paterson, Katherine. *The Great Gilly Hopkins*

Teachers of students at all levels must be familiar with the materials offered by the libraries in their own schools. Only then can they guide their students into appropriate selections for their social age and reading level development.

Adolescent literature, because of the age range of readers, is extremely diverse. Fiction for the middle group, usually ages 10–11 to 14–15, deals with issues of coping with internal and external changes in their lives. Because children's writers in the twentieth and twenty-first centuries have produced increasingly realistic fiction, adolescents can now find problems they can relate to being dealt with honestly in novels and short stories.

Teachers of middle/junior high school students see the greatest change in interests and reading abilities. Fifth- and sixth-graders, included in elementary grades in many schools, are viewed as older children, while seventh and eighth graders are seen as preadolescents. Ninth-graders, who are sometimes the highest class in junior high school and sometimes the lowest class in high school, definitely view themselves as teenagers. Their literature choices will often be governed more by interest than by ability; thus the wealth of high-interest, low-readability books that has flooded the market in recent years. Tenth- through twelfth-graders will still select high-interest books for pleasure reading but are also easily encouraged to stretch their abilities by reading more classics.

Because of rapid social changes, topics that once did not interest young people until they reached their teens—such as suicide, gangs, and homosexuality—are now subjects of books for younger readers. The plethora of high-interest books reveals how desperately schools have failed to produce on-level readers and how the market has adapted to that need. However, these high-interest books are now readable for younger children whose reading levels are at or above normal. No matter how tastefully written, some content is inappropriate for younger readers. The problem becomes not so much steering them toward books that they have the reading ability to handle but encouraging them toward books whose content is appropriate to their levels of cognitive and social development. A fifth-grader may be able to read V. C. Andrews' book *Flowers in the Attic* but not possess the social/moral development to handle the deviant behavior of the characters.

At the same time, because of the complex changes affecting adolescents, the teacher must be well versed in learning theory and child development, and be competent enough to teach the subject matter of language and literature.

Subarea IV: Integration of Knowledge & Understanding

OBJECTIVE 0015: PREPARE AN ORGANIZED, DEVELOPED ANALYSIS ON A TOPIC RELATED TO ONE OR MORE OF THE FOLLOWING: LITERATURE AND LANGUAGE; RHETORIC AND COMPOSITION; READING THEORY, RESEARCH, AND INSTRUCTION.

For example: research-based theories and practices relating to reading instruction; methods for planning, managing, and differentiating reading instruction to support students' reading development; the role of children's literature and young adult literature in promoting reading proficiency and motivating students to read independently; instructional strategies to promote development of particular reading skills (e.g., word analysis, vocabulary, comprehension); the adjustment of reading instruction based on ongoing assessment; strategies to promote independent reading; strategies for selecting and using meaningful reading materials at appropriate levels of difficulty for all students; and uses of instructional technologies to promote students' reading development.

When analyzing a text rhetorically, discuss the rhetorical structure—how the argument was formed and built. Also, identify the rhetorical devices the writer used to create an effective argument. For example, does the author rely largely on pathos to convince his reader or make his point and lack in any logic or logos? Which devices does he use to give his writing flow or balance? What diction does the writer employ? Is it low, medium, or elevated? How does the diction affect the reader?

Sample Analysis

Read the passage below from *The Diary of Anne Frank* (1947), and write a 150-300 word analysis.

Written on July 15, 1944, three weeks before the Frank family was arrested by the Nazis, Anne's diary entry explains her worldview and future hopes.

"It's difficult in times like these: ideals, dreams and cherished hopes rise within us, only to be crushed by grim reality. It's a wonder I haven't abandoned all my ideals, they seem so absurd and impractical. Yet I cling to them because I still believe, in spite of everything, that people are truly good at heart.

It's utterly impossible for me to build my life on a foundation of chaos, suffering and death. I see the world being slowly transformed into a wilderness, I hear the approaching thunder that, one day, will destroy us too, I feel the suffering of millions, And yet, when I look up at the sky, I somehow feel that everything will change for the better, that this cruelty too shall end, that peace and tranquility will return once more. In the meantime, I must hold on to my ideals. Perhaps the day will come when I will be able to realize them!"

Sample Weak Response

Anne Frank's ideals in this writing make readers clear on the point that she was strongly against Hitler and the Nazis. You can tell that she knows the Nazis are very dangerous and violent people who cause "the suffering of millions." Otherwise, why would she have written this? This fact of Nazis causing the suffering of millions of people, and killing them, is a large contrast to how much she believes "that people are truly good at heart." Anne Frank is right about her ideals. And that is why her whole book is such a large contrast to the conditions in which she lived in WWII, when everything was going wrong in the world. You can also tell from this passage that she is a lot smarter than Hitler was. That is another big contrast in the book.

Anne's sentences and paragraphs emphasize the above contrast. They are not fiction; they are her own real thoughts, and these thoughts don't cause "a grim reality" of "cruelty" or the "absurd and impractical" things that she talks about as the war's fault. No, Anne's words cause us to see what is true and real in her art and in her heart. She makes us see that love is not the fiction. Hitler and the Nazis are the ones who make the fiction. We can read this in between the line, which sometimes has to be done.

Back when Anne Frank wrote her words down on paper, everything was going wrong around her but she knew what to do, and she did it. She wrote a world classic story about her life. This story is a big contrast to what the Germans were doing.

Sample Strong Response

This excerpt from *The Diary of Anne Frank* juxtaposes Anne's hopes and fears and the evil and goodness that existed during WWII. Her words reveal the inner strength of a young girl who refuses, despite the wartime violence and danger surrounding her, to let her idealism be overcome by hatred and mass killing. This idealism is reflected, in part, by her emphases on universal human hopes such as peace, tranquility, and goodwill. Reflecting on her idealism in the context of the war raging around her, she matter-of-factly writes: "my dreams, they seem so absurd and impractical."

This indicates Anne Frank's awareness of not only her own predicament but also of human miseries that extend beyond the immediate circumstances of her life. For elsewhere she writes in a similar vein, "In times like these . . . I see the world being slowly transformed into a wilderness." Despite her own suffering she can "feel the suffering of millions."

And yet, Anne Frank believes "in spite of everything, that people are truly good at heart." This statement epitomizes the stark existential contrast of her worldview with the wartime reality that ultimately claimed her life.

The statement also exemplifies how Anne's literary form—her syntax and diction—mirror thematic content and contrasts. "In spite of everything" she still believes in people. She can "hear the approaching thunder . . . yet, when [she] look[s] up at the sky, [she] somehow feel[s] that everything will change for the better." At numerous points in this diary entry first-hand knowledge of violent tragedy stands side-by-side with belief in humanity and human progress.

"I must hold on to my ideals," Anne concludes. "Perhaps the day will come when I'll be able to realize them!" In her diary, she has done so, and more.

SUBAREA V: Sample Tests

Sample Test One

Section I

Questions 1-8. Read the following passage carefully before you decide on your answers to the questions.

THE BROAD-BACKED hippopotamus
Rests on his belly in the mud;
Although he seems so firm to us
He is merely flesh and blood.
Flesh and blood is weak and frail,
Susceptible to nervous shock;
While the True Church can never fail
For it is based upon a rock.

The hippo's feeble steps may err
In compassing material ends,
While the True Church need never stir
To gather in its dividends.

The potamus can never reach
The mango on the mango-tree;
But fruits of pomegranate and peach
Refresh the Church from over sea.

At mating time the hippos voice
Betrays inflexions hoarse and odd,
But every week we hear rejoice
The Church, at being one with God.

The hippopotamus's day
Is passed in sleep; at night he hunts;
God works in a mysterious way;
The Church can sleep and feed at once.

I saw the potamus take wing
Ascending from the damp savannas,
And quiring angels round him sing
The praise of God, in loud hosannas.
Blood of the Lamb shall wash him clean
And him shall heavenly arms enfold,
Among the saints he shall be seen
Performing on a harp of gold.
He shall be washed as white as snow,
By all the martyrd virgins kist,
While the True Church remains below
Wrapt in the old miasmal mist.

1. Who is the author of this poem?

A. William Faulkner

B. T.S. Eliot

C. William Blake

D. C.S. Lewis

E. William Shakespeare

2. What is the rhyme scheme in the second stanza?

A. ABAB

B. ABCD

C. ABCA

D. ADDA

E. None of the above

3. What literary device is used in this passage?

A. Alliteration

B. Allegory

C. Analogy

D. Anecdote

E. Anagram

4. What does the hippo represent?

A. The devil

B. Sinners

C. Animals

D. Heaven

E. Good luck

5. What does the mud represent?

A. Sin

B. Dirt

C. Home

D. Comfort

E. All of the above

6. What does "take wing" symbolize in the following line?
"I saw the potamus take wing"

A. Hunting a bird

B. Flying in a plane

C. Laying down on its side

D. Going to heaven

E. None of the above

7. What word does the author emphasize with repetition?

A. Church

B. Hippo

C. Hippopotamus

D. God

E. Mud

8. Which of the following best describes
"He shall be washed as white as snow"?

A. He will be washed by angels in heaven.

B. He will no longer rest in the mud

C. His sins will be forgiven.

D. His skin will be bleached.

E. He will become pure.

Questions 9-16. Read the following selection and answer the questions below, selecting the best choice of the options presented.

Two roads diverged in a yellow wood,
And sorry I could not travel both
And be one traveler, long I stood
And looked down one as far as I could
To where it bent in the undergrowth;

Then took the other, as just as fair,
And having perhaps the better claim,
Because it was grassy and wanted wear;
Though as for that the passing there
Had worn them really about the same,

And both that morning equally lay
In leaves no step had trodden black.
Oh, I kept the first for another day!
Yet knowing how way leads on to way,
I doubted if I should ever come back.

I shall be telling this with a sigh
Somewhere ages and ages hence:
Two roads diverged in a wood, and I—
I took the one less traveled by,
And that has made all the difference.

9. Who wrote this poem?

A. Robert Frost

B. Emily Dickinson

C. John Keats

D. William Wadsworth

E. Emily Bronte

10. When the author uses the phrase "wanted wear" in the third stanza, what does that mean?

A. It looked just as fair as the other path.

B. It was not as inviting.

C. The path didn't go the same way as the other one.

D. The path was less traveled than the other one.

E. You cannot determine what the author means.

11. The author says that he "took the one less traveled by"; what does that mean?

A. The other path looked like it was used more.

B. He did the right thing when others chose the wrong one.

C. He took the one on the left.

D. He took the one on the right.

E. It cannot be determined what the author meant by this short selection.

12. What is another way the author states his path was the "one less traveled by"?

A. "both that morning equally lay"

B. "no step had trodden black"

C. "Somewhere ages and ages hence"

D. "bent in the undergrowth"

E. "having perhaps the better claim"

13. What does the author imply since he took the path less traveled?

A. He has run into fewer people that try to bully him into doing what they want.

B. Life is tougher getting to see the light.

C. He was sorry he didn't chose to go the more well-trod path.

D. He didn't make as much money as the people that took the other path.

E. His life is better for choosing to go his own path.

14. What is the rhyme scheme?

A. ABBAB

B. ABABA

C. ABAAC

D. ABCAB

E. ABAAB

15. **Taking the road less traveled by made all the difference because ________.**

A. the decision shaped his life

B. it was a good hike

C. the character was able to find peace

D. he created a new path on the road

E. he will always be able to go back to walk on the more traveled path if he chooses to

16. **What literary device is used in this poem?**

A. Personification

B. Propaganda

C. Paradox

D. Parallelism

E. Pentameter

Questions 17-24. Read the following selection and answer the questions below, selecting the best choice of the options presented.

Fever 103°

Pure? What does it mean?
The tongues of hell
Are dull, dull as the triple

Tongues of dull, fat Cerberus
Who wheezes at the gate. Incapable
Of licking clean

The aguey tendon, the sin, the sin.
The tinder cries.
The indelible smell

Of a snuffed candle!
Love, love, the low smokes roll
From me like Isadora's scarves, I'm in a fright

One scarf will catch and anchor in thewheel,
Such yellow sullen smokes
Make their own element. They will not rise,

But trundle round the globe
Choking the aged and the meek,
The weak

Hothouse baby in its crib,
The ghastly orchid
Hanging its hanging garden in the air,

Devilish leopard!
Radiation turned it white
And killed it in an hour.

Greasing the bodies of adulterers
Like Hiroshima ash and eating in.
The sin. The sin.

17. Who is the author of this poem?

A. Margaret Atwood

B. Emily Dickinson

C. Sylvia Plath

D. Maya Angelou

E. Alice Walker

18. What imagery does "the tongues" create?

A. Flames

B. Gates

C. Sins

D. Lies

E. None of the above

19. Who is Cerberus?

A. A man entering the underworld

B. The guard of the underworld

C. The maid of the underworld

D. An angel

E. The devil

20. What does *aguey* mean?

A. Sinful

B. Torn

C. Deceitful

D. Beautiful

E. Burning

21. The word *trundle* is significant because ____.

A. It represents moving very slowly.

B. It is a roll out bed, used for camping.

C. it is not dark nor light.

D. it represents being instinctive.

E. None of the above.

22. What literary device is used in this poem?

A. Repetition

B. Onomatopoeia

C. Alliteration

D. Flashback

E. Flash forward

23. Which of the following best describes the setting?

A. Utopia

B. Dystopia

C. Promised land

D. Eden

E. Erotic

24. Why is the title substantial?

A. You can sweat out sins with a fever

B. It's the temperature in the underworld

C. This level of a fever would kill you

D. This is the temperature of fire

E. All of the above

Questions 25-32. Read the following selection and answer the questions below, selecting the best choice of the options presented.

"I went to work the next day, turning, so to speak, my back on that station. In that way only it seemed to me I could keep my hold on the redeeming facts of life. Still, one must look about sometimes; and then I saw this station, these men strolling aimlessly about in the sunshine of the yard. I asked myself sometimes what it all meant. They wandered here and there with their absurd long staves in their hands, like a lot of faithless pilgrims bewitched inside a rotten fence. The word 'ivory' rang in the air, was whispered, was sighed. You would think they were praying to it. A taint of imbecile rapacity blew through it all, like a whiff from some corpse. By Jove! I've never seen anything so unreal in my life. And outside, the silent wilderness surrounding this cleared speck on the earth struck me as something great and invincible, like evil or truth, waiting patiently for the passing away of this fantastic invasion.

—*Heart of Darkness*

25. Who wrote this novel?

A. Joseph Conrad

B. James Joyce

C. Jane Austen

D. Charlotte Brontë

E. Charles Dickens

26. What does the following line represent?
"I saw this station, these men strolling aimlessly about in the sunshine of the yard."

A. Soldiers enjoying their day

B. Men being unaware of the negativ,ity that surrounds them

C. Positivity is infectious

D. The station is a happy place

E. Embracing the weather before a storm hits

27. What does the word *staves* mean?

A. Machete

B. Axe

C. Gun

D. Bomb

E. Wooden club

28. What does the ivory represent?

A. Death

B. Prosperity

C. Jewelry

D. Trade

E. None of the above

29. What literary device is used when describing the ivory?

A. Alliteration

B. Allegory

C. Simile

D. Personification

E. Repetition

30. What does *rapacity* represent?

A. Greed

B. Rapid movement

C. Intelligent

D. Affluent

E. Generous

31. What literary device is used in this passage?

"And outside, the silent wilderness surrounding this cleared speck on the earth struck me as something great and invincible, like evil or truth, waiting patiently for the passing away of this fantastic invasion."

A. Simile

B. Metaphor

C. Illusion

D. Personification

E. Onomatopoeia

32. Which style of writing is represented in this novel?

A. Biographical

B. Autobiographical

C. Expository

D. Persuasive

E. None of the above

33. When students are given an assignment that is new to them, which of the following should almost always be discussed?

A. What the students can expect to learn from doing the assignment.

B. Whether the assignment will be graded in similar fashion to other assignments.

C. Whether the students can expect to be tested on the material presented.

D. The teacher's background with this type of assignment.

E. Samples of student work from this assignment in previous classes.

34. A high school classroom teacher is working with nonnative speakers of English. During class, students are asked to read aloud, and the teacher focuses on continuously correcting pronunciation errors. What has this teacher failed to take into account in regards to second language development?

A. Reading skills must be established prior to learning the syntax of a language.

B. The fastest way for a nonnative speaker is to imitate the way native speakers use the language.

C. Students should never be asked to read out loud before they can read and comprehend grade appropriate texts silently.

D. Nonnative speakers often understand what they are reading before they can accurately speak the language.

E. Oral punctuation corrections should only occur when the student is being assessed on pronunciation.

35. A middle school teacher gives her students a list of vocabulary words to use in their essay, intending for the list to act as a scaffold. If the students exhibit proficiency on a mastery level, which of the following would be the best 'next' step?

A. Give the students advanced words, and more of them, to include in the next essay.

B. Ask the students to work collectively to come up with a new list to use in the next essay.

C. Ask students to use the same vocabulary words in the next essay as well.

D. Give a new list of vocabulary terms and have them look up the definitions, then use them in the next essay.

E. Pair students up with a lower achieving peer in the class to help them explain the definitions.

36. An English teacher observes that a 10th grade student seems very upset about the idea of having to write a research paper. The teacher explains to the class as a whole, that the best approach for completing the assignment is to break the larger project into smaller tasks. Which of the following actions exemplify this methodology?

A. Having students write about a familiar topic, then contrasting it with the topic for the research paper.

B. Writing a rough draft of the paper, then handing it to a fellow student for feedback and a critical evaluation.

C. Finding at least two credible sources for the research paper's topic, and seeing which aspects they both agree on.

D. Compiling a bibliography of sources relating to the topic.

E. Write as much as you can think of and then schedule an individual conference with the instructor to discuss areas of improvement.

37. Why was it determined that students should be placed in the least restrictive educational environment?

A. Because placement in a 'least restrictive environment' would normalize children with disabilities, as opposed to being educated in isolation from others.

B. Because it was determined that classrooms should no longer be restrictive to minorities or females.

C. Because it would reduce the fiscal cost of providing additional classrooms.

D. Because adopting the least restrictive policies would increase funding to the school for special education.

E. Placing students in less restrictive environments makes grading easier on instructors.

38. In a crowded classroom with varying skill levels, how might the teacher best take advantage of the diversity of the learning styles?

A. Separate the students by reading levels.

B. Assess students individually, only, to mitigate potential anxiety for the students.

C. Incorporate opportunities for multilevel interaction through reciprocal learning events.

D. Assign students to learning centers for computer based learning.

E. Use a random number table to assign students to small groups.

39. When introducing a classic work of fiction to 8th graders, what is a significant factor in its presentation and study?

A. Whether the student finds that he or she can relate to the material.

B. Whether the material will include a test.

C. The material must be drawn from modern fiction sources.

D. Students must be able to read on grade level to be able to enjoy a classic work of literature.

E. The quality of the novels that are distributed for reading.

40. Classroom rules, when established correctly, require the teacher to do which of the following?

A. State the rules with a serious intent.

B. Quickly establish authority in the classroom.

C. Create as many rules as it takes to cover all of the possible issues that might arise.

D. Explain why the rules are needed.

E. Post the rules in a very obvious location in the classroom for students to reference.

41. If a teacher wanted to obtain data from a criterion-referenced test, as opposed to a norm-referenced test, which of the following would offer that information?

A. How much each student in the classroom already knows about a singular aspect of the subject.

B. How much each student in the classroom knows about a singular aspect as compared to other students on a national level.

C. How much each student in the classroom knows as compared to other students in the district.

D. How much each student in the classroom knows about a certain portion of the subject.

E. The average time spent on task for each test format.

42. Which of the following activities is a feature of an accelerated program as opposed to an enrichment activity?

A. Finishing an independent project.

B. Participating in simulations, role playing, playing games.

C. Taking an exam and receiving credit.

D. Enrolling and completing a summer program.

E. Participating in a team building activity.

43. When characterizing a student's creativity, which of the descriptors are most apt?

A. The student's solution is applicable in many areas, not just one domain.

B. The student's solutions, though seemingly unorthodox, upon further discovery prove sound.

C. The student's solutions are a collection of false starts, some of which end up being relevant.

D. The student's solutions do not deviate from the standard perspectives.

E. The student's interest in STEM topics in caparison with their interest in humanitarian topics.

44. When seeking to improve academic performance, as well as motivation of students, which of the following strategies are most likely to succeed?

A. Teachers appoint a liaison to work with the administration to create a 'best practices' set of rules.

B. Teachers present material as a team, standardizing presentation, and mapping academic progress.

C. Teacher collaboration to assess and monitor other classroom procedures offers successful solutions.

D. The classroom teacher must utilize management techniques with which he is familiar and comfortable.

E. Teachers are evaluated using a merit-based pay system.

45. For students learning the process of constructed response writing, what is the appropriate pedagogical process?

A. independent writing (summative), guided writing (formative), model/shadowing

B. Model/shadowing, guided writing (formative), independent writing (summative)

C. Guided writing (formative), model/shadowing, independent writing (summative)

D. Independent writing (summative), guided writing (formative), peer reviewed grouping

E. Guided writing (formative), peer reviewed grouping, individual conference.

46. An aspect of the reflective practice methodology is exemplified in which of the following?

A. The teacher limits the amount of peer review.

B. The teacher should limit student input that challenges or questions established teaching practices.

C. The teacher should allow peer review to take its natural course, offering very little framework to limit the problem solving process.

D. The teacher should establish a safe environment that allows reflection to take place among an accepted practice that is applicable for all learning situations.

E. The teacher should raise the stakes in the assignment by offering a peer assessment at the end of the peer review process.

47. When establishing the best way to assist students with comprehension skills, a teacher should focus on which of the following techniques as an informational text is read aloud?

A. Writing down questions as a text is read aloud

B. Creating an outline

C. Setting a purpose for reading

D. Encouraging students to make predictions

E. Telling students there will be a quiz at the end of a reading.

Questions 48-55. Read the following selection and answer the questions below, selecting the best choice of the options presented.

"If people bring so much courage to this world the world has to kill them to break them, so of course it kills them. The world breaks every one and afterward many are strong at the broken places. But those that will not break it kills. It kills the very good and the very gentle and the very brave impartially. If you are none of these you can be sure it will kill you too but there will be no special hurry."

—*A Farewell to Arms*

48. Who wrote this novel?

A. Henry David Thoreau

B. Ernest Hemingway

C. F. Scott Fitzgerald

D. Harper Lee

E. J.R.R. Tolkien

49. What is the theme of this novel?

A. Innocence

B. War

C. Love

D. Death

E. Grief

50. What does the title symbolize?

A. An amputation caused during war

B. Being discharged

C. Saying goodbye to the arms of someone you love

D. Saying goodbye to weaponry and warfare

E. C & D

51. Which literary device is used to describe war?

A. Personification

B. Alliteration

C. Simile

D. Metaphor

E. Idiom

52. What best describes the author's intention in the following line?
"It kills the very good and the very gentle and the very brave impartially."

A. Everyone will die sooner or later

B. Murderers target nice people

C. The good, gentle and brave are easier to kill

D. The good, gentle and brave die protecting others

E. War kills everyone, it doesn't have a bias

53. How does the world *break* people?

A. It creates challenging times

B. It represents being shot and not dying

C. It causes extreme wounds, mentally and physically

D. People can have broken bones

E. Physical objects and precious belongings can be broken

54. Which of the following best represents this passage?

A. Sarcasm

B. Resentment

C. Irony

D. Sympathy

E. Affectionate

55. Which literary period is this from?

A. Romanticism

B. Renaissance

C. The Enlightenment

D. Existentialism

E. Modernism

Questions 56-63. Read the following passage carefully before you decide on your answers to the questions.

O for a Muse of fire, that would ascend
The brightest heaven of invention,
A kingdom for a stage, princes to act
And monarchs to behold the swelling scene!
Then should the warlike Harry, like himself,
Assume the port of Mars; and at his heels,
Leash'd in like hounds, should famine sword and fire
Crouch for employment. But pardon, and gentles all,
The flat unraised spirits that have dared
On this unworthy scaffold to bring forth
So great an object: can this cockpit hold
The vasty fields of France? or may we cram
Within this wooden O the very casques
That did affright the air at Agincourt?
O, pardon! since a crooked figure may
Attest in little place a million;
And let us, ciphers to this great account,
On your imaginary forces work.
Suppose within the girdle of these walls
Are now confined two mighty monarchies,
Whose high upreared and abutting fronts
The perilous narrow ocean parts asunder:
Piece out our imperfections with your thoughts;
Into a thousand parts divide one man,
And make imaginary puissance;
Think when we talk of horses, that you see them
Printing their proud hoofs i' the receiving earth;
For 'tis your thoughts that now must deck our kings,
Carry them here and there; jumping o'er times,
Turning the accomplishment of many years
Into an hour-glass: for the which supply,
Admit me Chorus to this history;
Who prologue-like your humble patience pray,
Gently to hear, kindly to judge, our play.

56. The first four lines could best be described as...

A. A warning of violence to come.

B. A celebration of military victory.

C. An exultation of creative vision.

D. A lamentation of the inadequacy of mortals.

E. A plea for patience from the audience.

57. What can the reader infer from lines 5-8?

A. Harry was a man who inspired awe and fear.

B. Harry was a god.

C. Harry will soon rule over all people.

D. Harry is the villain of the play.

E. Harry was a sailor.

58. What is meant by the line "since a crooked figure may attest in little place a million"?

A. Small men can enact great change if they fulfill their potential.

B. A hand written number can evoke a massive value.

C. Trials can be overcome through perseverance.

D. Some tests are insurmountable to any man.

E. There are mysteries we cannot solve.

59. What does the narrator wish for the audience to do in lines 20-28?

A. Draw upon their own experiences at the theater.

B. Imagine the horror and glory of war.

C. Pretend the physical aspects of the theater reflect things far greater than can be shown onstage.

D. Appreciate history, both the good and bad aspects.

E. Understand their own smallness in the face of this epic tale.

60. What is the narrator's attitude towards the audience?

A. Egocentric disdain

B. Haughty dismissal

C. Meek terror

D. Wide-eyed fascination

E. Humble entreating

61. What is the "unworthy scaffold"?

A. A run-down building

B. A poorhouse

C. The barracks

D. The stage itself

E. A church

62. The narrator wishes to

A. Deceive the audience with propaganda.

B. Relay a tale too great for the stage to contain.

C. Repent for the sins committed by his people.

D. Slander the memory of a great leader.

E. Absolve himself of any guilt he may be feeling.

63. Who are the "ciphers to this great account"?

A. Soldiers

B. Actors

C. Women

D. Scholars

E. Royalty

Questions 64-71. Read the following passage carefully before you decide on your answers to the questions.

A child said, What is the grass? fetching it to me with full hands;
How could I answer the child?. . . .I do not know what it is any more than he.

I guess it must be the flag of my disposition, out of hopeful green stuff woven.

Or I guess it is the handkerchief of the Lord,
A scented gift and remembrancer designedly dropped,
Bearing the owner's name someway in the corners, that we may see and remark, and say Whose?

Or I guess the grass is itself a child. . . .the produced babe of the vegetation.

Or I guess it is a uniform hieroglyphic,
And it means, Sprouting alike in broad zones and narrow zones,
Growing among black folks as among white,
Kanuck, Tuckahoe, Congressman, Cuff, I give them the same, I receive them the same.

And now it seems to me the beautiful uncut hair of graves.

Tenderly will I use you curling grass,
It may be you transpire from the breasts of young men,
It may be if I had known them I would have loved them;
It may be you are from old people and from women, and
from offspring taken soon out of their mother's laps,
And here you are the mother's laps.

This grass is very dark to be from the white heads of old mothers,
Darker than the colorless beards of old men,
Dark to come from under the faint red roofs of mouths.

O I perceive after all so many uttering tongues!
And I perceive they do not come from the roofs of mouths for nothing.

I wish I could translate the hints about the dead young men and women,
And the hints about old men and mothers, and the offspring taken soon out of their laps.

What do you think has become of the young and old men?
What do you think has become of the women and children?

They are alive and well somewhere;
The smallest sprouts show there is really no death,
And if ever there was it led forward life, and does not wait at the end to arrest it,
And ceased the moment life appeared.

All goes onward and outward. . . .and nothing collapses,
And to die is different from what any one supposed, and luckier.

64. **What best describes the tone of this poem?**

A. Melancholic

B. Stream-of-consciousness

C. Bittersweet

D. Exuberant

E. Regretful

65. **Why does the author decide death is lucky?**

A. Death leads to new life, as evidenced by the grass.

B. People are immortal in the afterlife.

C. Children bring hope for the future, ever growing stronger.

D. Life is meaningless, and people are no worse off in death than cut grass.

E. Man's cruelty makes life not worth living.

66. **What does the speaker mean by "tenderly I will use you curling grass"?**

A. He will attempt to nurture a better generation.

B. He will ponder the implications and meanings of the grass.

C. He has no easy answers, the question is too complex to examine.

D. When he dies, he will become grass.

E. The grass connects him to all beings.

67. **What can we infer from the first stanza in context?**

A. The speaker is dim and uneducated.

B. The speaker has no mind for philosophy.

C. The child is cleverer than he appears.

D. The question is too complex for a simple answer.

E. The grass is a strange variety not seen in this location.

68. Who does the speaker decide is "the mother's laps"?

A. The child

B. Humanity

C. Himself

D. The grass

E. The dead

69. What is meant by lines 7-10?

A. The Lord works in mysterious ways.

B. The grass is an object, inanimate as a handkerchief.

C. The Lord created the grass, and it bears his signature.

D. There is no need for God with such natural beauty around us.

E. The answers to these questions float before us, like a handkerchief on the wind.

70. What can we infer that the author believes from stanza 5?

A. He is a mild racist.

B. All of humanity is fundamentally the same.

C. We are all united in death

D. Disharmony can be overcome through change.

E. Social class is a fact of life.

71. In context, what does the author mean by "I wish I could translate the hints about the dead young men and women"?

A. He wishes he could discern things about the people from the grass they became.

B. He wants to think no more of depressing matters like death.

C. He wishes he could speak to the dead to better understand what awaits him.

D. He wants to cure the suffering in the world.

E. He feels it is unnatural that mothers must lose their children.

Questions 72-79. Read the following passage carefully before you decide on your answers to the questions.

These pictures were in watercolors. The first represented clouds low and livid, rolling over a swollen sea: all the distance was in eclipse; so, too, was the foreground; or rather, the nearest billows, for there was no land. One gleam of light lifted into relief a half-submerged mast, on which sat a cormorant, dark and large, with wings flecked with foam; its beak held a gold bracelet set with gems, that I had touched with as brilliant tints as my palette could yield, and as glittering distinctness as my pencil could impart. Sinking below the bird and mast, a drowned corpse glanced through the green water; a fair arm was the only limb clearly visible, whence the bracelet had been washed or torn.

The second picture contained for foreground only the dim peak of a hill, with grass and some leaves slanting as if by a breeze. Beyond and above spread an expanse of sky, dark blue as at twilight: rising into the sky was a woman's shape to the bust, portrayed in tints as dusk and soft as I could combine. The dim forehead was crowned with a star; the lineaments below were seen as through the suffusion of vapour; the eyes shone dark and wild; the hair streamed shadowy, like a beamless cloud torn by storm or by electric travail. On the neck lay a pale reflection like moonlight; the same faint lustre touched the train of thin clouds from which rose and bowed this vision of the Evening Star.

The third showed the pinnacle of an iceberg piercing a polar winter sky: a muster of northern lights reared their dim lances, close serried, along the horizon. Throwing these into distance, rose, in the foreground, a head,--a colossal head, inclined towards the iceberg, and resting against it. Two thin hands, joined under the forehead, and supporting it, drew up before the lower features a sable veil, a brow quite bloodless, white as bone, and an eye hollow and fixed, blank of meaning but for the glassiness of despair, alone were visible. Above the temples, amidst wreathed turban folds of black drapery, vague in its character and consistency as cloud, gleamed a ring of white flame, gemmed with sparkles of a more lurid tinge. This pale crescent was "the likeness of a kingly crown;" what it diademed was "the shape which shape had none."

"Were you happy when you painted these pictures?" asked Mr. Rochester presently.

"I was absorbed, sir: yes, and I was happy. To paint them, in short, was to enjoy one of the keenest pleasures I have ever known."

"That is not saying much. Your pleasures, by your own account, have been few; but I daresay you did exist in a kind of artist's dreamland while you blent and arranged these strange tints. Did you sit at them long each day?"

"I had nothing else to do, because it was the vacation, and I sat at them from morning till noon, and from noon till night: the length of the midsummer days favoured my inclination to apply."

"And you felt self-satisfied with the result of your ardent labours?"

"Far from it. I was tormented by the contrast between my idea and my handiwork: in each case I had imagined something which I was quite powerless to realise."

"Not quite: you have secured the shadow of your thought; but no more, probably. You had not enough of the artist's skill and science to give it full being: yet the drawings are, for a school-girl, peculiar. As to the thoughts, they are elfish. These eyes in the Evening Star you must have seen in a dream. How could you make them look so clear, and yet not at all brilliant? for the planet above quells their rays. And what meaning is that in their solemn depth? And who taught you to paint wind. There is a high gale in that sky, and on this hill-top. Where did you see Latmos? For that is Latmos. There! put the drawings away!"

I had scarce tied the strings of the portfolio, when, looking at his watch, he said abruptly -

"It is nine o'clock: what are you about, Miss Eyre, to let Adele sit up so long? Take her to bed."

Adele went to kiss him before quitting the room: he endured the caress, but scarcely seemed to relish it more than Pilot would have done, nor so much.

"I wish you all good-night, now," said he, making a movement of the hand towards the door, in token that he was tired of our company, and wished to dismiss us. Mrs. Fairfax folded up her knitting: I took my portfolio: we curtseyed to him, received a frigid bow in return, and so withdrew.

72. What best describes Mr. Rochester's objective in the previous scene?

A. To break Jane down by insulting her art.

B. To determine her romantic interests and possibly woo her.

C. To discover more about her personality through her work.

D. To find something he can use against her family.

E. To establish his dominance over her and her household.

73. What is meant by the line "but scarcely seemed to relish it more than Pilot would have done"?

A. He despises the young Adele.

B. He dislikes such an expression of familiarity.

C. He is a sacrilegious man.

D. His depression prevents him from enjoying intimacy.

E. He is an antagonist.

74. Mr. Rochester feels Jane's paintings are...

A. Naïve and unskilled, but showing potential.

B. A frivolous waste of time.

C. Unique, perhaps disturbingly so.

D. Blasphemous, though well-made.

E. Extraordinary, though he struggles to express his admiration.

75. What is meant by the term "diademed" in this passage:
This pale crescent was "the likeness of a kingly crown;" what it diademed was "the shape which shape had none."

A. Illuminated

B. Exposed

C. Pierced

D. Crowned

E. Blended

76. The primary effect of the imagery in the description of Jane's second painting is to:

A. Emphasize the painting's religious themes

B. Explore its ethereal, supernatural quality

C. Determine its ill-formed concepts and amateurish execution

D. Characterize Jane as a hopeless romantic

E. Place the painting as an interpretation of Mr. Rochester

77. What is the primary subject of the first painting?

A. A bird holding a piece of jewelry

B. A Naval skirmish in full swing

C. A horrific murder and robbery

D. An abstract image of a woman shrouded in clouds

E. A religious ceremony

78. Inferring from the text, Jane must be Adele's…

A. Mother

B. Sister

C. Caretaker

D. Employer

E. Maid

79. What is Jane's attitude towards her paintings?

A. Loathing

B. Embarrassment

C. Pride

D. Dissatisfaction

E. Indifference

Questions 80-87. Read the following passage carefully before you decide on your answers to the questions.

"You've just told me some high spots in your memories. Want to hear mine? They're all connected with the sea.

Here's one. When I was on the Squarehead square rigger, bound for Buenos Aires. Full moon in the trades. The old hooker driving 14 knots. I lay on the bowsprit, facing astern, with the water foaming into spume under me. Every mast with sail white in the moonlight - towering high above me. I became drunk with the beauty and singing rhythm of it - and for a second I lost myself, actually lost my life. I was set free! I dissolved into the sea, became white sails and flying spray - became beauty and rhythm, became moonlight and the ship and the high dim-starred sky. I belonged, without past or future, within peace and unity and a wild joy, within something greater than my own life, or the life of man, to Life itself! To God if you want to put it that way.

Then another time, on the American line, when I was lookout in the crow's nest on the dawn watch. A calm sea that time. Only a lazy ground swell and a slow drousy roll of the ship. The passengers asleep and none of the crew in sight. No sound of man. Black smoke pouring from the funnels behind and beneath me. Dreaming, not keeping lookout, feeling alone, and above, and apart, watching the dawn creep like a painted dream over the sky and sea which slept together.

Then the moment of ecstatic freedom came. The peace, the end of the quest, the last harbor, the joy of belonging to a fulfillment beyond men's lousy, greedy fears and hopes and dreams! And several other times in my life, when I was swimming far out, or lying alone on the beach, I have had the same experience. Became the sun, the hot sand, green seaweed anchored to a rock, swaying in the tide. Like a saint's vision of beatitude. Like the veil of things as they seem drawn back by an unseen hand. For a second you see - and seeing the secret, are the secret. For a second there is meaning! Then the hand lets the veil fall and you are alone, lost in the fog again, stumbling on toward no where, for no good reason!

it was a great mistake, my being born a man. I would have been much more successful as a seagull or fish. As it is, I will always be a stranger who never feels at home, who does not want and is not really wanted, who can never belong, who must always be a little in love with death."

80. What adjective best describes Edmund's tone in this piece?

A. Disaffected

B. Morose

C. Longing

D. Celebratory

E. Inspired

81. This piece can best be described as…

A. A poem

B. A dramatic monologue

C. Prose fiction

D. An ode

E. A dirge

82. What are the two primary contrasts of this piece?

A. The sea with the land; drunkenness with sobriety.

B. Depression and joy; sailing with being "anchored".

C. The wild sea with the calm sea; ecstasy with numbness.

D. Edmund with his father; freedom with responsibility.

E. Humanity with nature; godlessness with holiness.

83. The author conveys the sea using what primary technique?

A. Analogy

B. Assonance

C. Simile

D. Personification

E. Imagery

84. The phrase "like a saint's vision of beatitude" serves to reinforce what idea?

A. Edmund's desire to die.

B. Edmund finds spirituality in nature.

C. Edmund wishes to sail again.

D. Edmund wishes to repent

E. Edmund dislikes religion.

85. In the first paragraph, the author characterizes this piece as a…

A. Story-within-a-story

B. Memory

C. Soliloquy

D. Ballad

E. Fabrication

86. Where does the primary shift in tone occur in this piece?

A. Paragraph two, "I became drunk with the beauty…"

B. Paragraph three, "The another time, on the American line…"

C. Paragraph four, "Then that moment of ecstatic freedom came!"

D. Paragraph four, "Then the hand lets the veil fall…"

E. Paragraph five, "I will always be a stranger…"

87. What natural image does the author use to contrast the sea and its feelings of freedom?

A. Black smoke

B. Fog

C. Spray

D. Seagull

E. Waves

Questions 88-95. Read the following passage carefully before you decide on your answers to the questions.

In a village of La Mancha, the name of which I have no desire to call to mind, there lived not long since one of those gentlemen that keep a lance in the lance-rack, an old buckler, a lean hack, and a greyhound for coursing. An olla of rather more beef than mutton, a salad on most nights, scraps on Saturdays, lentils on Fridays, and a pigeon or so extra on Sundays, made away with three-quarters of his income. The rest of it went in a doublet of fine cloth and velvet breeches and shoes to match for holidays, while on week-days he made a brave figure in his best homespun. He had in his house a housekeeper past forty, a niece under twenty, and a lad for the field and market-place, who used to saddle the hack as well as handle the bill-hook. The age of this gentleman of ours was bordering on fifty; he was of a hardy habit, spare, gaunt-featured, a very early riser and a great sportsman. They will have it his surname was Quixada or Quesada (for here there is some difference of opinion among the authors who write on the subject), although from reasonable conjectures it seems plain that he was called Quexana. This, however, is of but little importance to our tale; it will be enough not to stray a hair's breadth from the truth in the telling of it.

You must know, then, that the above-named gentleman whenever he was at leisure (which was mostly all the year round) gave himself up to reading books of chivalry with such ardour and avidity that he almost entirely neglected the pursuit of his field-sports, and even the management of his property; and to such a pitch did his eagerness and infatuation go that he sold many an acre of tillage land to buy books of chivalry to read, and brought home as many of them as he could get. But of all there were none he liked so well as those of the famous Feliciano de Silva's composition, for their lucidity of style and complicated conceits were as pearls in his sight, particularly when in his reading he came upon courtships and cartels, where he often found passages like "the reason of the unreason with which my reason is afflicted so weakens my reason that with reason I murmur at your beauty;" or again, "the high heavens, that of your divinity divinely fortify you with the stars, render you deserving of the desert your greatness deserves." Over conceits of this sort the poor gentleman lost his wits, and used to lie awake striving to understand them and worm the meaning out of them; what Aristotle himself could not have made out or extracted had he come to life again for that special purpose. He was not at all easy about the wounds which Don Belianis gave and took, because it seemed to him that, great as were the surgeons who had cured him, he must have had his face and body covered all over with seams and scars. He commended, however, the author's way of ending his book with the promise of that interminable adventure, and many a time was he tempted to take up his pen and finish it properly as is there proposed, which no doubt he would have done, and made a successful piece of work of it too, had not greater and more absorbing thoughts prevented him.

88. The author's tone in this piece can best be described as…

A. Heroic

B. Comedic

C. Florid

D. Epic

E. Mysterious

89. The line "were as pearls to his site" is an example of a...

A. Metaphor

B. Analogy

C. Simile

D. Allegory

E. Conceit

90. Our main character's attitude towards reading can best be described as...

A. Lackadaisical

B. Unusual

C. Illiterate

D. Obsessive

E. Joyous

91. The passage "the high heavens, that of your divinity divinely fortify you with the stars, render you deserving of the desert your greatness deserves" contains several examples what poetic device?

A. Alliteration

B. Onomatopoeia

C. Diction

D. Resonance

E. Enjambment

92. According to the text, who is Count Belianis?

A. A historical champion

B. A fictional character

C. A competing nobleman

D. A romantic rival

E. A dead family member

93. The passage "it will be enough not to stray a hair's breadth from the truth in the telling of it" characterizes the previous passage as...

A. Essential

B. Metaphorical

C. Unimportant

D. Esoteric

E. Bland

94. What are the two defining traits of the main character described above?

A. Laziness and obsessiveness

B. Ignorance and piousness

C. Diligence and valor

D. Prideful and vain

E. Curious and kindhearted

95. The final sentence of this excerpt is an example of...

A. Satire

B. Foreshadowing

C. Interstitial

D. Subtext

E. Premonition

Questions 96-100. Read the following passage carefully before you decide on your answers to the questions.

O wild West Wind, thou breath of Autumn's being,
Thou, from whose unseen presence the leaves dead
Are driven, like ghosts from an enchanter fleeing,

Yellow, and black, and pale, and hectic red,
Pestilence-stricken multitudes: O thou,
Who chariotest to their dark wintry bed

The winged seeds, where they lie cold and low,
Each like a corpse within its grave, until
Thine azure sister of the Spring shall blow

Her clarion o'er the dreaming earth, and fill
(Driving sweet buds like flocks to feed in air)
With living hues and odors plain and hill:

Wild Spirit, which art moving everywhere;
Destroyer and preserver; hear, oh, hear!

Thou on whose stream, 'mid the steep sky's commotion,
Loose clouds like earth's decaying leaves are shed,
Shook from the tangled boughs of Heaven and Ocean,

Angels of rain and lightning: there are spread
On the blue surface of thine aery surge,
Like the bright hair uplifted from the head

Of some fierce Maenad, even from the dim verge
Of the horizon to the zenith's height,
The locks of the approaching storm. Thou dirge

Of the dying year, to which this closing night
Will be the dome of a vast sepulchre,
Vaulted with all thy congregated might

Of vapors, from whose solid atmosphere
Black rain, and fire, and hail will burst: oh, hear!

96. The first line of this poem exhibits what poetic devices?

I. Alliteration

II. Personification

III. Onomatopoeia

A. Only I

B. Only II

C. Only III

D. I and II

E. I, II, and III

97. What best describes the final stanza of this selection?

A. Slant rhyme

B. Heroic couplet

C. Hyperbole

D. Irony

E. Blank verse

98. "Wild Spirit, which art moving everywhere; Destroyer and preserver; hear, oh, hear!" This passage displays a…

A. Enjambment

B. Slant rhyme

C. Simile

D. Iamb

E. Allegory

99. This poem is written in what style?

A. Vers libre

B. Heroic couplet

C. Epic saga

D. Imagist soliloquy

E. Iambic pentameter

100. What in the poem is compared to "Angels of rain and lightning"?

A. The wind

B. Maenads

C. Clouds

D. Human souls

E. Autumn

Free Response Essay Sample Questions

Section II

Question 1.

Read the following passage from Huckleberry Finn. Education in literature can have a variety of outcomes for characters. Analyze how the author describes in the passage the way the protagonist was educated and discuss in an essay how this affected the character. Do not summarize the plot.

> Her sister, Miss Watson, a tolerable slim old maid, with goggles on, had just come to live with her, and took a set at me now with a spelling-book. She worked me middling hard for about an hour, and then the widow made her ease up. I couldn't stood it much longer. Then for an hour it was deadly dull, and I was fidgety. Miss Watson would say, "Don't put your feet up there, Huckleberry - set up straight;" and pretty soon she would say, "Don't gap and stretch like that, Huckleberry - why don't you try to behave?" Then she told me all about the bad place, and I said I wished I was there. She got mad then, abut I didn't mean no harm. All I wanted was to go somewheres; all I wanted was a change, I warn't particular. She said it as wicked to say what I said; said she wouldn't say it for the whole world; she was going to live so as to go to the good place. Well, I couldn't see no advantage in going where she was going, so I made up my mind I wouldn't try for it. But I never said so, because it would only make trouble, and wouldn't do no good.

Question 2.

Choose a character from a novel or play who responds in some significant way to a life-changing incident. Then write a well-developed essay in which you analyze the way that incident was used by the author to make a change in either the character's life or the community that surrounds the character, describe the way the event influences justice or injustice being served.

Sample Test One: ANSWER KEY

Question Number	Correct Answer	Your Answer
1.	B	
2.	A	
3.	B	
4.	B	
5.	A	
6.	D	
7.	A	
8.	C	
9.	A	
10.	D	
11.	A	
12.	B	
13.	E	
14.	E	
15.	A	
16.	D	
17.	C	
18.	A	
19.	B	
20.	E	
21.	A	
22.	A	
23.	B	
24.	A	
25.	A	
26.	B	
27.	E	
28.	B	
29.	D	
30.	A	
31.	A	
32.	D	
33.	A	
34.	D	

Question Number	Correct Answer	Your Answer
35.	B	
36.	C	
37.	A	
38.	C	
39.	A	
40.	D	
41.	D	
42.	C	
43.	B	
44.	C	
45.	B	
46.	D	
47.	A	
48.	B	
49.	B	
50.	E	
51.	A	
52.	E	
53.	C	
54.	B	
55.	E	
56.	C	
57.	A	
58.	B	
59.	C	
60.	E	
61.	D	
62.	B	
63.	B	
64.	C	
65.	A	
66.	B	
67.	D	

Question Number	Correct Answer	Your Answer
68.	D	
69.	C	
70.	B	
71.	A	
72.	C	
73.	B	
74.	A	
75.	D	
76.	B	
77.	A	
78.	C	
79.	D	
80.	C	
81.	B	
82.	C	
83.	E	
84.	B	
85.	B	
86.	D	
87.	B	
88.	B	
89.	C	
90.	D	
91.	A	
92.	B	
93.	C	
94.	A	
95.	B	
96.	D	
97.	B	
98.	B	
99.	E	
100.	C	

Answer Key and Rationale

If there are words that are options for answers that you do not know, now is the time to look them up and prepare yourself for the exam! Many answer options includes words or phrases used in literary discussions, and some may not be familiar. It is possible they will be on the actual exam, so you should familiarize yourself with them now.

Questions 1-8. Read the following passage carefully before you decide on your answers to the questions.

THE BROAD-BACKED hippopotamus
Rests on his belly in the mud;
Although he seems so firm to us
He is merely flesh and blood.
Flesh and blood is weak and frail,
Susceptible to nervous shock;
While the True Church can never fail
For it is based upon a rock.

The hippo's feeble steps may err
In compassing material ends,
While the True Church need never stir
To gather in its dividends.

The potamus can never reach
The mango on the mango-tree;
But fruits of pomegranate and peach
Refresh the Church from over sea.

At mating time the hippos voice
Betrays inflexions hoarse and odd,
But every week we hear rejoice
The Church, at being one with God.

The hippopotamus's day
Is passed in sleep; at night he hunts;
God works in a mysterious way;
The Church can sleep and feed at once.

I saw the potamus take wing
Ascending from the damp savannas,
And quiring angels round him sing
The praise of God, in loud hosannas.
Blood of the Lamb shall wash him clean
And him shall heavenly arms enfold,
Among the saints he shall be seen
Performing on a harp of gold.

He shall be washed as white as snow,
By all the martyrd virgins kist,
While the True Church remains below
Wrapt in the old miasmal mist.

1. Who is the author of this poem?

A. William Faulkner

B. T.S. Eliot

C. William Blake

D. C.S. Lewis

E. William Shakespeare

The answer is B.

T.S. Eliot is the author of this poem.

2. What is the rhyme scheme in the second stanza?

A. ABAB

B. ABCD

C. ABCA

D. ADDA

E. None of the above

The answer is A.

The rhyme scheme in the second stanza follows ABAB. The first and third lines rhyme, and the second and fourth lines rhyme.

3. What literary device is used in this passage?

A. Alliteration

B. Allegory

C. Analogy

D. Anecdote

E. Anagram

The answer is B.

An allegory is a literary device that includes hidden meaning in a poem or short story. Because the hippo represents sinners in this poem, B is the best answer.

4. What does the hippo represent?

A. The devil

B. Sinners

C. Animals

D. Heaven

E. Good luck

The answer is B.

The hippo represents sinners in this poem. Given the religious context of the poem, sinners is the most appropriate answer.

5. What does the mud represent?

A. Sin

B. Dirt

C. Home

D. Comfort

E. All of the above

The answer is A.

Because the hippo represents sinners, the mud represents sin. The hippo may be dirty (B), and could feel at home (C) or comforted by the mud (D), but this does not parallel the symbolism within the writing.

6. What does "take wing" symbolize in the following line?
"I saw the potamus take wing"

A. Hunting a bird

B. Flying in a plane

C. Laying down on its side

D. Going to heaven

E. None of the above

The answer is D.

Taking wing is a representation of going to the heavens in the sky. Flying a plane and laying on its side are obviously incorrect and it's easy to narrow down to A and D. The literal interpretation, A, is incorrect and does not represent the symbolism embedded in the writing.

7. **What word does the author emphasize with repetition?**

A. Church

B. Hippo

C. Hippopotamus

D. God

E. Mud

The answer is A.

The only word that is emphasized in this poem with repetition is church; therefore, A is the most appropriate answer.

8. **Which of the following best describes "He shall be washed as white as snow"?**

A. He will be washed by angels in heaven.

B. He will no longer rest in the mud

C. His sins will be forgiven.

D. His skin will be bleached.

E. He will become pure.

The answer is C.

Washing is a representation of cleansing one of their sins. The symbolism in this quote represents the forgiveness of sins. C is the correct answer for this question.

Questions 9-16. Read the following selection and answer the questions below, selecting the best choice of the options presented.

Two roads diverged in a yellow wood,
And sorry I could not travel both
And be one traveler, long I stood
And looked down one as far as I could
To where it bent in the undergrowth;

Then took the other, as just as fair,
And having perhaps the better claim,
Because it was grassy and wanted wear;
Though as for that the passing there
Had worn them really about the same,

And both that morning equally lay
In leaves no step had trodden black.
Oh, I kept the first for another day!
Yet knowing how way leads on to way,
I doubted if I should ever come back.

I shall be telling this with a sigh
Somewhere ages and ages hence:
Two roads diverged in a wood, and I—
I took the one less traveled by,
And that has made all the difference.

9. **Who wrote this poem?**

   A. Robert Frost

   B. Emily Dickinson

   C. John Keats

   D. William Wadsworth

   E. Emily Bronte

   The answer is A.

   Robert Frost is the author of this poem.

10. When the author uses the phrase "wanted wear" in the third stanza, what does that mean?

A. It looked just as fair as the other path.

B. It was not as inviting.

C. The path didn't go the same way as the other one.

D. The path was less traveled than the other one.

E. You cannot determine what the author means.

The answer is D.

One path had obviously been walked on, or "worn" more than the other. By stating that one of the paths "wanted wear," the author is implying that this path had not been trav-eled on often. Therefore, D is the best answer.

11. The author says that he "took the one less traveled by"; what does that mean?

A. The other path looked like it was used more.

B. He did the right thing when others chose the wrong one.

C. He took the one on the left.

D. He took the one on the right.

E. It cannot be determined what the author meant by this short selection.

The answer is A.

Just as we learned in the previous question, one of the paths had been walked on far more frequently. The author took the one "less traveled by," meaning it had a minimal path already carved out. This makes A the best answer.

12. What is another way the author states his path was the "one less traveled by"?

A. "both that morning equally lay"

B. "no step had trodden black"

C. "Somewhere ages and ages hence"

D. "bent in the undergrowth"

E. "having perhaps the better claim"

The answer is B.

B is the only reference to travel, as the author suggests with a step.

13. What does the author imply since he took the path less traveled?

A. He has run into fewer people that try to bully him into doing what they want.

B. Life is tougher getting to see the light.

C. He was sorry he didn't chose to go the more well-trod path.

D. He didn't make as much money as the people that took the other path.

E. His life is better for choosing to go his own path.

The answer is E.

The author implies that he has had a better life due to the decisions that he's made on his own. He believes his life is better for choosing to go his own path.

14. What is the rhyme scheme?

A. ABBAB

B. ABABA

C. ABAAC

D. ABCAB

E. ABAAB

The answer is E.

This poem follows the ABAAB rhyme scheme.

15. Taking the road less traveled by made all the difference because ________.

A. the decision shaped his life

B. it was a good hike

C. the character was able to find peace

D. he created a new path on the road

E. he will always be able to go back to walk on the more traveled path if he chooses to

The answer is A.

Going on the other path would have led to a different life for this character. The best answer is A because choosing the road less traveled by has been a decision that has shaped his life. While B, C, D, and E may have partial truths, A is the best answer for this question.

16. What literary device is used in this poem?

A. Personification

B. Propaganda

C. Paradox

D. Parallelism

E. Pentameter

The answer is D.

Because we know the path represents roads the author has taken in life, it's easy to determine that parallelism is the literary device used in this poem.

Questions 17-24. Read the following selection and answer the questions below, selecting the best choice of the options presented.

Fever 103°

Pure? What does it mean?
The tongues of hell
Are dull, dull as the triple

Tongues of dull, fat Cerberus
Who wheezes at the gate. Incapable
Of licking clean

The aguey tendon, the sin, the sin.
The tinder cries.
The indelible smell

Of a snuffed candle!
Love, love, the low smokes roll
From me like Isadora's scarves, I'm in a fright

One scarf will catch and anchor in thewheel,
Such yellow sullen smokes
Make their own element. They will not rise,

But trundle round the globe
Choking the aged and the meek,
The weak

Hothouse baby in its crib,
The ghastly orchid
Hanging its hanging garden in the air,

Devilish leopard!
Radiation turned it white
And killed it in an hour.

Greasing the bodies of adulterers
Like Hiroshima ash and eating in.
The sin. The sin.

17. Who is the author of this poem?

A. Margaret Atwood

B. Emily Dickinson

C. Sylvia Plath

D. Maya Angelou

E. Alice Walker

The answer is C.

Sylvia Plath wrote this poem.

18. What imagery does "the tongues" create?

A. Flames

B. Gates

C. Sins

D. Lies

E. None of the above

The answer is A.

There is a strong connection to the afterlife in this poem, and the tongues create im-agery of flames. A is the best answer for this question.

19. Who is Cerberus?

A. A man entering the underworld

B. The guard of the underworld

C. The maid of the underworld

D. An angel

E. The devil

The answer is B.

A, C, and D are easy to eliminate because they are general and there are no refer-ences to point to them being correct. E can be eliminated because the description would have been much more detailed and powerful if Cerberus was the devil. Be-cause he is the guard of the underworld, B is the correct answer.

20. What does *aguey* mean?

A. Sinful

B. Torn

C. Deceitful

D. Beautiful

E. Burning

The answer is E.

Keeping the theme with the temperature in the title and the descriptions of the hellish afterlife, this should be an easy question. E is the obvious answer.

21. The word *trundle* is significant because ____.

A. It represents moving very slowly.

B. It is a roll out bed, used for camping.

C. it is not dark nor light.

D. it represents being instinctive.

E. None of the above.

The answer is A.

Trundle is the word for a bed that is used for camping, but it also represents moving very slowly. In the context of this piece, trundle represents traveling around the world very slowly. C and D are easy to mark off as incorrect for this question.

22. What literary device is used in this poem?

A. Repetition

B. Onomatopoeia

C. Alliteration

D. Flashback

E. Flash forward

The answer is A.

This is an obvious answer. "The sin." is repeated several times.

23. Which of the following best describes the setting?

A. Utopia

B. Dystopia

C. Promised land

D. Eden

E. Erotic

The answer is B.

Unlike utopia, where everything is perceived to be beautiful and happy, dystopia is the complete opposite. It represents a very negative, unpleasant environment. Because the poem represents a hell-like environment, it's easy to eliminate C and D. There are no sexual references, so E can also be eliminated. This leaves B as the best answer.

24. Why is the title substantial?

A. You can sweat out sins with a fever

B. It's the temperature in the underworld

C. This level of a fever would kill you

D. This is the temperature of fire

E. All of the above

The answer is A.

While it's assumed that the underworld is a hot place, we are not aware of the exact temperature; therefore, B can be eliminated. The temperature of fire is much higher, and can reach as high as 1500 degrees. This level of a fever would be dangerous, but not necessarily deadly. This leaves A as the best answer, as it represents a cleanse of sins by sweating them out with a fever.

Questions 25-32. Read the following selection and answer the questions below, selecting the best choice of the options presented.

"I went to work the next day, turning, so to speak, my back on that station. In that way only it seemed to me I could keep my hold on the redeeming facts of life. Still, one must look about sometimes; and then I saw this station, these men strolling aimlessly about in the sunshine of the yard. I asked myself sometimes what it all meant. They wandered here and there with their absurd long staves in their hands, like a lot of faithless pilgrims bewitched inside a rotten fence. The word 'ivory' rang in the air, was whispered, was sighed. You would think they were praying to it. A taint of imbecile rapacity blew through it all, like a whiff from some corpse. By Jove! I've never seen anything so unreal in my life. And outside, the silent wilderness surrounding this cleared speck on the earth struck me as something great and invincible, like evil or truth, waiting patiently for the passing away of this fantastic invasion.

—*Heart of Darkness*

25. Who wrote this novel?

A. Joseph Conrad

B. James Joyce

C. Jane Austen

D. Charlotte Brontë

E. Charles Dickens

The answer is A.

Joseph Conrad is the author of *Heart of Darkness.*

26. What does the following line represent?
"I saw this station, these men strolling aimlessly about in the sunshine of the yard."

A. Soldiers enjoying their day

B. Men being unaware of the negativ,ity that surrounds them

C. Positivity is infectious

D. The station is a happy place

E. Embracing the weather before a storm hits

The answer is B.

The sunshine represents happiness and the fact that they are strolling around aimless-ly implies they are unaware of their surroundings. Given the representation of this symbolism, B is the best option for this question.

27. What does the word *staves* mean?

A. Machete

B. Axe

C. Gun

D. Bomb

E. Wooden club

The answer is E.

Because of the invasion mentioned, it can be determined that the characters are walk-ing around with staves in order to protect themselves. Although each of the options for this question are weapons, E is the correct answer. It's a word that is most common to the time period in which this book was written.

28. What does the ivory represent?

A. Death

B. Prosperity

C. Jewelry

D. Trade

E. None of the above

The answer is B.

Ivory has historically been very valuable. While it can be viewed as representing trade, D is incorrect because this piece includes symbolism. B is the best answer because ivory best represents prosperity. A and C are easy to knock out as incorrect options.

29. What literary device is used when describing the ivory?

A. Alliteration

B. Allegory

C. Simile

D. Personification

E. Repetition

The answer is B.

An allegory represents a piece of writing with hidden meaning or significant hidden symbolism. This is the only option that makes sense for this question.

30. What does *rapacity* represent?

A. Greed

B. Rapid movement

C. Intelligent

D. Affluent

E. Generous

The answer is A.

Rapacity represents greed; therefore, A is the correct answer.

31. What literary device is used in this passage?

"And outside, the silent wilderness surrounding this cleared speck on the earth struck me as something great and invincible, like evil or truth, waiting patiently for the passing away of this fantastic invasion."

A. Simile

B. Metaphor

C. Illusion

D. Personification

E. Onomatopoeia

The answer is A.

A simile is a comparison or description that uses "like" or "as." Because this passage uses "like evil or truth" to describe the wilderness, A is the best answer.

32. Which style of writing is represented in this novel?

A. Biographical

B. Autobiographical

C. Expository

D. Persuasive

E. None of the above

The answer is D.

The story being told is fiction, so A and B can be eliminated from the start. C is incorrect because the writing does not intend to give information. The writing is intended to persuade the reader, leaving D as the best answer.

33. **When students are given an assignment that is new to them, which of the following should almost always be discussed?**

A. What the students can expect to learn from doing the assignment.

B. Whether the assignment will be graded in similar fashion to other assignments.

C. Whether the students can expect to be tested on the material presented.

D. The teacher's background with this type of assignment.

E. Samples of student work from this assignment in previous classes.

The answer is A.

According to many studies, students learn best when they are motivated. To be motivated, students must draw conclusions that are meaningful and worthwhile, leading toward larger goals instead of performance goals. By discussing why something is being done, and what they can gain from learning it, students will be more motivated to attempt something new.

34. **A high school classroom teacher is working with nonnative speakers of English. During class, students are asked to read aloud, and the teacher focuses on continuously correcting pronunciation errors. What has this teacher failed to take into account in regards to second language development?**

A. Reading skills must be established prior to learning the syntax of a language.

B. The fastest way for a nonnative speaker is to imitate the way native speakers use the language.

C. Students should never be asked to read out loud before they can read and comprehend grade appropriate texts silently.

D. Nonnative speakers often understand what they are reading before they can accurately speak the language.

E. Oral punctuation corrections should only occur when the student is being assessed on pronunciation.

The answer is D.

Learning should focus on comprehension and formal accuracy, as well as usage.

35. **A middle school teacher gives her students a list of vocabulary words to use in their essay, intending for the list to act as a scaffold. If the students exhibit proficiency on a mastery level, which of the following would be the best 'next' step?**

A. Give the students advanced words, and more of them, to include in the next essay.

B. Ask the students to work collectively to come up with a new list to use in the next essay.

C. Ask students to use the same vocabulary words in the next essay as well.

D. Give a new list of vocabulary terms and have them look up the definitions, then use them in the next essay.

E. Pair students up with a lower achieving peer in the class to help them explain the definitions.

The answer is B.

Scaffolding is, at best, a temporary framework to assist students toward the goal of being independent learners. Thus, once the skill has been mastered, the scaffold needs to be withdrawn. Having the students become responsible for providing their own vocabulary words not only withdraws the scaffold, but it encourages independent, as well as reciprocal, learning. None of the other answers meet these two criteria.

36. **An English teacher observes that a 10th grade student seems very upset about the idea of having to write a research paper. The teacher explains to the class as a whole, that the best approach for completing the assignment is to break the larger project into smaller tasks. Which of the following actions exemplify this methodology?**

A. Having students write about a familiar topic, then contrasting it with the topic for the research paper.

B. Writing a rough draft of the paper, then handing it to a fellow student for feedback and a critical evaluation.

C. Finding at least two credible sources for the research paper's topic, and seeing which aspects they both agree on.

D. Compiling a bibliography of sources relating to the topic.

E. Write as much as you can think of and then schedule an individual conference with the instructor to discuss areas of improvement.

The answer is C.

A larger task can often overwhelm a student, so breaking the task into smaller subtasks is a way of lessening a student's anxiety about a long term assignment. Both A and B involve creating the whole work first, and D and E are both large tasks and may only serve to overwhelm the student further.

37. **Why was it determined that students should be placed in the least restrictive educational environment?**

A. Because placement in a 'least restrictive environment' would normalize children with disabilities, as opposed to being educated in isolation from others.

B. Because it was determined that classrooms should no longer be restrictive to minorities or females.

C. Because it would reduce the fiscal cost of providing additional classrooms.

D. Because adopting the least restrictive policies would increase funding to the school for special education.

E. Placing students in less restrictive environments makes grading easier on instructors.

The answer is A.

The idea of 'least restrictive' was based on the legislation that stated that the education of divergent learners, and learners with disabilities should only be segregated if necessary, and that permanent placement within a regular classroom setting would be of more benefit to all students. The legislation is based on P.L 94-142.

38. **In a crowded classroom with varying skill levels, how might the teacher best take advantage of the diversity of the learning styles?**

A. Separate the students by reading levels.

B. Assess students individually, only, to mitigate potential anxiety for the students.

C. Incorporate opportunities for multilevel interaction through reciprocal learning events.

D. Assign students to learning centers for computer based learning.

E. Use a random number table to assign students to small groups.

The answer is C.

Students who work within varying level environments all benefit. Those who are in the lower quartile may be motivated or encouraged by their peers, while those who are in the upper quartile will synthesize the material in a way that allows them to apply what they have learned.

39. When introducing a classic work of fiction to 8th graders, what is a significant factor in its presentation and study?

A. Whether the student finds that he or she can relate to the material.

B. Whether the material will include a test.

C. The material must be drawn from modern fiction sources.

D. Students must be able to read on grade level to be able to enjoy a classic work of literature.

E. The quality of the novels that are distributed for reading.

The answer is A.

Many studies exist which indicate that students who are interested, and who feel that the material has some relevance to their lives will be motivated to learn a subject. Literature whose themes and relevancy to modern life are indicated by the teacher can play a significant factor in the successful completion of a unit of study.

40. Classroom rules, when established correctly, require the teacher to do which of the following?

A. State the rules with a serious intent.

B. Quickly establish authority in the classroom.

C. Create as many rules as it takes to cover all of the possible issues that might arise.

D. Explain why the rules are needed.

E. Post the rules in a very obvious location in the classroom for students to reference.

The answer is D.

Classroom management is achieved by having a few rules that make sense to students. When students in this age group are given reasons for the rules, they are more likely to comply.

41. If a teacher wanted to obtain data from a criterion-referenced test, as opposed to a norm-referenced test, which of the following would offer that information?

A. How much each student in the classroom already knows about a singular aspect of the subject.

B. How much each student in the classroom knows about a singular aspect as compared to other students on a national level.

C. How much each student in the classroom knows as compared to other students in the district.

D. How much each student in the classroom knows about a certain portion of the subject.

E. The average time spent on task for each test format.

Answer: D.

Criterion-referenced tests determine the comprehension of a specific competency. These types of tests judge the student against the standard, and not against others in the state, nation, or district. Since the goal is to determine comprehension and knowledge, a group based performance (norm referenced) is not indicated. A is not the answer because it does not measure the student's gained knowledge, only knowledge that was preexisting.

42. Which of the following activities is a feature of an accelerated program as opposed to an enrichment activity?

A. Finishing an independent project.

B. Participating in simulations, role playing, playing games.

C. Taking an exam and receiving credit.

D. Enrolling and completing a summer program.

E. Participating in a team building activity.

The answer is C.

Students who take an exam and are able to receive credit for that class, or subject, are able to skip out of that class, this is seen when a person passes a CLEP exam and no longer needs to take that class. Thus, they have accelerated their learning process. The other options offer students enrichment activities designed to supplement learning.

43. **When characterizing a student's creativity, which of the descriptors are most apt?**

A. The student's solution is applicable in many areas, not just one domain.

B. The student's solutions, though seemingly unorthodox, upon further discovery prove sound.

C. The student's solutions are a collection of false starts, some of which end up being relevant.

D. The student's solutions do not deviate from the standard perspectives.

E. The student's interest in STEM topics in caparison with their interest in humanitarian topics.

The answer is B.

With the exception of B, the other answers are common misconceptions about creative thinkers. Divergent thinkers typically arrive at their conclusions from different perspectives and angles.

44. **When seeking to improve academic performance, as well as motivation of students, which of the following strategies are most likely to succeed?**

A. Teachers appoint a liaison to work with the administration to create a 'best practices' set of rules.

B. Teachers present material as a team, standardizing presentation, and mapping academic progress.

C. Teacher collaboration to assess and monitor other classroom procedures offers successful solutions.

D. The classroom teacher must utilize management techniques with which he is familiar and comfortable.

E. Teachers are evaluated using a merit-based pay system.

The answer is C.

When teachers collaborate, share experiences, and assess one another on a routine basis, all are made stronger and benefit from the collaboration. New teachers often benefit from a veteran teacher's experience, while the veteran teacher can benefit by embracing new techniques and processes employed by the new teacher.

45. For students learning the process of constructed response writing, what is the appropriate pedagogical process?

A. independent writing (summative), guided writing (formative), model/shadowing

B. Model/shadowing, guided writing (formative), independent writing (summative)

C. Guided writing (formative), model/shadowing, independent writing (summative)

D. Independent writing (summative), guided writing (formative), peer reviewed grouping

E. Guided writing (formative), peer reviewed grouping, individual conference

The answer is B.

Writing is a skill and as such must be presented in a logical manner, and in a manner which does not promote student anxiety or apprehension. Thus, showing the students how something is written, having them imitate the process, then guiding them through the process, culminating in independent attempts is the best method for acquisition of a new skill, in particular, writing.

46. An aspect of the reflective practice methodology is exemplified in which of the following?

A. The teacher limits the amount of peer review.

B. The teacher should limit student input that challenges or questions established teaching practices.

C. The teacher should allow peer review to take its natural course, offering very little framework to limit the problem solving process.

D. The teacher should establish a safe environment that allows reflection to take place among an accepted practice that is applicable for all learning situations.

E. The teacher should raise the stakes in the assignment by offering a peer assessment at the end of the peer review process.

The answer is D.

Trust is the foundation upon which peer review and reflective practice must be built. B and C are useful only in a limited capacity, as creativity may be hampered. The classroom teacher must establish a set context upon which each assignment will draw, especially when peer interaction, reflection, or critique are involved.

47. When establishing the best way to assist students with comprehension skills, a teacher should focus on which of the following techniques as an informational text is read aloud?

A. Writing down questions as a text is read aloud

B. Creating an outline

C. Setting a purpose for reading

D. Encouraging students to make predictions

E. Telling students there will be a quiz at the end of a reading

The answer is A.

If a student is able to write down questions about what is being read, then comprehension must follow. This type of metacognition is evident when a relevant question is asked about the text that is read. C and D are used as pre-reading strategies.

Questions 48-55. Read the following selection and answer the questions below, selecting the best choice of the options presented.

"If people bring so much courage to this world the world has to kill them to break them, so of course it kills them. The world breaks every one and afterward many are strong at the broken places. But those that will not break it kills. It kills the very good and the very gentle and the very brave impartially. If you are none of these you can be sure it will kill you too but there will be no special hurry."

—*A Farewell to Arms*

48. Who wrote this novel?

A. Henry David Thoreau

B. Ernest Hemingway

C. F. Scott Fitzgerald

D. Harper Lee

E. J.R.R. Tolkien

The answer is B.

A Farewell to Arms was written by Ernest Hemmingway.

49. What is the theme of this novel?

A. Innocence

B. War

C. Love

D. Death

E. Grief

The answer is B.

Arms represents guns, making the connection of the theme and the title of the book very obvious. While love, death, and grief may be involved in the book, war is the theme.

50. What does the title symbolize?

A. An amputation caused during war

B. Being discharged

C. Saying goodbye to the arms of someone you love

D. Saying goodbye to weaponry and warfare

E. C & D

The answer is E.

The word arms represents war, and the title symbolizes saying goodbye to warfare, weaponry, and love. A and B are literal translations and do not include symbolism.

51. Which literary device is used to describe war?

A. Personification

B. Alliteration

C. Simile

D. Metaphor

E. Idiom

The answer is A.

Personification is used to describe the war, particularly in the statement "it will kill you."

52. What best describes the author's intention in the following line? "It kills the very good and the very gentle and the very brave impartially."

A. Everyone will die sooner or later

B. Murderers target nice people

C. The good, gentle and brave are easier to kill

D. The good, gentle and brave die protecting others

E. War kills everyone, it doesn't have a bias

The answer is E.

While it's true that everyone will die sooner or later (A), and the good, gentle and brave die protecting others (D), the author's intention was to show that there is no bias when it comes to death during war. B and C are easy to eliminate, leaving E as the best answer.

53. How does the world *break* people?

A. It creates challenging times

B. It represents being shot and not dying

C. It causes extreme wounds, mentally and physically

D. People can have broken bones

E. Physical objects and precious belongings can be broken

The answer is C.

The war leaves soldiers with many wounds, both mentally and physically. C is the best answer because it covers both of these scenarios.

54. Which of the following best represents this passage?

A. Sarcasm

B. Resentment

C. Irony

D. Sympathy

E. Affectionate

The answer is B.

The author is resentful in his tone throughout this passage, so B is the best answer of these options.

55. Which literary period is this from?

A. Romanticism

B. Renaissance

C. The Enlightenment

D. Existentialism

E. Modernism

The answer is E.

Because it was written in the 19th century, this passage is from the Modernism period. The reference to war should be an obvious reference to this era, making it easy to eliminate A-D.

Questions 56-63. Read the following passage carefully before you decide on your answers to the questions.

O for a Muse of fire, that would ascend
The brightest heaven of invention,
A kingdom for a stage, princes to act
And monarchs to behold the swelling scene!
Then should the warlike Harry, like himself,
Assume the port of Mars; and at his heels,
Leash'd in like hounds, should famine sword and fire
Crouch for employment. But pardon, and gentles all,
The flat unraised spirits that have dared
On this unworthy scaffold to bring forth
So great an object: can this cockpit hold
The vasty fields of France? or may we cram
Within this wooden O the very casques
That did affright the air at Agincourt?
O, pardon! since a crooked figure may
Attest in little place a million;
And let us, ciphers to this great account,
On your imaginary forces work.
Suppose within the girdle of these walls
Are now confined two mighty monarchies,
Whose high upreared and abutting fronts
The perilous narrow ocean parts asunder:
Piece out our imperfections with your thoughts;
Into a thousand parts divide one man,
And make imaginary puissance;
Think when we talk of horses, that you see them
Printing their proud hoofs i' the receiving earth;
For 'tis your thoughts that now must deck our kings,
Carry them here and there; jumping o'er times,
Turning the accomplishment of many years
Into an hour-glass: for the which supply,
Admit me Chorus to this history;
Who prologue-like your humble patience pray,
Gently to hear, kindly to judge, our play.

56. The first four lines could best be described as...

A. A warning of violence to come.

B. A celebration of military victory.

C. An exultation of creative vision.

D. A lamentation of the inadequacy of mortals.

E. A plea for patience from the audience.

The answer is C.

The "Muse of fire" is understood to be figurative, referencing the "muse" of inspiration that will allow the speaker to spin his tale. The entire monologue centers around the author explaining the limitations of his storytelling capabilities, so C is the safest answer.

57. What can the reader infer from lines 5-8?

A. Harry was a man who inspired awe and fear.

B. Harry was a god.

C. Harry will soon rule over all people.

D. Harry is the villain of the play.

E. Harry was a sailor.

The answer is A.

Lines 5 through 8 exult Harry's fearsome figure, comparing Harry to the war god Mars and explaining how even the concepts of famine, sword and fire must bow to him like obedient dogs. The other answers require assumptions not present in the text, A is the safest answer.

58. What is meant by the line "since a crooked figure may attest in little place a million"?

A. Small men can enact great change if they fulfill their potential.

B. A hand written number can evoke a massive value.

C. Trials can be overcome through perseverance.

D. Some tests are insurmountable to any man.

E. There are mysteries we cannot solve.

The answer is B.

"Crooked figure" refers to a number. The speaker is explaining that even a small, handwritten numeral can be understood to evoke a huge number, and so can their play be understood to represent a titanic struggle.

59. What does the narrator wish for the audience to do in lines 20-28?

A. Draw upon their own experiences at the theater.

B. Imagine the horror and glory of war.

C. Pretend the physical aspects of the theater reflect things far greater than can be shown onstage.

D. Appreciate history, both the good and bad aspects.

E. Understand their own smallness in the face of this epic tale.

The answer is C.

With lines such as "into a thousand parts divide one man", the author is requesting that the audience use their imaginations to fill in the gaps of their tale. C is the best answer.

60. What is the narrator's attitude towards the audience?

A. Egocentric disdain

B. Haughty dismissal

C. Meek terror

D. Wide-eyed fascination

E. Humble entreating

The answer is E.

E is the best answer. The raconteur even uses the word "humble" towards the end of the piece. He does not wish to talk down to the audience in any way.

61. What is the "unworthy scaffold"?

A. A run-down building

B. A poorhouse

C. The barracks

D. The stage itself

E. A church

The answer is D.

The "flat, unraised spirits" are the actors, and their "unworthy scaffold" is the stage upon which they are performing.

62. The narrator wishes to

A. Deceive the audience with propaganda.

B. Relay a tale too great for the stage to contain.

C. Repent for the sins committed by his people.

D. Slander the memory of a great leader.

E. Absolve himself of any guilt he may be feeling.

The answer is B.

The speaker states many times that, though this tale is grander than we can comprehend, he wishes to make his best effort at telling it.

63. Who are the "ciphers to this great account"?

A. Soldiers

B. Actors

C. Women

D. Scholars

E. Royalty

The answer is B.

The speaker refers to the ciphers as "us". This line also connects with the "crooked figure" line, as the "figure" he refers to is the numeral for one million, and since "cipher" means "zero", the actors likewise are zeros in the figure evoking a far greater value.

Questions 64-71. Read the following passage carefully before you decide on your answers to the questions.

A child said, What is the grass? fetching it to me with full hands;
How could I answer the child?. . . .I do not know what it is any more than he.

I guess it must be the flag of my disposition, out of hopeful green stuff woven.

Or I guess it is the handkerchief of the Lord,
A scented gift and remembrancer designedly dropped,
Bearing the owner's name someway in the corners, that we may see and remark, and say Whose?

Or I guess the grass is itself a child. . . .the produced babe of the vegetation.

Or I guess it is a uniform hieroglyphic,
And it means, Sprouting alike in broad zones and narrow zones,
Growing among black folks as among white,
Kanuck, Tuckahoe, Congressman, Cuff, I give them the same, I receive them the same.

And now it seems to me the beautiful uncut hair of graves.

Tenderly will I use you curling grass,
It may be you transpire from the breasts of young men,
It may be if I had known them I would have loved them;
It may be you are from old people and from women, and
from offspring taken soon out of their mother's laps,
And here you are the mother's laps.

This grass is very dark to be from the white heads of old mothers,
Darker than the colorless beards of old men,
Dark to come from under the faint red roofs of mouths.

O I perceive after all so many uttering tongues!
And I perceive they do not come from the roofs of mouths for nothing.

I wish I could translate the hints about the dead young men and women,
And the hints about old men and mothers, and the offspring taken soon out of their laps.

What do you think has become of the young and old men?
What do you think has become of the women and children?

They are alive and well somewhere;
The smallest sprouts show there is really no death,
And if ever there was it led forward life, and does not wait at the end to arrest it,
And ceased the moment life appeared.

All goes onward and outward. . . .and nothing collapses,
And to die is different from what any one supposed, and luckier.

64. What best describes the tone of this poem?

A. Melancholic

B. Stream-of-consciousness

C. Bittersweet

D. Exuberant

E. Regretful

The answer is C.

The poem discusses topics relating to innocence and joy for life, counterbalanced by musings on the inevitability of death. Though ultimately positive in message, it could not be characterized as exuberant (D), nor does its acceptance of death suggest any regret (E) or melancholy (A). The style is not stream-of-consciousness.

65. Why does the author decide death is lucky?

A. Death leads to new life, as evidenced by the grass.

B. People are immortal in the afterlife.

C. Children bring hope for the future, ever growing stronger.

D. Life is meaningless, and people are no worse off in death than cut grass.

E. Man's cruelty makes life not worth living.

The answer is A.

The author makes no reference to the afterlife (B), and is not preoccupied with the future (C). D and E likewise do not apply, the poem exhibits no such pessimism.

66. What does the speaker mean by "tenderly I will use you curling grass"?

A. He will attempt to nurture a better generation.

B. He will ponder the implications and meanings of the grass.

C. He has no easy answers, the question is too complex to examine.

D. When he dies, he will become grass.

E. The grass connects him to all beings.

The answer is B.

The author makes this statement and then proceeds to explore the implications of grass for life, death, and divinity. He does not give up, as referenced by answer C, nor does he make any firm statements about any future generations (A). He does understand he will become grass like all things (D and E) but these notions are not connected to the quote in the question.

67. What can we infer from the first stanza in context?

A. The speaker is dim and uneducated.

B. The speaker has no mind for philosophy.

C. The child is cleverer than he appears.

D. The question is too complex for a simple answer.

E. The grass is a strange variety not seen in this location.

The answer is D.

As the poem features an author philosophically overthinking the question about grass, A and B do not apply. The child also does not exhibit undue cleverness by asking such a typical question (C). The author also makes no mention of this particular grass being unique (E). D is the correct answer.

68. Who does the speaker decide is "the mother's laps"?

A. The child

B. Humanity

C. Himself

D. The grass

E. The dead

The answer is D.

The author is referring to grass when he makes this statement.

69. What is meant by lines 7-10?

A. The Lord works in mysterious ways.

B. The grass is an object, inanimate as a handkerchief.

C. The Lord created the grass, and it bears his signature.

D. There is no need for God with such natural beauty around us.

E. The answers to these questions float before us, like a handkerchief on the wind.

The answer is C.

The author spins a metaphor about God leaving his signature in the grass in much the same way a dropped handkerchief might feature its owner's initials. The author characterizes the grass as alive, so B is inaccurate, and A is a vagary the inquisitive author would not be satisfied with. D is inaccurate as the author sees God IN the natural beauty.

70. What can we infer that the author believes from stanza 5?

A. He is a mild racist.

B. All of humanity is fundamentally the same.

C. We are all united in death

D. Disharmony can be overcome through change.

E. Social class is a fact of life.

The answer is B.

The author is suggesting that we all come from the same source and all return to the same dirt. It could be considered a political statement, but from the poem itself we cannot infer enough for the other answers to be appropriate.

71. In context, what does the author mean by "I wish I could translate the hints about the dead young men and women"?

A. He wishes he could discern things about the people from the grass they became.

B. He wants to think no more of depressing matters like death.

C. He wishes he could speak to the dead to better understand what awaits him.

D. He wants to cure the suffering in the world.

E. He feels it is unnatural that mothers must lose their children.

The answer is A.

B is inaccurate as the author is delving into the subject of death headlong. C is close but still inaccurate, he does not ask what awaits him in the afterlife. D is untrue, he makes no mention of curing suffering, and E is also inaccurate, as he suggests that all of these occurrences are in fact completely natural, albeit sad.

Questions 72-79. Read the following passage carefully before you decide on your answers to the questions.

These pictures were in watercolors. The first represented clouds low and livid, rolling over a swollen sea: all the distance was in eclipse; so, too, was the foreground; or rather, the nearest billows, for there was no land. One gleam of light lifted into relief a half-submerged mast, on which sat a cormorant, dark and large, with wings flecked with foam; its beak held a gold bracelet set with gems, that I had touched with as brilliant tints as my palette could yield, and as glittering distinctness as my pencil could impart. Sinking below the bird and mast, a drowned corpse glanced through the green water; a fair arm was the only limb clearly visible, whence the bracelet had been washed or torn.

The second picture contained for foreground only the dim peak of a hill, with grass and some leaves slanting as if by a breeze. Beyond and above spread an expanse of sky, dark blue as at twilight: rising into the sky was a woman's shape to the bust, portrayed in tints as dusk and soft as I could combine. The dim forehead was crowned with a star; the lineaments below were seen as through the suffusion of vapour; the eyes shone dark and wild; the hair streamed shadowy, like a beamless cloud torn by storm or by electric travail. On the neck lay a pale reflection like moonlight; the same faint lustre touched the train of thin clouds from which rose and bowed this vision of the Evening Star.

The third showed the pinnacle of an iceberg piercing a polar winter sky: a muster of northern lights reared their dim lances, close serried, along the horizon. Throwing these into distance, rose, in the foreground, a head,--a colossal head, inclined towards the iceberg, and resting against it. Two thin hands, joined under the forehead, and supporting it, drew up before the lower features a sable veil, a brow quite bloodless, white as bone, and an eye hollow and fixed, blank of meaning but for the glassiness of despair, alone were visible. Above the temples, amidst wreathed turban folds of black drapery, vague in its character and consistency as cloud, gleamed a ring of white flame, gemmed with sparkles of a more lurid tinge. This pale crescent was "the likeness of a kingly crown;" what it diademed was "the shape which shape had none."

"Were you happy when you painted these pictures?" asked Mr. Rochester presently.

"I was absorbed, sir: yes, and I was happy. To paint them, in short, was to enjoy one of the keenest pleasures I have ever known."

"That is not saying much. Your pleasures, by your own account, have been few; but I daresay you did exist in a kind of artist's dreamland while you blent and arranged these strange tints. Did you sit at them long each day?"

"I had nothing else to do, because it was the vacation, and I sat at them from morning till noon, and from noon till night: the length of the midsummer days favoured my inclination to apply."

"And you felt self-satisfied with the result of your ardent labours?"

"Far from it. I was tormented by the contrast between my idea and my handiwork: in each case I had imagined something which I was quite powerless to realise."

"Not quite: you have secured the shadow of your thought; but no more, probably. You had not enough of the artist's skill and science to give it full being: yet the drawings are, for a school-girl, peculiar. As to the thoughts, they are elfish. These eyes in the Evening Star you must have seen in a dream. How could you make them look so clear, and yet not at all brilliant? for the planet above quells their rays. And what meaning is that in their solemn depth? And who taught you to paint wind. There is a high gale in that sky, and on this hill-top. Where did you see Latmos? For that is Latmos. There! put the drawings away!"

I had scarce tied the strings of the portfolio, when, looking at his watch, he said abruptly -

"It is nine o'clock: what are you about, Miss Eyre, to let Adele sit up so long? Take her to bed."

Adele went to kiss him before quitting the room: he endured the caress, but scarcely seemed to relish it more than Pilot would have done, nor so much.

"I wish you all good-night, now," said he, making a movement of the hand towards the door, in token that he was tired of our company, and wished to dismiss us. Mrs. Fairfax folded up her knitting: I took my portfolio: we curtseyed to him, received a frigid bow in return, and so withdrew.

72. What best describes Mr. Rochester's objective in the previous scene?

A. To break Jane down by insulting her art.

B. To determine her romantic interests and possibly woo her.

C. To discover more about her personality through her work.

D. To find something he can use against her family.

E. To establish his dominance over her and her household.

The answer is C.

Rochester is terse with Jane, but he does not directly insult her work. He makes no motion towards romantic interest (B), and D and E are inaccurate as Rochester is already very dominant in this context and has no need to exert force over the family.

73. What is meant by the line "but scarcely seemed to relish it more than Pilot would have done"?

A. He despises the young Adele.

B. He dislikes such an expression of familiarity.

C. He is a sacrilegious man.

D. His depression prevents him from enjoying intimacy.

E. He is an antagonist.

The answer is B.

"Despise" (A) is too strong a word, he has tolerated Adele's presence for the entire scene, indeed, a moment earlier he exhibits concern for her being up so late. We don't have enough information to ascertain D or E's accuracy, and though Pilot is a biblical reference, we learn nothing from this comparison about his sacrilege (C).

74. Mr. Rochester feels Jane's paintings are…

A. Naïve and unskilled, but showing potential.

B. A frivolous waste of time.

C. Unique, perhaps disturbingly so.

D. Blasphemous, though well-made.

E. Extraordinary, though he struggles to express his admiration.

The answer is A.

Even grumpy Mr. Rochester allows that the paintings display some talent, though not much. The answer is A.

75. What is meant by the term "diademed" in this passage:
This pale crescent was "the likeness of a kingly crown;" what it diademed was "the shape which shape had none."

A. Illuminated

B. Exposed

C. Pierced

D. Crowned

E. Blended

The answer is D.

A diadem is a circlet worn by royalty. In verb form, this supports the royal aspects of the image.

76. The primary effect of the imagery in the description of Jane's second painting is to:

A. Emphasize the painting's religious themes

B. Explore its ethereal, supernatural quality

C. Determine its ill-formed concepts and amateurish execution

D. Characterize Jane as a hopeless romantic

E. Place the painting as an interpretation of Mr. Rochester

The answer is B.

The picture is described as dreamlike, replete with clouds and moonbeams. It is described in great detail, so C would not apply, and D is too great an assumption to draw from a single painting. E would not apply, the painting is of a cloudy woman, nor would A, as there are no clear religious motifs in the painting.

77. What is the primary subject of the first painting?

A. A bird holding a piece of jewelry

B. A Naval skirmish in full swing

C. A horrific murder and robbery

D. An abstract image of a woman shrouded in clouds

E. A religious ceremony

The answer is A.

A bird is clearly identified as the prominent foreground image of the picture. Though it seems to feature a sunken ship, we see no Naval battle (B), and it features a corpse, but no indications of murder or robbery (C). D refers to the second painting, not the first, and there is no religious ceremony in this picture.

78. Inferring from the text, Jane must be Adele's…

A. Mother

B. Sister

C. Caretaker

D. Employer

E. Maid

The answer is C.

Rochester clearly suggests Jane is responsible for Adele's well-being by letting her stay up so late. We have no proof of the other answers, so C is the safest.

79. What is Jane's attitude towards her paintings?

A. Loathing

B. Embarrassment

C. Pride

D. Dissatisfaction

E. Indifference

The answer is D.

Jane clearly says she was "tormented" by her inability to capture the full idea of each painting. Though she enjoyed painting them, she is not proud of them (C), nor is she embarrassed by them (B) as she speaks freely about their creation. Loathing (A) is too strong a term, and she is anything but indifferent towards her paintings (E).

Questions 80-87. Read the following passage carefully before you decide on your answers to the questions.

"You've just told me some high spots in your memories. Want to hear mine? They're all connected with the sea.

Here's one. When I was on the Squarehead square rigger, bound for Buenos Aires. Full moon in the trades. The old hooker driving 14 knots. I lay on the bowsprit, facing astern, with the water foaming into spume under me. Every mast with sail white in the moonlight - towering high above me. I became drunk with the beauty and singing rhythm of it - and for a second I lost myself, actually lost my life. I was set free! I dissolved into the sea, became white sails and flying spray - became beauty and rhythm, became moonlight and the ship and the high dim-starred sky. I belonged, without past or future, within peace and unity and a wild joy, within something greater than my own life, or the life of man, to Life itself! To God if you want to put it that way.

Then another time, on the American line, when I was lookout in the crow's nest on the dawn watch. A calm sea that time. Only a lazy ground swell and a slow drousy roll of the ship. The passengers asleep and none of the crew in sight. No sound of man. Black smoke pouring from the funnels behind and beneath me. Dreaming, not keeping lookout, feeling alone, and above, and apart, watching the dawn creep like a painted dream over the sky and sea which slept together.

Then the moment of ecstatic freedom came. The peace, the end of the quest, the last harbor, the joy of belonging to a fulfillment beyond men's lousy, greedy fears and hopes and dreams! And several other times in my life, when I was swimming far out, or lying alone on the beach, I have had the same experience. Became the sun, the hot sand, green seaweed anchored to a rock, swaying in the tide. Like a saint's vision of beatitude. Like the veil of things as they seem drawn back by an unseen hand. For a second you see - and seeing the secret, are the secret. For a second there is meaning! Then the hand lets the veil fall and you are alone, lost in the fog again, stumbling on toward no where, for no good reason!

it was a great mistake, my being born a man. I would have been much more successful as a seagull or fish. As it is, I will always be a stranger who never feels at home, who does not want and is not really wanted, who can never belong, who must always be a little in love with death."

80. What adjective best describes Edmund's tone in this piece?

A. Disaffected

B. Morose

C. Longing

D. Celebratory

E. Inspired

The answer is C.

This monologue is a memory piece describing Edmund's happiest days. "Longing" best describes this tone.

81. This piece can best be described as...

A. A poem

B. A dramatic monologue

C. Prose fiction

D. An ode

E. A dirge

The answer is B.

The piece is a monologue from Eugene O'Neill's "Long Day's Journey Into Night". It contains few poetic elements, and is not a prose piece, as it's written in first person and does not break this form.

82. What are the two primary contrasts of this piece?

A. The sea with the land; drunkenness with sobriety.

B. Depression and joy; sailing with being "anchored".

C. The wild sea with the calm sea; ecstasy with numbness.

D. Edmund with his father; freedom with responsibility.

E. Humanity with nature; godlessness with holiness.

The answer is C.

Edmund uses the sea to characterize his own emotional ups and downs. C is the best answer.

83. The author conveys the sea using what primary technique?

A. Analogy

B. Assonance

C. Simile

D. Personification

E. Imagery

The answer is E.

Edmund does not describe the sea with an analogy, nor with any specific poetic devices beyond imagery. He describes how it looks, sounds, and how that makes him feel.

84. The phrase "like a saint's vision of beatitude" serves to reinforce what idea?

A. Edmund's desire to die.

B. Edmund finds spirituality in nature.

C. Edmund wishes to sail again.

D. Edmund wishes to repent

E. Edmund dislikes religion.

The answer is B.

"Beatitudes" are saintly blessings. In this sentence, Edmund is describing how he finds such things only in nature, specifically the sea.

85. In the first paragraph, the author characterizes this piece as a...

A. Story-within-a-story

B. Memory

C. Soliloquy

D. Ballad

E. Fabrication

The answer is B.

Right off the bat, Edmund characterizes this piece as a memory tale.

86. Where does the primary shift in tone occur in this piece?

A. Paragraph two, "I became drunk with the beauty..."

B. Paragraph three, "The another time, on the American line..."

C. Paragraph four, "Then that moment of ecstatic freedom came!"

D. Paragraph four, "Then the hand lets the veil fall..."

E. Paragraph five, "I will always be a stranger..."

The answer is D.

"The hand lets the veil fall" is the "climax" of this piece. Until that point, Edmund's story is happy, building up to pure ecstasy. With that line, the piece becomes somber and regretful.

87. What natural image does the author use to contrast the sea and its feelings of freedom?

A. Black smoke

B. Fog

C. Spray

D. Seagull

E. Waves

The answer is B.

Edmund describes the fog as his counter to the sea. The sea makes him feel alive and open, the fog makes him feel numb and depressed.

Questions 88-95. Read the following passage carefully before you decide on your answers to the questions.

In a village of La Mancha, the name of which I have no desire to call to mind, there lived not long since one of those gentlemen that keep a lance in the lance-rack, an old buckler, a lean hack, and a greyhound for coursing. An olla of rather more beef than mutton, a salad on most nights, scraps on Saturdays, lentils on Fridays, and a pigeon or so extra on Sundays, made away with three-quarters of his income. The rest of it went in a doublet of fine cloth and velvet breeches and shoes to match for holidays, while on week-days he made a brave figure in his best homespun. He had in his house a housekeeper past forty, a niece under twenty, and a lad for the field and market-place, who used to saddle the hack as well as handle the bill-hook. The age of this gentleman of ours was bordering on fifty; he was of a hardy habit, spare, gaunt-featured, a very early riser and a great sportsman. They will have it his surname was Quixada or Quesada (for here there is some difference of opinion among the authors who write on the subject), although from reasonable conjectures it seems plain that he was called Quexana. This, however, is of but little importance to our tale; it will be enough not to stray a hair's breadth from the truth in the telling of it.

You must know, then, that the above-named gentleman whenever he was at leisure (which was mostly all the year round) gave himself up to reading books of chivalry with such ardour and avidity that he almost entirely neglected the pursuit of his field-sports, and even the management of his property; and to such a pitch did his eagerness and infatuation go that he sold many an acre of tillage land to buy books of chivalry to read, and brought home as many of them as he could get. But of all there were none he liked so well as those of the famous Feliciano de Silva's composition, for their lucidity of style and complicated conceits were as pearls in his sight, particularly when in his reading he came upon courtships and cartels, where he often found passages like "the reason of the unreason with which my reason is afflicted so weakens my reason that with reason I murmur at your beauty;" or again, "the high heavens, that of your divinity divinely fortify you with the stars, render you deserving of the desert your greatness deserves." Over conceits of this sort the poor gentleman lost his wits, and used to lie awake striving to understand them and worm the meaning out of them; what Aristotle himself could not have made out or extracted had he come to life again for that special purpose. He was not at all easy about the wounds which Don Belianis gave and took, because it seemed to him that, great as were the surgeons who had cured him, he must have had his face and body covered all over with seams and scars. He commended, however, the author's way of ending his book with the promise of that interminable adventure, and many a time was he tempted to take up his pen and finish it properly as is there proposed, which no doubt he would have done, and made a successful piece of work of it too, had not greater and more absorbing thoughts prevented him.

88. The author's tone in this piece can best be described as...

A. Heroic

B. Comedic

C. Florid

D. Epic

E. Mysterious

The answer is B.

The passage contains several wry commentaries and witty asides to the audience which characterize the piece as comedic in tone, such as the author's insistence that he does not wish to remember specific names. The actions of the person described, likewise, are absurd, as he spends his time not working, spending his money on ridiculous finery, and reading unrealistic novels.

89. The line "were as pearls to his site" is an example of a...

A. Metaphor

B. Analogy

C. Simile

D. Allegory

E. Conceit

The answer is C.

A simile almost always contains the words "like" or "as" to indicate similarity.

90. Our main character's attitude towards reading can best be described as...

A. Lackadaisical

B. Unusual

C. Illiterate

D. Obsessive

E. Joyous

The answer is D.

The author explains the main character reads with "ardour and avidity" such that he neglects other household chores. A, B, and C do not apply, and though he certainly could be said to enjoy reading, the piece clearly characterizes this behavior as obsessive and not joyous (E).

91. The passage "the high heavens, that of your divinity divinely fortify you with the stars, render you deserving of the desert your greatness deserves" contains several examples what poetic device?

A. Alliteration

B. Onomatopoeia

C. Diction

D. Resonance

E. Enjambment

The answer is A.

The selection features repeated D and H sounds.

92. According to the text, who is Count Belianis?

A. A historical champion

B. A fictional character

C. A competing nobleman

D. A romantic rival

E. A dead family member

The answer is B.

The piece mentions Belianis as being a character created by Feliciano de Silva, one who is often harmed in the course of his adventures and is likely covered in scars.

93. The passage "it will be enough not to stray a hair's breadth from the truth in the telling of it" characterizes the previous passage as...

A. Essential

B. Metaphorical

C. Unimportant

D. Esoteric

E. Bland

The answer is C.

The quoted passage is one of the author's wry asides. A moment earlier he was describing the surname of the main character, but he cannot recall the correct name, explaining that it doesn't matter anyway.

94. What are the two defining traits of the main character described above?

A. Laziness and obsessiveness

B. Ignorance and piousness

C. Diligence and valor

D. Prideful and vain

E. Curious and kindhearted

The answer is A.

The character is said to rarely work nor even to play outside, hiring servants to take care of him. Yet he reads obsessively, even to the point of it affecting his mental health. He exhibits no piousness, so B is inaccurate, nor does he exhibit pride, diligence, or kindheartedness. Indeed, he seems rather aloof and disconnected.

95. The final sentence of this excerpt is an example of…

A. Satire

B. Foreshadowing

C. Interstitial

D. Subtext

E. Premonition

The answer is B.

The main character finds pleasure in how the author always ends with the promise of a new adventure, suggesting he will go on one himself. The entire selection could be considered satirical, but the last sentence in particular holds no special satirical value, so A is inaccurate. The sentence is not an interstitial (C) nor does it hold subtextual value (D). Since we do not know where the story goes from here, we cannot say for certain if this is a premonition (E).

Questions 96-100. Read the following passage carefully before you decide on your answers to the questions.

O wild West Wind, thou breath of Autumn's being,
Thou, from whose unseen presence the leaves dead
Are driven, like ghosts from an enchanter fleeing,

Yellow, and black, and pale, and hectic red,
Pestilence-stricken multitudes: O thou,
Who chariotest to their dark wintry bed

The winged seeds, where they lie cold and low,
Each like a corpse within its grave, until
Thine azure sister of the Spring shall blow

Her clarion o'er the dreaming earth, and fill
(Driving sweet buds like flocks to feed in air)
With living hues and odors plain and hill:

Wild Spirit, which art moving everywhere;
Destroyer and preserver; hear, oh, hear!

Thou on whose stream, 'mid the steep sky's commotion,
Loose clouds like earth's decaying leaves are shed,
Shook from the tangled boughs of Heaven and Ocean,

Angels of rain and lightning: there are spread
On the blue surface of thine aery surge,
Like the bright hair uplifted from the head

Of some fierce Maenad, even from the dim verge
Of the horizon to the zenith's height,
The locks of the approaching storm. Thou dirge

Of the dying year, to which this closing night
Will be the dome of a vast sepulchre,
Vaulted with all thy congregated might

Of vapors, from whose solid atmosphere
Black rain, and fire, and hail will burst: oh, hear!

96. The first line of this poem exhibits what poetic devices?

I. Alliteration

II. Personification

III. Onomatopoeia

A. Only I

B. Only II

C. Only III

D. I and II

E. I, II, and III

The answer is D.

"Wild West wind" is an alliteration and "breath" is a personification of the wind the poem goes on to describe.

97. What best describes the final stanza of this selection?

A. Slant rhyme

B. Heroic couplet

C. Hyperbole

D. Irony

E. Blank verse

The answer is B.

The final line is a classic heroic couplet, it contains an AA rhyme and has ten syllables per line. "Rhyme" is too vague for this question (A), and it exhibits no hyperbole (C), irony (D), or blank verse (E).

98. "Wild Spirit, which art moving everywhere; Destroyer and preserver; hear, oh, hear!" This passage displays a...

A. Enjambment

B. Slant rhyme

C. Simile

D. Iamb

E. Allegory

The answer is B.

"Everywhere" and "hear" are not "true" rhymes, though they are close. The selection features no enjambment (A), simile (C), iamb (D), or allegory (E).

99. This poem is written in what style?

A. Vers libre

B. Heroic couplet

C. Epic saga

D. Imagist soliloquy

E. Iambic pentameter

The answer is E.

The piece features ten syllables per line divided into five iambs, suggesting similarities to a sonnet.

100. What in the poem is compared to "Angels of rain and lightning"?

A. The wind

B. Maenads

C. Clouds

D. Human souls

E. Autumn

The answer is C.

Two lines earlier the poem describes "loose clouds" which are later likened to angels of rain and lightning.

Sample Test Two

Section I

1. A teacher is planning a lesson on T.S. Eliot's "The Hollow Men" for his eleventh grade English class. This is an excerpt from the poem:

The eyes reappear
As the perpetual star
Multifoliate rose
Of death's twilight kingdom
The hope only
Of empty men.

What strategy, of those listed below, best allows for identification and understanding of the word 'multifoliate'?

A. Structural analysis

B. Contextual analysis

C. Graphophonic analysis

D. Syntactical analysis

E. Comprehensive analysis

2. A teacher is working with a class that includes an ELL (English Language Learner) student. When assigning an informational essay to the class, which of the following techniques would assist the ELL in an understanding of the text?

A. Have all students create an illustration of some part of the text that they found interesting.

B. Have the class use a graphic organizer to write down main ideas in the article.

C. Hand out a list of most often used sentence stems to the entire classroom to use.

D. Provide a list of words to the ELL that are familiar synonyms to the words that he or she is likely to encounter in the article assigned.

E. Define all difficult vocabulary words and phrases aloud at the start of the class.

3. An 8th grade English teacher notices that each day when she asks a couple of questions about the previous day's lesson, the same handful of students always answer. Which of the following would promote active engagement by a larger percentage of the students?

A. Encouraging those who are not answering, to do so.

B. Allowing all students to create two questions about the day's assignment, to be asked the next day.

C. Giving a participation grade that is not dependent on the correct answer.

D. Having students evaluate their peers' responses using a rubric.

E. Call on students at random.

4. Which of the following indicators would suggest that a student has developed strong communication skills when placed in a small group to discuss a novel?

A. Taking charge of the group and directing the conversation.

B. Making comments that build upon statements made by others in the group.

C. Asking questions of the group members that diverges from the topic of conversation.

D. Asking whomever is talking to explain what they mean by their statements.

E. Speaking loudly and assertively within the group.

5. In a high school classroom, a teacher has had students complete rough drafts of an expository essay, and has placed them in pairs to peer review each other's work. As a guideline, what should the teacher have students read to discern first?

A. Transitions

B. Supporting details

C. Biased language

D. Varied sentence lengths

E. Grammar and punctuation errors

Questions 6-13. Read the following passage carefully before you decide on your answers to the questions.

William Wordsworth — "I Wandered Lonely As A Cloud"

I wandered lonely as a cloud
That floats on high o'er vales and hills,
When all at once I saw a crowd,
A host, of golden daffodils;
Beside the lake, beneath the trees,
Fluttering and dancing in the breeze.

Continuous as the stars that shine
And twinkle on the milky way,
They stretched in never-ending line
Along the margin of a bay:
Ten thousand saw I at a glance,
Tossing their heads in sprightly dance.

The waves beside them danced; but they
Out-did the sparkling waves in glee:
A poet could not but be gay,
In such a jocund company:
I gazed—and gazed—but little thought
What wealth the show to me had brought:

For oft, when on my couch I lie
In vacant or in pensive mood,
They flash upon that inward eye
Which is the bliss of solitude;
And then my heart with pleasure fills,
And dances with the daffodils.

6. **What type of passage is the above selection?**

A. Lyrical poem

B. Haiku poem

C. Acrostic poem

D. Limerick poem

E. Cinquain poem

7. **The permanence of stars as compared with flowers emphasizes**

   A. the impermanence of life.

   B. the permanence of memory for the poet.

   C. the earlier comparison of the sky to the lake.

   D. that stars are frozen above and daffodils dance below.

   E. the similarity of the inward eye with the fleeting bliss of solitude.

8. **The scheme of the poem is**

   A. ballad.

   B. Scottish stanza.

   C. Spenserian stanza.

   D. quatrain-couplet.

   E. sonnet.

9. **This poem uses the ________ metric pattern.**

   A. dactylic tetrameter

   B. trochaic pentameter

   C. trochaic tetrameter

   D. iambic pentameter

   E. iambic tetrameter

10. **What is a literary device used in the last two lines of the first two stanzas?**

    A. Simile.

    B. Metaphor.

    C. Personification.

    D. Allegory.

    E. Paradox.

11. In what literary period did this author write?

A. Edwardian Movement.

B. Romanticism.

C. Existentialism.

D. Renaissance Literature.

E. Victorian Movement.

12. As used in this poem, the best choice for a synonym of jocund means

A. pleasant.

B. vapid.

C. lonely.

D. jovial.

E. sad.

13. What literary device is used in line 9. "They stretched in never-ending line."

A. hyperbole.

B. onomatopoeia.

C. epithet.

D. irony.

E. anecdote.

Questions 14-21. Read the following selection and answer the questions below, selecting the best choice of the options presented.

My Bondage and My Freedom

Disappearing from the kind reader, in a flying cloud or balloon (pardon the figure), driven by the wind, and knowing not where I should land—whether in slavery or in freedom—it is proper that I should remove, at once, all anxiety, by frankly making known where I alighted. The flight Disappearing from the kind reader, in a flying cloud or balloon (pardon the figure), driven by the wind, and knowing not where I should land--whether in slavery or in freedom--it is proper that I should remove, at once, all anxiety, by frankly making known where I alighted. The flight was a bold and perilous one; but here I am, in the great city of New York, safe and sound, without loss of blood or bone. In less than a week after leaving Baltimore, I was walking amid the hurrying throng, and gazing upon the dazzling wonders of Broadway. The dreams of my childhood and the purposes of my manhood were now fulfilled. A free state around me, and a free earth under my feet! What a moment was this to me! A whole year was pressed into a single day. A new world burst upon my agitated vision. I have often been asked, by kind friends to whom I have told my story, how I felt when first I found myself beyond the limits of slavery; and I must say here, as I have often said to them, there is scarcely anything about which I could not give a more satisfactory answer. It was a moment of joyous excitement, which no words can describe. In a letter to a friend, written soon after reaching New York. I said I felt as one might be supposed to feel, on escaping from a den of hungry lions.

14. In what literary period did this author write?

A. Transcendentalism.

B. Realism.

C. Victorian.

D. Modernism.

E. Naturalism.

15. When the author writes "escaping from a den of hungry lions," what type of literary device is he using?

A. Simile

B. Personification.

C. Metaphor.

D. Hyperbole.

E. Irony.

16. **What is the author's theme in this passage?**

    A. Anger at being a slave.

    B. Numb, as one might be supposed to feel.

    C. Confusion at the new things he is seeing.

    D. Self-discovery after flight from slavery.

    E. None of these describe his tone.

17. **In context of the passage, the opening phrase "to the kind reader" used by the author sets what kind of opening tone?**

    A. Friendly

    B. Condescending

    C. Boisterous

    D. Prideful

    E. Meek

18. **The author of this book relays his own experiences fighting slavery. Why does he fight against it (i.e. what is the theme of the book)?**

    A. Slavery is unnatural.

    B. Slavery wasn't needed as an economic engine.

    C. Slavery was morally acceptable.

    D. Slavery enabled him to see the light of day.

    E. Slavery made time move too quickly.

19. **What does the author figuratively mean by "hurrying throng"?**

    A. The people that bump into him walking past him.

    B. His blurred vision from bright sunlight.

    C. The New York tradesmen rushing to their jobs.

    D. The busy middle class.

    E. The bustling crowd of free people.

20. What is the author's tone?

A. Cautious

B. Enlightened

C. Exuberant

D. Nervous

E. None of these apply

21. Who wrote this novel?

A. E.B. White

B. Francis Scott

C. Frederick Douglass

D. Harriet Beecher Stowe

E. Ralph Waldo Emerson

Questions 22-29. Read the following poem by Emily Dickenson and answer the questions below, selecting the best choice of the options presented.

IN THE GARDEN

A bird came down the walk:
He did not know I saw;
He bit an angle-worm in halves
And ate the fellow, raw.

And then, he drank a dew
From a convenient grass,
And then hopped sidewise to the wall
To let a beetle pass.

He glanced with rapid eyes
That hurried all abroad,—
They looked like frightened beads, I thought;
He stirred his velvet head

Like one in danger; cautious,
I offered him a crumb,
And he unrolled his feathers
And rowed him softer home

Than oars divide the ocean,
Too silver for a seam,
Or butterflies, off banks of noon,
Leap, splashless, as they swim.

22. What type of literary device is used in the author's phrase, "drank a dew"?

A. Allusion.

B. Foreshadowing.

C. Juxtaposition.

D. Satire.

E. Alliteration.

23. The author describes action beginning in line 15 of the bird's flight. What type of literary device is used?

A. Simile.

B. Metaphor.

C. Irony.

D. Satire.

E. None of these are correct.

24. The rhyme scheme of the poem (except the final three stanzas) is

A. XAXA or Ghazal.

B. Scottish stanza.

C. Spenserian stanza.

D. quatrain-couplet.

E. Petrarchan sonnet.

25. This poem uses a particular metric pattern throughout the poem, except in the third line of each stanza. What is the main metric pattern?

A. dactylic tetrameter

B. trochaic trimeter

C. trochaic tetrameter

D. iambic pentameter

E. iambic trimeter

26. What literary device is used when the bird's eyes are compared to frightened beads?

A. Reverse Personification.

B. Metaphor.

C. Simile.

D. Allegory.

E. Paradox.

27. What does the dash at the end of line 12 represent?

A. A change in focus from the bird to the water.

B. An abrupt change for the bird.

C. An emotional shift from fear to fascination.

D. It only shows the middle of the poem.

E. None of these accurately describe the meaning of the dash.

28. What is the author's tone in this poem?

A. She takes the perspective of the bird.

B. The author's tone is harsh toward potential prey.

C. The tone is factual, describing the actions of a bird.

D. Ornithology fascinated the author and she uses flowery language to describe it.

E. The author's tone is gentle and respectful demeanor regarding nature.

29. What is a potential meaning of the allegory used by the author?

A. It could reveal the author's perceptions of God.

B. The allegory could be looking at the author's view of marriage.

C. The author could reveal the hierarchy between man and beast.

D. Descriptions of the forces of nature could parallel emotions.

E. There is no allegory used as a literary device in this poem.

Questions 30-37. Read the following selection and answer the questions below, selecting the best choice of the options presented.

There is no frigate like a book
To take us lands away,
Nor any coursers like a page
Of prancing poetry;
This traverse may the poorest take
Without oppress of toll;
How frugal is the chariot
That bears the human soul!

30. Authors use particular literary structures for descriptions. What best explains the type that Emily Dickinson employs in this poem?

A. Connotative

B. Argumentative

C. Narrative

D. Rhetoric

E. Expository

31. How many types of transport does the author incorporate?

A. Two

B. Three

C. Four

D. Five

E. None

32. If the words 'frigate, coursers, and traverse' were replaced with synonyms, what would the best choice of the following options include?

A. Train, car, carriage

B. Train, horse, carriage

C. Ship, car, carriage

D. Ship, car, train

E. Ship, horse, carriage

33. Which of the following descriptions more closely describes the author's intended meaning of poem?

A. Difficulties at work

B. The importance of books

C. Confessions for the soul

D. Poverty makes things difficult

E. Describing modes of transportation

34. There are very descriptive and strong feelings conveyed by the poet. Which of the following is not the definition of what she shares?

A. Overstatement

B. Paradox

C. Understatement

D. Irony

E. Sarcasm

35. What kind of poetry form is utilized by Ms. Dickinson in this poem?

A. Alexandrine

B. Didactic poetry

C. Ballad stanza

D. Epitaph

E. Rondel

36. Who is the author of this poem?

A. Emily Dickinson

B. Emily Brontë

C. Emily Mortimer

D. Lord Byron

E. William Blake

37. When the boat is compared to a book, that is an example of:

A. a metaphor.

B. personification.

C. a simile.

D. an extended metaphor.

E. none of these.

Questions 38-45. Read the following selection and answer the questions below, selecting the best choice of the options presented.

"A man is born into this world with only a tiny spark of goodness in him. The spark is God, it is the soul; the rest is ugliness and evil, a shell. The spark must be guarded like a treasure, it must be nurtured, it must be fanned into flame. It must learn to seek out other sparks, it must dominate the shell. Anything can be a shell, Reuven. Anything. Indifference, laziness, brutality, and genius. Yes, even a great mind can be a shell and choke the spark.

"Reuven, the Master of the Universe blessed me with a brilliant son. And he cursed me with all the problems of raising him. Ah, what it is to have a Daniel, whose mind is like a pearl, like a sun. Reuben, when my Daniel was four years old, I saw him reading a story from a book. And I was frightened. He did not read the story, he swallowed it, as one swallows food or water. There was no soul in my four-year-old Daniel, there was only his mind. He was a mind in a body without a soul. It was a story in a Yiddish book about a poor Jew and his struggles to get to Eretz Yisroel before he died. Ah, how that man suffered! And my Daniel *enjoyed* the story, he *enjoyed* the last terrible page, because when he finished it he realized for the first time what a memory he had. He looked at me proudly and told me back the story from memory, and I cried inside my heart. I went away and cried to the Master of the Universe, 'What have you done to me? A mind like this I need for a son? A *heart* I need for a son, a *soul* I need for a son, *compassion* I want for my son, righteousness, mercy, strength to suffer and carry pain, *that* I want from my son, not a mind without a soul!'"

Reb Saunders paused and took a deep, trembling breath. I tried to swallow; my mouth was sand-dry. Danny sat with his right hand over his eyes, his glasses pushed up on his forehead. He was crying silently, his shoulders quivering. Reb Saunders did not look at him.

38. According to the passage, what was the goal behind raising Danny in silence?

A. For the speaker to be cruel.

B. The speaker thought he was being noble.

C. The narrator believed by being harsh, he was right.

D. The speaker wanted other people to think they were normal.

E. He wanted to develop Danny's compassion and soul.

39. When the narrator describes Danny "swallowing" the story, what kind of literary device is employed?

A. A simile.

B. A metaphor.

C. An allusion.

D. Personification.

E. An alliteration.

40. What is the author doing when using italics?

A. The author is using short words to mean big things.

B. The author signifies the important things in a person's life.

C. The speaker is listing the attributes of his son.

D. The speaker shows what his son understood in the stories.

E. None of these things apply to those words.

41. When Reb's mouth went "sand-dry," this is an example of:

A. a parody.

B. an allusion.

C. a synecdoche.

D. a metaphor.

E. an oxymoron.

42. Throughout the book, Reuven had been the peripheral narrator. Who is the narrator in this section?

A. It is still Reuven.

B. It is Reb.

C. It is Danny.

D. It is a third person narrator.

E. It is Eretz Yisroel.

43. This passage is written as:

A. the denouement.

B. the complication.

C. the climax.

D. the suspense.

E. the introduction.

44. What is the theme of this passage?

A. Recounting the last moments of an old man's life.

B. The discussion of coming marriage of Danny.

C. The symbolism of reading as an alternative for family interactions.

D. The adoption of Reuven by Reb.

E. Another example of Jews suffering to get further in life.

45. What is the writing style used by this author in this passage?

A. Expository

B. Didactic

C. Persuasive

D. Descriptive

E. Theatrical

Questions 46-53. Read the following selection and answer the questions below, selecting the best choice of the options presented.

Okonkwo and his fellow prisoners were set free as soon as the fine was paid. The District Commissioner spoke to them again about the great queen, and about peace and good government. But the men did not listen. They just sat and looked at him and at his interpreter. In the end they were given back their bags and sheathed machetes and told to go home. They rose and left the courthouse. They neither spoke to anyone nor among themselves.

The courthouse, like the church, was but a little way outside the village. The footpath that linked them was a very busy one because it also led to the stream, beyond the court. It was open and sandy. Footpaths were open and sandy in the dry season. But when the rains came the bush grew thick on either side and closed in on the path. It was now dry season.

As they made their way to the village the six men met women and children going to the stream with their waterpots. But them wore such heavy and fearsome looks to them, but edged out of the way to let them pass. In the village little groups of men joined them until they became a sizable company. They walked silently. As each of the six men got to his compound, he turned in, taking some of the crowd with him. The village was air in a silent, suppressed way.

Ezinma had prepared some food for her father as soon as news spread that the six men would be released. She took it to him in his obi. He ate absentmindedly. He had no appetite, he only ate to please her. His male relations and friends had gathered in his obi, and Obierika was urging him to eat. Nobody else spoke, but they noticed the log stripes on Okonkwo's back where the warder's whip had cut into his flesh.

46. Who is the protagonist of this story?

A. Obierika

B. Ezinma

C. Okonkwo

D. The District Commissioner

E. Okonkwo's wife

47. What is the name of this book?

A. Obi

B. Things Fall Apart

C. Let the Circle Be Unbroken

D. Ashes and Dust

E. The rainy season

48. What category of literature does this book represent?

A. Romantic.

B. Victorian.

C. Modernism.

D. Transcendentalism.

E. Post Colonial.

49. The main character of the book appears to have what occur throughout the book?

A. He is a champion of his village.

B. He shows that he is good provider for his family.

C. He represents the disintegration of his society against the change.

D. The village doesn't support him.

E. The courthouse is targeting him to get rid of the village.

50. The narrative structure of this passage is:

A. simple narrative.

B. cause and effect.

C. chronological.

D. inductive.

E. deductive.

51. The literary style of the book is:

A. comedy.

B. tragedy.

C. drama.

D. exploration.

E. quest.

52. How is this passage narrated?

A. First person.

B. Second person.

C. Third person.

D. Omniscient observer.

E. None of these.

53. What is the main idea of this passage?

A. The village members continue to carry out the traditions of their ancestors.

B. There is a drought affecting crops and village life.

C. The interpreter was sharing with them a new way of life.

D. The government and church were coming together for the people.

E. People are resistant to change, and the village and protagonist illustrate it.

Questions 54-60. Read the following selection and answer the questions below, selecting the best choice of the options presented.

Mornings, he likes to sit in his new leather chair by his new living room window, looking out across the rooftops and chimney pots, the clotheslines and telegraph lines and office towers. It's the first time Manhattan, from high above, hasn't crushed him with desire. On the contrary the view makes him feel smug. All those people down there, striving, hustling, pushing, shoving, busting to get what Willie's already got. In spades. He lights a cigarette, blows a jet of smoke against the window. Suckers.

54. The subject in this passage is:

A. a character, and seems to be the lead of the story.

B. a supporting character.

C. has an attitude of a criminal.

D. is female.

E. has been poor his whole life.

55. What kind of description is the author providing of this scene?

A. Backstory of the character.

B. A characterization of what the character is like.

C. A narrative in the first person.

D. The unreliable narrative about a character.

E. The author is using a persuasive argument.

56. What types of words are "striving, hustling, pushing, shoving, bustling"?

A. Adjectives

B. Adverbs

C. Nouns

D. Gerunds

E. Verbs

57. If you had to explain the phrase "crushed him" in the paragraph above and context of the paragraph, what would be the best appropriate explanation?

A. The city sustained him with all the opportunity available.

B. The city called to him to be part of its life.

C. The city complimented him for everything he has achieved.

D. The city had energized him to get what he felt he deserved.

E. The city smothered him with all its offerings.

58. Replacing the word "smug" with an antonym in context would have which of the following used?

A. Sleepy

B. Prideful

C. Humble

D. Self-satisfied

E. Elated

59. When the author uses the phrase, "In spades," which of the following is best representing what he is referencing?

A. The apartment where Willie is living.

B. The personal satisfaction of accumulated wealth.

C. Modern comforts in his home.

D. The loved ones surrounding him.

E. None of these is representative.

60. By using the introductory word "Mornings," the author achieves what?

A. An optimistic tone for the passage.

B. A simple description of time of day, or chronology for the passage.

C. It's the start of the book, so he sets the passage at "day one."

D. A and C.

E. None of these.

61. A ninth grade English teacher is attempting to develop strategies that will promote a reading community in his classroom. Which of the following would be the least effective way of accomplishing this task?

A. Students bring in books from home to include in a classroom library.

B. The teacher assigns book reports on books that are to be selected from a list.

C. Students work with the teacher to create a list of favorite books to read.

D. The teacher will institute a 'drop everything and read' program for thirty minutes each week.

E. Students are allowed to select texts from the classroom library at their leisure.

62. What best describes a type of formative evaluation for writing education?

A. Making careful readings of the text for mechanics, usage, spelling, and content.

B. Marking mechanical errors with a colored pen.

C. Asks students to turn in all work pertaining to the writing assignment, including outlines.

D. Teacher makes comments on the goals that are being met by the student as the student works.

E. Giving pop quizzes after reviewing writing concepts in class.

63. **When utilizing a computer in the classroom for writing assignments, the teacher must be aware of which of the following drawbacks when writing on a computer?**

A. The writer may be unable to focus on the details and become distracted by the technology.

B. The ability of a computer to quickly correct mistakes, often automatically, takes away from the aspect of writing that calls for reflection.

C. Spell check programs do not assist students in learning to spell correctly, or select proper grammatical choices in their writing.

D. Students tend to overlook glaring errors on the page because of the print type.

E. Students will lose the ability to refine their handwriting skills.

64. **When attempting to introduce a unit on poetry to freshmen students in a regular classroom, which of the following is the most ineffective technique?**

A. Students are encouraged to bring their favorite song lyrics to class to discuss poetic devices used.

B. Students will bring in their favorite poems to read aloud to the class.

C. Students will work in groups to try to apply poetic devices in creating a popular song.

D. Students will work in groups to illustrate a given poem.

E. Students will lose the ability to refine their handwriting skills.

65. **A new teacher is experiencing his first ELL student and wonders what type of activity would help this student the most. Which of the following might be suggested?**

A. Provide the ELL student with more opportunities to write in English.

B. Provide opportunities for the class, as well as the ELL student, to listen to the language via various media.

C. Provide a wide range of activities that promote exposure to the language in all of its various modes (speaking, writing, reading).

D. Make an assignment requiring students to make oral presentations in front of the class.

E. Assign the student extra homework to allow them to practice reading, writing, listening, and speaking in their home environment.

Questions 66-73. Read the following passage carefully before you decide on your answers to the questions.

"Mother," said little Pearl, "the sunshine does not love you. It runs away and hides itself, because it is afraid of something on your bosom. . . . It will not flee from me, for I wear nothing on my bosom yet!"

"Nor ever will, my child, I hope," said Hester.

"And why not, mother?" asked Pearl, stopping short. . . . "Will it not come of its own accord, when I am a woman grown?"

—*The Scarlett Letter*

66. Who is the author of this book?

A. William Faulkner

B. Nathaniel Hawthorne

C. William Blake

D. William Shakespeare

E. Frederick Douglass

67. What is the relationship between these two characters?

A. Mother and daughter

B. Sisters

C. Aunt and niece

D. Cousins

E. Grandmother and grandchild

68. What kind of description is the author providing of this scene?

A. A symbolic, metaphorical description that provides a backstory of the main character

B. A characterization of what the character is like

C. A narrative, with the end of the selection giving thoughts in the first person

D. The unreliable narrative about a character

E. The author is using a persuasive argument

69. What does the "sunshine" represent?

A. Light

B. Hope

C. Purity

D. Heaven

E. Good luck

70. Why doesn't Pearl have anything on her bosom?

A. Only one person in the village wears the symbol at a time.

B. The symbol is used to signify divorce, and Pearl is not yet married.

C. It represents pregnancy and she is too young to be pregnant.

D. She will inherit the symbol to wear when her mother dies.

E. It's a symbol of womanhood, and Pearl is still considered a child.

71. The author portrays the attitude of the character Pearl as:

A. condescending

B. loving

C. disrespectful

D. innocent

E. resentful

72. "Will it not come of its own accord, when I am a woman grown?" What is the author implying that Pearl is asking for?

A. If the scarlet letter will be handed down to her when she becomes a woman.

B. If she will become pregnant when she becomes mature enough.

C. Whether or not she will get divorced when she marries.

D. If she will find true love when she grows up.

E. If her mother will share this symbol with her when she is old enough.

73. Which of the following best describes the author's message?

A. Little girls are oblivious to the world around them.

B. Daughters always question things that their mothers do.

C Growing up means losing your innocence.

D. The world will know when you have sinned.

E. None of the above.

Questions 74-81. Read the following passage carefully before you decide on your answers to the questions.

Death, be not proud

Death, be not proud, though some have called thee
Mighty and dreadful, for thou art not so;
For those whom thou think'st thou dost overthrow
Die not, poor Death, nor yet canst thou kill me.
From rest and sleep, which but thy pictures be,
Much pleasure; then from thee much more must flow,
And soonest our best men with thee do go,
Rest of their bones, and soul's delivery.

Thou art slave to fate, chance, kings, and desperate men,
And dost with poison, war, and sickness dwell,
And poppy or charms can make us sleep as well
And better than thy stroke; why swell'st thou then?
One short sleep past, we wake eternally
And death shall be no more;
Death, thou shalt die.

74. Who wrote this poem, titled "Death, be not Proud?"

A. John Donne

B. William Shakespeare

C. Emily Dickinson

D. Edgar Allen Poe

E. William Wordsworth

75. What type of poem is this?

A. Ballad

B. Epic

C. Haiku

D. Prose

E. Sonnet

76. What is the rhyme scheme in the first stanza?

A. ABBAABBA

B. AABBABBA

C. ABCABCBC

D. AABBCCAA

E. ABBBAAAB

77. What is the author implying in the following line?
"Die not, poor Death, nor yet canst thou kill me."

A. He/She is invincible.

B. His/Her soul will go to heaven; therefore, death does not end life.

C. Death does not decide when he/she will die.

D. Poor people do not decide when they will die.

E. He/she will defend themselves against a murderer.

78. What does the following line represent?
"One short sleep past, we wake eternally"

A. Being buried

B. A coma

C. Fighting off disease

D. A dream

E. Resurrection

79. The last line of the poem tries to explain ________.

A. That heaven/the afterlife defeats death.

B. that death dies when the human body dies.

C. that death can be defeated with death.

D. that death is only a threat to those that are alive.

E. None of the above.

80. Why are poison, war, and sickness mentioned?

A. To give examples of cowardly death scenarios.

B. To show that you can be killed by others or in a passive way.

C. To provoke memories from the reader.

D. To personify death as a bully.

E. None of the above.

81. The author speaks about death as if it's a/an ______.

A. theory

B. legacy

C. person

D. threat

E. imaginary concept

Questions 82-89. Read the following passage carefully before you decide on your answers to the questions.

"You boys know what tropism is, it's what makes a plant grow toward the light. Everything aspires to the light. You don't have to chase down a fly to get rid of it —you just darken the room, leave a crack of light in a window, and out he goes. Works every time. We all have that instinct, that aspiration. Science can't — what was your word? *Dim?* — science can't dim that. All science can do is turn out the false lights so the true light can get us home."

—*Old School*

82. Who is the author of the novel *Old School*?

A. Ernest Hemingway

B. Tobias Wolff

C. Geoffrey Chaucer

D. William Blake

E. William Wordsworth

83. Which point of view is this written in?

A. First-person

B. Second-person

C. Third-person

D. Third-person plural

E. None of the above

84. Tropism is ____.

A. photosynthesis

B. always caused by light

C. the moving of an organism in response to a stimulus

D. an imaginary concept

E. survival of the fittest

85. **Why would the author mention tropism as an instinct or aspiration?**

A. All organisms are instinctive when they are hunting.

B. All organisms use strategies like this to attract prey.

C. It represents being able to flee.

D. Everyone wants to be attractive.

E. It represents moving towards a goal.

86. **The word *dim* is significant because ____.**

A. Light is necessary for tropism to occur.

B. Bad influences

C. Dim lights

D. Lights that prompt tropism

E. Parents

87. **What do the false lights mentioned in the last line represent?**

A. Bad influences

B. Dim lights

C. Lights that prompt tropism

D. Parents

E. All great persons wear silk.

88. **What does this passage imply about the main character?**

A. He questions scientific theories.

B. He doesn't believe science has all the answers.

C. He is highly intelligent.

D. Science is his favorite subject.

E. All of the above.

89. The literal interpretation of this passage is science. The symbolic interpretation is:

A. Religion

B. Motivation

C. Instinct

D. Aspiration

E. Economics

Questions 90-94. Read the following passage carefully before you decide on your answers to the questions.

"Then you must tell 'em dat love ain't somethin' lak uh grindstone dat's de same thing everywhere and do de same thing tuh everything it touch. Love is lak de sea. It's uh movin' thing, but still and all, it takes its shape from de shore it meets, and it's different with every shore."

—*Their Eyes Were Watching God*

90. In what form is this written?

A. Phonetic

B. Informal

C. With an accent

D. Vernacular

E. Stream of consciousness

91. ______ is used to describe the sea.

A. Imagery

B. Alliteration

C. Action

D. Personification

E. All of the above

Sample Test Two

92. **How does the author portray love?**

A. It's different for each relationship.

B. It's unobtainable.

C. It causes waves in your life.

D. It comes and goes like the tide.

E. None of the above.

93. **What is a grindstone?**

A. A stone made of sand

B. A workday

C. A square stone used to grind sediment

D. A round stone used to sharpen tools

E. A plantation

94. **What best describes love in this passage?**

A. Grindstone

B. Uh movin' thing

C. Still

D. Same thing

E. Everyone

Questions 95-100. Read the following passage carefully before you decide on your answers to the questions.

"Oh, Jake," Brett said, "we could have had such a damned good time together."

Ahead was a mounted policeman in khaki directing traffic. He raised his baton. The car slowed suddenly pressing Brett against me.

"Yes," I said. "Isn't it pretty to think so?"

—*The Sun Also Rises*

95. What is the significance of the policeman waiting his baton?

A. It symbolizes that it's time to move along

B. Their love will never be legal

C. If they get caught they will go to jail

D. It shows their love stuck, as if in traffic

E. All of the above

96. Which is true about Brett?

A. She has always been in love with Jake.

B. She refuses to go anywhere without Jake.

C. She sees Jake in her future.

D. She regrets the past.

E. All of the above.

97. Which is true about Jake?

A. He sees Brett in his future.

B. He wants to marry Brett.

C. He doesn't think their relationship would ever work out.

D. He loves Brett as a friend.

E. He thinks Brett is pretty.

98. **Which is the best description of this dialogue and its placement in the story?**

A. Introduction

B. Cliffhanger

C. Frame story

D. Backstory

E. Setting

99. **Why did the car slow down?**

A. There was traffic.

B. The policeman waved his baton.

C. The driver needed directions.

D. The driver was picking up another passenger.

E. It was time to get out.

100. **Which literatry device would be most appropriate after this dialogue?**

A. Flashforward

B. Foreshadowing

C. Backflash

D. Metaphor

E. Flashback

Free Response Essay Sample Questions
Section II

Question 1.

Chose a literary work that describes a perception of utopia. In your analysis, describe impacts of that perception on a particular character and experiences or choices made because of that perception or devotion to a utopian ideal. In your essay, do not merely summarize the plot.

Question 2.

Prompt: Ms. Payne lists the goals for the lesson that is to be observed, stating that she has made some modifications for various students, and level of students. Review the comments about the modifications that were employed. For each of these modifications and the students it impacted, describe an alternative modification that might have yielded better results. Include an explanation of accommodations for different types of learning styles in your response.

Ms. Payne teaches freshman English to a class of 30 students, ranging in ages from 14-16. Working with her new teacher mentor, Mr. Smith, Ms. Payne is planning for her first observation from the school's principal. As part of this observation process, Ms. Payne is also required to complete a self-evaluation, which will be utilized on the final observation in the late spring. Mr. Smith assisted her in keeping a portfolio of her students which would assist in the self-evaluation in the spring.

Ms. Payne's notes on three students:

James

James has been attending school in the county for 10 years, and he has had to repeat both fifth and sixth grade. He is older than his classmates, but he seems to get along with most of them well. He offered to help me work with the younger students in class, but also added in that he knew I was a good teacher and that I shouldn't take it badly if he failed the class, stating that he was just born 'dumb'.

Brooke

Brooke comes from a family whose roots in this county run deeply. Her family is well off and they do a lot of traveling internationally during the summer months. Brooke has determined that she is going to go into intentional affairs and hopes to one day become a US ambassador. She is quiet, yet highly intelligent, often preferring to sit with students who are also focused on academics. Brooke is friends with Amanda, one of the students in the class who is in the lower quartile. They have been friends since kindergarten. They walk into class together, but don't sit with one another.

Keri

Keri is often dishevelled and disorganized and it is reflected in her work. In the past she's been a C student, but seems as if she could do better if motivated to try. The other students dislike her for some reason, and during class she spends her time looking out of the window, as if

Sample Test Two

she'd give anything to be there. I spoke with her counsellor about the problem, but it backfired when Keri confronted me the next day after class stating that the counsellor had lectured her about daydreaming in English class. Keri was openly hostile, swore, and walked away from our conversation.

Self-Analysis Report Given Prior to the Observation

Though I did well in school and during student teaching, using some of the same instructional techniques with this class has proven difficult. When I initially divided students into small groups, it was a disaster. Only a few students in each group completed the work and the others contributed nothing. Brooke was nearly in tears because her group participants had pushed all of the work on her, and she'd stayed up all night to complete it. The lower achieving students, if not being disruptive, sit silently and 'check out'. This is the case with Keri, notably. Every time I attempt to use a creative teaching style, diverting from lecture, workbook, text readings, it tends to fall apart, classroom management is compromised, and only the higher quartile students seem motivated, interested, or learn anything.

Lesson to be Observed

Goals:

- Introduce students to important facts about the Elizabethan Period in literature.
- Incorporate outside sources in the discovery of Shakespeare and his time period.
- Give students practical writing applications on the topics being studied.
- Improve note taking skills, both from written and oral sources.

Before beginning a novel study of Romeo & Juliet, students need to understand the time period in which it was written and how men and women viewed one another. I've assigned a couple of websites for students to look up and take notes on. With James, however, I offered a different website, one that was a graphic depiction of Elizabethan England, and of Shakespeare. There was no accommodation offered to Brooke, as she was more than capable of enjoying and completing the assignment. I offered to assist Keri as she went through the websites and took notes, but she asked me to leave her alone. I will address particular facts and information in my next lecture to make certain that all students took enough information down so that they can pass next week's quiz.

Principal's Observation Notes

Ms. Payne's Freshman English class started on time, and she gave a short lecture on Shakespeare's England. She had reserved the laptop cart for the day and had them set up on a table at the back of the classroom. Ms. Payne instructed the students to take careful notes when going to the websites listed on the handout that she gave to each student. She stated that the quiz that would be given would include information from her lecture and the information that they took down from the websites. Ms. Payne recorded her lecture on her phone, though she did not tell the classroom that she was doing so. When asked about it later, Ms. Payne stated that she wanted to record the lecture so that the students could refer back to it after class if they needed to. She mentioned that a student named Keri might benefit from it. She didn't mention that she was recording anything prior to class as she didn't want it to interfere with the assignment. While students are working, Ms. Payne supervises, walks around, stops to ask students questions and to point out good note taking skills, and attempts to assist a student who continues to look out of the windows.

Ms. Payne's Follow-Up Observations and Conclusions

The students were eager to use the computers, though it became evident that not all of the students were particularly proficient with using a laptop. Since some of them were battling the technology, the completeness of the notes was not good. Tomorrow I will go over the notes that they should have been taking, asking them to highlight information that they did write down. I will also place the recording on my class webpage for those who want to access it, and offer time at the end of class for students to listen to it in class. I'm hopeful that Keri will take advantage of it.

Sample Test Two: ANSWER KEY

Question Number	Correct Answer	Your Answer
1.	A	
2.	D	
3.	B	
4.	B	
5.	A	
6.	A	
7.	B	
8.	D	
9.	E	
10.	C	
11.	B	
12.	D	
13.	A	
14.	A	
15.	C	
16.	C	
17.	B	
18.	A	
19.	E	
20.	C	
21.	C	
22.	E	
23.	B	
24.	A	
25.	E	
26.	C	
27.	B	
28.	E	
29.	A	
30.	A	
31.	B	
32.	E	
33.	B	
34.	E	

Question Number	Correct Answer	Your Answer
35.	C	
36.	A	
37.	C	
38.	E	
39.	C	
40.	B	
41.	B	
42.	B	
43.	A	
44.	A	
45.	C	
46.	C	
47.	B	
48.	C	
49.	A	
50.	C	
51.	B	
52.	D	
53.	A	
54.	A	
55.	C	
56.	C	
57.	D	
58.	C	
59.	B	
60.	A	
61.	C	
62.	D	
63.	B	
64.	D	
65.	D	
66.	B	
67.	A	

Question Number	Correct Answer	Your Answer
68.	A	
69.	C	
70.	C	
71.	D	
72.	B	
73.	C	
74.	A	
75.	E	
76.	A	
77.	C	
78.	E	
79.	A	
80.	B	
81.	C	
82.	B	
83.	B	
84.	C	
85.	E	
86.	B	
87.	A	
88.	B	
89.	A	
90.	D	
91.	D	
92.	C	
93.	D	
94.	B	
95.	A	
96.	D	
97.	C	
98.	B	
99.	A	
100.	A	

Answer Key and Rationale

1. A teacher is planning a lesson on T.S. Eliot's "The Hollow Men" for his eleventh grade English class. This is an excerpt from the poem:

The eyes reappear
As the perpetual star
Multifoliate rose
Of death's twilight kingdom
The hope only
Of empty men.

What strategy, of those listed below, best allows for identification and understanding of the word 'multifoliate'?

A. Structural analysis

B. Contextual analysis

C. Graphophonic analysis

D. Syntactical analysis

E. Comprehensive analysis

The answer is A.

Structural analysis is the most effective way to analyze the prefix, and the root. Graphophonic requires a student to create a definition based on the sounds, and does not provide enough context for figuring out the meaning of the word. B is partially useful only in that the word, rose, offers some clues to the meaning of the word, but it does not offer enough context to come to a determination of its meaning. Syntactical analysis (D) is incorrect because this type of analysis will only determine that the word in question is being used as an adjective and nothing more.

2. A teacher is working with a class that includes an ELL (English Language Learner) student. When assigning an informational essay to the class, which of the following techniques would assist the ELL in an understanding of the text?

A. Have all students create an illustration of some part of the text that they found interesting.

B. Have the class use a graphic organizer to write down main ideas in the article.

C. Hand out a list of most often used sentence stems to the entire classroom to use.

D. Provide a list of words to the ELL that are familiar synonyms to the words that he or she is likely to encounter in the article assigned.

E. Define all difficult vocabulary words and phrases aloud at the start of the class.

The answer is D.

The answer is D because the ELL is provided some context for the words that he or she is likely to encounter in the reading. Sentence stems (C) may be helpful when the ELL begins to write but it does not assist with comprehension in reading. (B) is incorrect because the student would have to already have an understanding of the content and context. (A) is incorrect because it does not perpetuate language development comprehension.

3. An 8th grade English teacher notices that each day when she asks a couple of questions about the previous day's lesson, the same handful of students always answer. Which of the following would promote active engagement by a larger percentage of the students?

A. Encouraging those who are not answering, to do so.

B. Allowing all students to create two questions about the day's assignment, to be asked the next day.

C. Giving a participation grade that is not dependent on the correct answer.

D. Having students evaluate their peers' responses using a rubric.

E. Call on students at random.

The answer is B.

Having students create a bank of questions each day allows the teacher to use questions from students whom do not normally risk answering a question. Not only does this promote interaction, but it also creates an opportunity for students to create relevant questions, and adds one more evaluative model for a teacher to assess comprehension.

4. Which of the following indicators would suggest that a student has developed strong communication skills when placed in a small group to discuss a novel?

A. Taking charge of the group and directing the conversation.

B. Making comments that build upon statements made by others in the group.

C. Asking questions of the group members that diverges from the topic of conversation.

D. Asking whomever is talking to explain what they mean by their statements.

E. Speaking loudly and assertively within the group.

The answer is B.

While many of the other answers may be indicators of someone who is able to communicate, (B) indicates that the student not only comprehends what is being said, but is also able to be a constructive listener. (C) is incorrect because students who diverge from the topic at hand are not effectively listening. (A) is incorrect because the student may be more interested in garnering attention without furthering the goal of the group, while (D) is incorrect because if someone is asking for a lot of explanation it is clear that they are not listening, or that there may be comprehension issues.

5. **In a high school classroom, a teacher has had students complete rough drafts of an expository essay, and has placed them in pairs to peer review each other's work. As a guideline, what should the teacher have students read to discern first?**

A. Transitions

B. Supporting details

C. Biased language

D. Varied sentence lengths

E. Grammar and punctuation errors

The answer is A.

While all of these are good aspects to evaluate, the first to be evaluated should be the use of adequate transitions. If a student has used transitions, shifts from one idea to the next, then the student has internalized the concept of 'flow' and 'voice' within their writing. The other aspects must certainly be considered, but as a first evaluative assessment, (A) is the starting point.

Questions 6-13. Read the following passage carefully before you decide on your answers to the questions.

William Wordsworth — "I Wandered Lonely As A Cloud"

I wandered lonely as a cloud
That floats on high o'er vales and hills,
When all at once I saw a crowd,
A host, of golden daffodils;
Beside the lake, beneath the trees,
Fluttering and dancing in the breeze.

Continuous as the stars that shine
And twinkle on the milky way,
They stretched in never-ending line
Along the margin of a bay:
Ten thousand saw I at a glance,
Tossing their heads in sprightly dance.

The waves beside them danced; but they
Out-did the sparkling waves in glee:
A poet could not but be gay,
In such a jocund company:
I gazed—and gazed—but little thought
What wealth the show to me had brought:

For oft, when on my couch I lie
In vacant or in pensive mood,
They flash upon that inward eye
Which is the bliss of solitude;
And then my heart with pleasure fills,
And dances with the daffodils.

6. What type of passage is the above selection?

A. Lyrical poem

B. Haiku poem

C. Acrostic poem

D. Limerick poem

E. Cinquain poem

The answer is A.

This is where literary terms are important. In poetry, many of the devices and nomenclature need to be memorized and understood so you can answer these questions quickly and accurate.

7. The permanence of stars as compared with flowers emphasizes

A. the impermanence of life.

B. the permanence of memory for the poet.

C. the earlier comparison of the sky to the lake.

D. that stars are frozen above and daffodils dance below.

E. the similarity of the inward eye with the fleeting bliss of solitude.

The answer is B.

The key word in option A is opposite in meaning and the relationship of the verbs in D are not correctly aligned for the comparison. E is not part of the poem at all. If you don't know the answer between B and C, look back at the poem - and there is no comparison of sky to lake, so that gives you the right answer.

8. The scheme of the poem is

A. ballad.

B. Scottish stanza.

C. Spenserian stanza.

D. quatrain-couplet.

E. sonnet.

The answer is D.

While this may not be one of the typical questions on the test, it is incorporated so you remember to look at general literary definitions. You can also figure this out by looking at quatrain, which has the base that means "four" and couplet means "two" - that is the same pattern as the poem. E isn't right because a sonnet is one verse of specific length; a ballad is the manner of telling a story so it isn't A. There are particular components of B and C, but if you get to this stage and use the root words, you may be able to guess the right answer if you don't know.

9. **This poem uses the ________ metric pattern.**

   A. dactylic tetrameter

   B. trochaic pentameter

   C. trochaic tetrameter

   D. iambic pentameter

   E. iambic tetrameter

   The answer is E.

   Similar to the rationale of the first question, you need to know these terms. You can "break them down" into tetra - meaning four - and meter,or beat. Iambic is a rhythm of two, so there are four sets of two beats

10. **What is a literary device used in the last two lines of the first two stanzas?**

   A. Simile.

   B. Metaphor.

   C. Personification.

   D. Allegory.

   E. Paradox.

   The answer is C.

   When an inanimate or non-human objects is given person-like traits, it's call personification. You should be familiar with all of the words that are given as options in this multiple choice question - review them in the guide for refresher.

11. **In what literary period did this author write?**

   A. Edwardian Movement.

   B. Romanticism.

   C. Existentialism.

   D. Renaissance Literature.

   E. Victorian Movement.

   The answer is B.

   In an AP situation, your understanding of when great writers of literature wrote, and the context of their writing - when they wrote - often gives additional insights to the meaning of their work or the themes.

12. As used in this poem, the best choice for a synonym of jocund means

A. pleasant.

B. vapid.

C. lonely.

D. jovial.

E. sad.

The answer is D.

This is a question that tests vocabulary - you should be able to eliminate choices A, C, and E. If you don't know what jocund means, or either vapid or jovial, this is how they are testing for reading comprehension. Jovial is happy and that fits into the structure of the passage within context.

13. What literary device is used in line 9. "They stretched in never-ending line."

A. hyperbole.

B. onomatopoeia.

C. epithet.

D. irony.

E. anecdote.

The answer is A.

Knowing what common literary terms mean will allow you to eliminate at least D and E, if not also B. Between C and A, you could guess, but if you understand either of the definitions, you will pick the correct answer. Review definitions if you can't eliminate at least three of the word answer choices.

Questions 14-21. Read the following selection and answer the questions below, selecting the best choice of the options presented.

My Bondage and My Freedom

Disappearing from the kind reader, in a flying cloud or balloon (pardon the figure), driven by the wind, and knowing not where I should land—whether in slavery or in freedom—it is proper that I should remove, at once, all anxiety, by frankly making known where I alighted. The flight Disappearing from the kind reader, in a flying cloud or balloon (pardon the figure), driven by the wind, and knowing not where I should land--whether in slavery or in freedom--it is proper that I should remove, at once, all anxiety, by frankly making known where I alighted. The flight was a bold and perilous one; but here I am, in the great city of New York, safe and sound, without loss of blood or bone. In less than a week after leaving Baltimore, I was walking amid the hurrying throng, and gazing upon the dazzling wonders of Broadway. The dreams of my childhood and the purposes of my manhood were now fulfilled. A free state around me, and a free earth under my feet! What a moment was this to me! A whole year was pressed into a single day. A new world burst upon my agitated vision. I have often been asked, by kind friends to whom I have told my story, how I felt when first I found myself beyond the limits of slavery; and I must say here, as I have often said to them, there is scarcely anything about which I could not give a more satisfactory answer. It was a moment of joyous excitement, which no words can describe. In a letter to a friend, written soon after reaching New York. I said I felt as one might be supposed to feel, on escaping from a den of hungry lions.

14. In what literary period did this author write?

A. Transcendentalism.

B. Realism.

C. Victorian.

D. Modernism.

E. Naturalism.

The correct answer is A.

15. When the author writes "escaping from a den of hungry lions," what type of literary device is he using?

A. Simile

B. Personification.

C. Metaphor.

D. Hyperbole.

E. Irony.

The correct answer is C.

16. **What is the author's theme in this passage?**

A. Anger at being a slave.

B. Numb, as one might be supposed to feel.

C. Confusion at the new things he is seeing.

D. Self-discovery after flight from slavery.

E. None of these describe his tone.

The correct answer is C.

The author is in a storm of new sensations.

17. In context of the passage, the opening phrase "to the kind reader" used by the author sets what kind of opening tone?

A. Friendly

B. Condescending

C. Boisterous

D. Prideful

E. Meek

The correct answer is B.

If you were answering too quickly, you may think A is the correct answer. But look at the context. The speaker is pandering to the listener.

18. The author of this book relays his own experiences fighting slavery. Why does he fight against it (i.e. what is the theme of the book)?

A. Slavery is unnatural.

B. Slavery wasn't needed as an economic engine.

C. Slavery was morally acceptable.

D. Slavery enabled him to see the light of day.

E. Slavery made time move too quickly.

The correct answer is A.

There is no proof that the author believes B is true, nor any of the other answers. Remember, it's not what you believe but what the author is stating or leading you to believe and that's how you must answer. If you read too fast, you may have thought B was the correct answer, but notice the answer is actually negative. Read carefully.

19. What does the author figuratively mean by "hurrying throng"?

A. The people that bump into him walking past him.

B. His blurred vision from bright sunlight.

C. The New York tradesmen rushing to their jobs.

D. The busy middle class.

E. The bustling crowd of free people.

The correct answer is E.

The middle three options are not correct, but A could possibly be accurate. However, there is nothing in the passage that should lead you to think he was bumped into by people passing him. Don't make assumptions or you won't select the right answer.

20. What is the author's tone?

A. Cautious

B. Enlightened

C. Exuberant

D. Nervous

E. None of these apply

The correct answer is C.

While the feeling of the character may be D, there are more cues that point to C being the right answer.

21. Who wrote this novel?

A. E.B. White

B. Francis Scott

C. Frederick Douglass

D. Harriet Beecher Stowe

E. Ralph Waldo Emerson

The correct answer is C.

Some of the main pieces of literature are listed for you in the book, and it would be wise to know some of the main and often used authors and their high profile works.

Questions 22-29. Read the following poem by Emily Dickenson and answer the questions below, selecting the best choice of the options presented.

IN THE GARDEN

A bird came down the walk:
He did not know I saw;
He bit an angle-worm in halves
And ate the fellow, raw.

And then, he drank a dew
From a convenient grass,
And then hopped sidewise to the wall
To let a beetle pass.

He glanced with rapid eyes
That hurried all abroad,—
They looked like frightened beads, I thought;
He stirred his velvet head

Like one in danger; cautious,
I offered him a crumb,
And he unrolled his feathers
And rowed him softer home

Than oars divide the ocean,
Too silver for a seam,
Or butterflies, off banks of noon,
Leap, splashless, as they swim.

22. What type of literary device is used in the author's phrase, "drank a dew"?

A. Allusion.

B. Foreshadowing.

C. Juxtaposition.

D. Satire.

E. Alliteration.

The correct answer is E.

These are all basic literary device words and you should know the definitions of these most-frequently used terms.

23. **The author describes action beginning in line 15 of the bird's flight. What type of literary device is used?**

A. Simile.

B. Metaphor.

C. Irony.

D. Satire.

E. None of these are correct.

The correct answer is B.

Remember, absolute answers, such as ones that give "always" or "never" or "none" are typically incorrect. Of the remaining options, you should know these definitions, especially the difference between simile and metaphor.

24. **The rhyme scheme of the poem (except the final three stanzas) is**

A. XAXA or Ghazal.

B. Scottish stanza.

C. Spenserian stanza.

D. quatrain-couplet.

E. Petrarchan sonnet.

The correct answer is A.

Even if you don't know the terms (which you should have memorized for poetry), the pattern is usually listed for you. As long as you know how to use those abbreviations, you can get any poetry scheme question correct.

25. This poem uses a particular metric pattern throughout the poem, except in the third line of each stanza. What is the main metric pattern?

A. dactylic tetrameter

B. trochaic trimeter

C. trochaic tetrameter

D. iambic pentameter

E. iambic trimeter

The correct answer is E.

Using the logic explained in earlier rational, iambic is "rhythm of two and tri- means three. You should be able to get to the root of any of these words and determine the correct answer if you don't know it, so practice!

26. What literary device is used when the bird's eyes are compared to frightened beads?

A. Reverse Personification.

B. Metaphor.

C. Simile.

D. Allegory.

E. Paradox.

The correct answer is C.

While these types of questions are not likely to come back-to-back in the actual exam, they were placed in repetitive order here to show you that you need to remain focus, answer each question and move forward.

27. What does the dash at the end of line 12 represent?

A. A change in focus from the bird to the water.

B. An abrupt change for the bird.

C. An emotional shift from fear to fascination.

D. It only shows the middle of the poem.

E. None of these accurately describe the meaning of the dash.

The correct answer is B.

In context, the bird goes from drinking and allowing a beetle to pass to abruptly being wary. That is the opposite of C, but many students who rush through the test may select that option. Literally, D is not accurate nor is A.

28. **What is the author's tone in this poem?**

    A. She takes the perspective of the bird.

    B. The author's tone is harsh toward potential prey.

    C. The tone is factual, describing the actions of a bird.

    D. Ornithology fascinated the author and she uses flowery language to describe it.

    E. The author's tone is gentle and respectful demeanor regarding nature.

    The correct answer is E.

    If you know basics about various authors, you would know that Ms. Dickenson wrote during an era of respecting nature and promoting its good features to the masses.

29. **What is a potential meaning of the allegory used by the author?**

    A. It could reveal the author's perceptions of God.

    B. The allegory could be looking at the author's view of marriage.

    C. The author could reveal the hierarchy between man and beast.

    D. Descriptions of the forces of nature could parallel emotions.

    E. There is no allegory used as a literary device in this poem.

    The correct answer is A.

    Knowing your definitions, E can be removed as correct because you would have identified the allegory previously. While D is a fair choice, A is a better one - again, known the traits of the era, you would be able to most easily identify the right choice.

Questions 30-37. Read the following selection and answer the questions below, selecting the best choice of the options presented.

There is no frigate like a book
To take us lands away,
Nor any coursers like a page
Of prancing poetry;
This traverse may the poorest take
Without oppress of toll;
How frugal is the chariot
That bears the human soul!

30. Authors use particular literary structures for descriptions. What best explains the type that Emily Dickinson employs in this poem?

A. Connotative

B. Argumentative

C. Narrative

D. Rhetoric

E. Expository

The correct answer is A.

You need to know the definitions of literary terms.

31. How many types of transport does the author incorporate?

A. Two

B. Three

C. Four

D. Five

E. None

The correct answer is B.

You can see the next question to identify the three options.

Sample Test Two

32. **If the words 'frigate, coursers, and traverse' were replaced with synonyms, what would the best choice of the following options include?**

A. Train, car, carriage

B. Train, horse, carriage

C. Ship, car, carriage

D. Ship, car, train

E. Ship, horse, carriage

The correct answer is E.

You can see them listed in the poem.

33. **Which of the following descriptions more closely describes the author's intended meaning of poem?**

A. Difficulties at work

B. The importance of books

C. Confessions for the soul

D. Poverty makes things difficult

E. Describing modes of transportation

The correct answer is B.

The main idea of the poem is stated in the first line.

34. **There are very descriptive and strong feelings conveyed by the poet. Which of the following is not the definition of what she shares?**

A. Overstatement

B. Paradox

C. Understatement

D. Irony

E. Sarcasm

The correct answer is E.

The other four selections are used at various times in the poem and you must read carefully as the question asks for the one that isn't used.

35. What kind of poetry form is utilized by Ms. Dickinson in this poem?

A. Alexandrine

B. Didactic poetry

C. Ballad stanza

D. Epitaph

E. Rondel

The correct answer is C.

You should be able to eliminate B, D, and E immediately. Alexandrine is a French style that has twelve syllables. If you didn't know that, and you probably won't, a ballad stanza is four line verses - and that should be enough to get it right.

36. Who is the author of this poem?

A. Emily Dickinson

B. Emily Brontë

C. Emily Mortimer

D. Lord Byron

E. William Blake

The correct answer is A.

Sometimes they give you the answer in another question or in the passage - it checks to see if you are actually reading!

37. When the boat is compared to a book, that is an example of:

A. a metaphor.

B. personification.

C. a simile.

D. an extended metaphor.

E. none of these.

The correct answer is C.

You should know the definitions of these literary terms.

Questions 38-45. Read the following selection and answer the questions below, selecting the best choice of the options presented.

"A man is born into this world with only a tiny spark of goodness in him. The spark is God, it is the soul; the rest is ugliness and evil, a shell. The spark must be guarded like a treasure, it must be nurtured, it must be fanned into flame. It must learn to seek out other sparks, it must dominate the shell. Anything can be a shell, Reuven. Anything. Indifference, laziness, brutality, and genius. Yes, even a great mind can be a shell and choke the spark.

"Reuven, the Master of the Universe blessed me with a brilliant son. And he cursed me with all the problems of raising him. Ah, what it is to have a Daniel, whose mind is like a pearl, like a sun. Reuben, when my Daniel was four years old, I saw him reading a story from a book. And I was frightened. He did not read the story, he swallowed it, as one swallows food or water. There was no soul in my four-year-old Daniel, there was only his mind. He was a mind in a body without a soul. It was a story in a Yiddish book about a poor Jew and his struggles to get to Eretz Yisroel before he died. Ah, how that man suffered! And my Daniel *enjoyed* the story, he *enjoyed* the last terrible page, because when he finished it he realized for the first time what a memory he had. He looked at me proudly and told me back the story from memory, and I cried inside my heart. I went away and cried to the Master of the Universe, 'What have you done to me? A mind like this I need for a son? A *heart* I need for a son, a *soul* I need for a son, *compassion* I want for my son, righteousness, mercy, strength to suffer and carry pain, *that* I want from my son, not a mind without a soul!'"

Reb Saunders paused and took a deep, trembling breath. I tried to swallow; my mouth was sand-dry. Danny sat with his right hand over his eyes, his glasses pushed up on his forehead. He was crying silently, his shoulders quivering. Reb Saunders did not look at him.

38. According to the passage, what was the goal behind raising Danny in silence?

A. For the speaker to be cruel.

B. The speaker thought he was being noble.

C. The narrator believed by being harsh, he was right.

D. The speaker wanted other people to think they were normal.

E. He wanted to develop Danny's compassion and soul.

The correct answer is E.

The intention of the speaker wasn't to be cruel or noble, and there was no indication that the speaker wanted to appear "normal" to his neighbors. This is an example of when your ability to infer is tested. By the repetition of the italics, that should give you an indication those are the important traits that Reb wanted to develop in Danny.

39. When the narrator describes Danny "swallowing" the story, what kind of literary device is employed?

A. A simile.

B. A metaphor.

C. An allusion.

D. Personification.

E. An alliteration.

The correct answer is C.

Know your literary term

40. What is the author doing when using italics?

A. The author is using short words to mean big things.

B. The author signifies the important things in a person's life.

C. The speaker is listing the attributes of his son.

D. The speaker shows what his son understood in the stories.

E. None of these things apply to those words.

The correct answer is B.

Option C is not correct - it is actually the opposite. It also isn't the explanation of his son's attributes, but the ones Danny was lacking. A is not correct, either, and you should know by now to be skeptical of answers like E.

41. When Reb's mouth went "sand-dry," this is an example of:

A. a parody.

B. an allusion.

C. a synecdoche.

D. a metaphor.

E. an oxymoron.

The correct answer is B.

These are definitions you should know and thus be able to recognize examples in literature.

42. Throughout the book, Reuven had been the peripheral narrator. Who is the narrator in this section?

A. It is still Reuven.

B. It is Reb.

C. It is Danny.

D. It is a third person narrator.

E. It is Eretz Yisroel.

The correct answer is B.

This is clear in the beginning of the last paragraph.

43. This passage is written as:

A. the denouement.

B. the complication.

C. the climax.

D. the suspense.

E. the introduction.

The correct answer is A.

By knowing the stages used in literature, you should be able to answer the question. You can also infer the meaning from the poignant phrases in the passage to help you pick the right option.

44. What is the theme of this passage?

A. Recounting the last moments of an old man's life.

B. The discussion of coming marriage of Danny.

C. The symbolism of reading as an alternative for family interactions.

D. The adoption of Reuven by Reb.

E. Another example of Jews suffering to get further in life.

The correct answer is A.

This question should have been easy to answer. There is no mention of Danny's marriage. Reading was not an alternative for attributes, but Reb believed it was a replacement for personality traits. There is no discussion that supports option D and E is not correct, either.

45. What is the writing style used by this author in this passage?

A. Expository

B. Didactic

C. Persuasive

D. Descriptive

E. Theatrical

The correct answer is C.

If you can't tell from the description being given by the speaker, then if you know the basic definitions of these terms then you would be able to pick the right answer.

Questions 46-53. Read the following selection and answer the questions below, selecting the best choice of the options presented.

Okonkwo and his fellow prisoners were set free as soon as the fine was paid. The District Commissioner spoke to them again about the great queen, and about peace and good government. But the men did not listen. They just sat and looked at him and at his interpreter. In the end they were given back their bags and sheathed machetes and told to go home. They rose and left the courthouse. They neither spoke to anyone nor among themselves.

The courthouse, like the church, was but a little way outside the village. The footpath that linked them was a very busy one because it also led to the stream, beyond the court. It was open and sandy. Footpaths were open and sandy in the dry season. But when the rains came the bush grew thick on either side and closed in on the path. It was now dry season.

As they made their way to the village the six men met women and children going to the stream with their waterpots. But them wore such heavy and fearsome looks to them, but edged out of the way to let them pass. In the village little groups of men joined them until they became a sizable company. They walked silently. As each of the six men got to his compound, he turned in, taking some of the crowd with him. The village was air in a silent, suppressed way.

Ezinma had prepared some food for her father as soon as news spread that the six men would be released. She took it to him in his obi. He ate absentmindedly. He had no appetite, he only ate to please her. His male relations and friends had gathered in his obi, and Obierika was urging him to eat. Nobody else spoke, but they noticed the log stripes on Okonkwo's back where the warder's whip had cut into his flesh.

46. Who is the protagonist of this story?

A. Obierika

B. Ezinma

C. Okonkwo

D. The District Commissioner

E. Okonkwo's wife

The correct answer is C.

If you are unfamiliar with the book, you can still read carefully and pick the right main character. If you didn't recognize the word protagonist, brush up on your literary device vocabulary.

47. What is the name of this book?

A. Obi

B. Things Fall Apart

C. Let the Circle Be Unbroken

D. Ashes and Dust

E. The rainy season

The correct answer is B.

We mentioned in the chapters that you should have familiarity with era and types of literature, such as some key writers and books in American, British and World Literature.

48. What category of literature does this book represent?

A. Romantic.

B. Victorian.

C. Modernism.

D. Transcendentalism.

E. Post Colonial.

The correct answer is C.

Knowing the literary eras are important. If you forget during the test, look at the keys of each word. Romantic era as well as Victorian are much older - and a book about Africa from the native resident's perspective would not likely have been widely published early in literature. Post-colonial refers to British colonies and usually Indian pieces. Narrowed down to Transcendentalism and Modernism, you may recall the first is written by American authors and in particular Ralph Waldo Emerson.

49. The main character of the book appears to have what occur throughout the book?

A. He is a champion of his village.

B. He shows that he is good provider for his family.

C. He represents the disintegration of his society against the change.

D. The village doesn't support him.

E. The courthouse is targeting him to get rid of the village.

The correct answer is A.

Neither D nor E are correct, and that can be known from the passage. He is a tragic hero, and nothing in the passage represents C being accurate. Of the two remaining, while both A and B are true, option A is supported by the characterization in the passage.

50. The narrative structure of this passage is:

A. simple narrative.

B. cause and effect.

C. chronological.

D. inductive.

E. deductive.

The correct answer is C.

While it is a narration, and yes because of their release there is food waiting at the village, it is a chronological stepwise piece and that is the best answer.

51. The literary style of the book is:

A. comedy.

B. tragedy.

C. drama.

D. exploration.

E. quest.

The correct answer is B.

It describes the downfall of the main character due to his own choices. While C is a tempting answer, it is not the best option.

52. **How is this passage narrated?**

A. First person.

B. Second person.

C. Third person.

D. Omniscient observer.

E. None of these.

The correct answer is D.

Third person may seem like a desirable option, but it only gives the point of view from one particular person and there are two "inside thoughts" here. Omniscient means they see everything. You should have been able to discount A and B quite easily.

53. **What is the main idea of this passage?**

A. The village members continue to carry out the traditions of their ancestors.

B. There is a drought affecting crops and village life.

C. The interpreter was sharing with them a new way of life.

D. The government and church were coming together for the people.

E. People are resistant to change, and the village and protagonist illustrate it.

The correct answer is A.

This is the best option for the passage and though E may be accurate for the book, you must answer according to what's in the passage.

Questions 54-60. Read the following selection and answer the questions below, selecting the best choice of the options presented.

Mornings, he likes to sit in his new leather chair by his new living room window, looking out across the rooftops and chimney pots, the clotheslines and telegraph lines and office towers. It's the first time Manhattan, from high above, hasn't crushed him with desire. On the contrary the view makes him feel smug. All those people down there, striving, hustling, pushing, shoving, busting to get what Willie's already got. In spades. He lights a cigarette, blows a jet of smoke against the window. Suckers.

54. The subject in this passage is:

A. a character, and seems to be the lead of the story.

B. a supporting character.

C. has an attitude of a criminal.

D. is female.

E. has been poor his whole life.

The correct answer is A.

The female pronoun is used, so D is inaccurate. B is not accurate as he is the focus of the passage. You can not infer E is correct. Of A and C, there is no support for this character being a criminal. Remember not to make assumptions when you answer questions.

55. What kind of description is the author providing of this scene?

A. Backstory of the character.

B. A characterization of what the character is like.

C. A narrative in the first person.

D. The unreliable narrative about a character.

E. The author is using a persuasive argument.

The correct answer is C.

Backstory isn't accurate because a current scene is described. B uses the same root-word twice, which is usually an indication that it is not a correct guess. There is nothing to suggest the character is unreliable. This leaves options C and E and neither the author nor character are persuading the reader toward a conclusion.

56. What types of words are "striving, hustling, pushing, shoving, bustling"?

A. Adjectives

B. Adverbs

C. Nouns

D. Gerunds

E. Verbs

The correct answer is C.

Backstory isn't accurate because a current scene is described. B uses the same root-word twice, which is usually an indication that it is not a correct guess. There is nothing to suggest the character is unreliable. This leaves options C and E and neither the author nor character are persuading the reader toward a conclusion.

57. If you had to explain the phrase "crushed him" in the paragraph above and context of the paragraph, what would be the best appropriate explanation?

A. The city sustained him with all the opportunity available.

B. The city called to him to be part of its life.

C. The city complimented him for everything he has achieved.

D. The city had energized him to get what he felt he deserved.

E. The city smothered him with all its offerings.

The correct answer is D.

This tests your reading comprehension.

58. Replacing the word "smug" with an antonym in context would have which of the following used?

A. Sleepy

B. Prideful

C. Humble

D. Self-satisfied

E. Elated

The correct answer is C.

This involves knowing the words meanings as well as reading carefully as the question asked for antonym.

59. **When the author uses the phrase, "In spades," which of the following is best representing what he is referencing?**

A. The apartment where Willie is living.

B. The personal satisfaction of accumulated wealth.

C. Modern comforts in his home.

D. The loved ones surrounding him.

E. None of these is representative.

The correct answer is B.

The context and reading comprehension bring you to the correct answer. Nothing implying loved ones, modern comforts or the mere large apartment relate to the question.

60. **By using the introductory word "Mornings," the author achieves what?**

A. An optimistic tone for the passage.

B. A simple description of time of day, or chronology for the passage.

C. It's the start of the book, so he sets the passage at "day one."

D. A and C.

E. None of these.

The correct answer is A.

Context of the tone of the passage shows the character speaking is in a good mood, but it does not mean that it actually is morning and there is no indication that it is the start of the book.

61. **A ninth grade English teacher is attempting to develop strategies that will promote a reading community in his classroom. Which of the following would be the least effective way of accomplishing this task?**

A. Students bring in books from home to include in a classroom library.

B. The teacher assigns book reports on books that are to be selected from a list.

C. Students work with the teacher to create a list of favorite books to read.

D. The teacher will institute a 'drop everything and read' program for thirty minutes each week.

E. Students are allowed to select texts from the classroom library at their leisure.

Answer: C.

Rationale: (C) is the least likely technique to improve or promote a sense of community as it is teacher-centric rather than student-centric. Students are motivated and readily participate on a larger percentage when there has been active participation in the process. Additionally, (D) is a type of modelling behavior where the teacher actively promotes reading for enjoyment, and it opens up a ready platform for a dialogue about reading, thus motivating reluctant readers to attempt reading more frequently.

62. **What best describes a type of formative evaluation for writing education?**

A. Making careful readings of the text for mechanics, usage, spelling, and content.

B. Marking mechanical errors with a colored pen.

C. Asks students to turn in all work pertaining to the writing assignment, including outlines.

D. Teacher makes comments on the goals that are being met by the student as the student works.

E. Giving pop quizzes after reviewing writing concepts in class.

Answer: D.

Rationale: In formative evaluation the teacher continues to give insight to the student on those goals that are being met, thus supporting behaviors and skills that are wanted, and focusing on achieving the goal rather than focusing on those skills that are lacking.

63. **When utilizing a computer in the classroom for writing assignments, the teacher must be aware of which of the following drawbacks when writing on a computer?**

A. The writer may be unable to focus on the details and become distracted by the technology.

B. The ability of a computer to quickly correct mistakes, often automatically, takes away from the aspect of writing that calls for reflection.

C. Spell check programs do not assist students in learning to spell correctly, or select proper grammatical choices in their writing.

D. Students tend to overlook glaring errors on the page because of the print type.

E. Students will lose the ability to refine their handwriting skills.

Answer: B.

Rationale: One of the largest components of learning to write is to take the time to consider what will be written. Because of various social media interactions, the quick aspect of the computer to automatically correct problems, the contemplation factor is removed, and the process of revising may break down.

64. When attempting to introduce a unit on poetry to freshmen students in a regular classroom, which of the following is the most ineffective technique?

A. Students are encouraged to bring their favorite song lyrics to class to discuss poetic devices used.

B. Students will bring in their favorite poems to read aloud to the class.

C. Students will work in groups to try to apply poetic devices in creating a popular song.

D. Students will work in groups to illustrate a given poem.

E. Students will research autobiographical elements for each poet that will be covered in the unit.

Answer: D.

Rationale: Students may enjoy illustrating a poem, but it does not facilitate or accomplish the goal. The goal is to encourage students to learn to appreciate poetry and to try to write their own poems. Allowing students to bring in poems that they already like, or song lyrics they are familiar with, are better methods for promoting interest and motivating students to attempt the new skill.

65. A new teacher is experiencing his first ELL student and wonders what type of activity would help this student the most. Which of the following might be suggested?

A. Provide the ELL student with more opportunities to write in English.

B. Provide opportunities for the class, as well as the ELL student, to listen to the language via various media.

C. Provide a wide range of activities that promote exposure to the language in all of its various modes (speaking, writing, reading).

D. Make an assignment requiring students to make oral presentations in front of the class.

E. Assign the student extra homework to allow them to practice reading, writing, listening, and speaking in their home environment.

Answer: D.

Rationale: While this may be initially a difficult assignment, the ELL student will benefit from hearing the language and thus understand phonologically the differences in the sounds. Correlations and contextual meanings of words are understood when heard and viewed, than when read.

Questions 66-73. Read the following passage carefully before you decide on your answers to the questions.

"Mother," said little Pearl, "the sunshine does not love you. It runs away and hides itself, because it is afraid of something on your bosom. . . . It will not flee from me, for I wear nothing on my bosom yet!"

"Nor ever will, my child, I hope," said Hester.

"And why not, mother?" asked Pearl, stopping short. . . . "Will it not come of its own accord, when I am a woman grown?"

—*The Scarlett Letter*

66. Who is the author of this book?

A. William Faulkner

B. Nathaniel Hawthorne

C. William Blake

D. William Shakespeare

E. Frederick Douglass

The correct answer is B.

The very famous novel, *The Scarlett Letter*, was written by Nathaniel Hawthorne.

67. **What is the relationship between these two characters?**

A. Mother and daughter

B. Sisters

C. Aunt and niece

D. Cousins

D. Grandmother and grandchild

The correct answer is A.

For this question, the word "mother" is a dead giveaway to the characters' relationship.

68. **What kind of description is the author providing of this scene?**

A. A symbolic, metaphorical description that provides a backstory of the main character

B. A characterization of what the character is like

C. A narrative, with the end of the selection giving thoughts in the first person

D. The unreliable narrative about a character

E. The author is using a persuasive argument

The correct answer is A.

The author provides details through symbolism to describe the main character's past.

69. **What does the "sunshine" represent?**

A. Light

B. Hope

C. Purity

D. Heaven

E. Good luck

The correct answer is C.

Sunshine representing light is a literal interpretation, which can be quickly eliminated. Sunshine symbolizing hope, heaven, or good luck is possible for another passage, but the context should point to the correct answer. For this particular question, sunshine represents purity.

70. Why doesn't Pearl have anything on her bosom?

A. Only one person in the village wears the symbol at a time.

B. The symbol is used to signify divorce, and Pearl is not yet married.

C. It represents pregnancy and she is too young to be pregnant.

D. She will inherit the symbol to wear when her mother dies.

E. It's a symbol of womanhood, and Pearl is still considered a child.

The correct answer is C.

The scarlet letter on her mother's bosom represents pregnancy. The daughter is too young to be pregnant.

71. The author portrays the attitude of the character Pearl as:

A. condescending

B. loving

C. disrespectful

D. innocent

E. resentful

The correct answer is D.

Pearl is very respectful, and in no way condescending or resentful of her mother, which quickly eliminates A, C, and E. While loving could be a quality used to describe Pearl, D is the best answer.

72. "Will it not come of its own accord, when I am a woman grown?" What is the author implying that Pearl is asking for?

A. If the scarlet letter will be handed down to her when she becomes a woman.

B. If she will become pregnant when she becomes mature enough.

C. Whether or not she will get divorced when she marries.

D. If she will find true love when she grows up.

E. If her mother will share this symbol with her when she is old enough.

The correct answer is B.

The daughter is questioning at what point she will be able to wear a similar letter on her bosom, as she wants to be like her mother. The symbolism behind this question represents her inquiry as to whether or not she'll become pregnant when she is mature enough.

73. Which of the following best describes the author's message?

A. Little girls are oblivious to the world around them.

B. Daughters always question things that their mothers do.

C Growing up means losing your innocence.

D. The world will know when you have sinned.

E. None of the above.

The correct answer is C.

A and B can be ruled out quickly, due to the deep level of symbolism in The Scarlett Letter. While it may be true that this novel represents the world recognizing sin, it's more evident that the author's intention was to portray losing innocence as one grows older.

Questions 74-81. Read the following passage carefully before you decide on your answers to the questions.

Death, be not proud

Death, be not proud, though some have called thee
Mighty and dreadful, for thou art not so;
For those whom thou think'st thou dost overthrow
Die not, poor Death, nor yet canst thou kill me.
From rest and sleep, which but thy pictures be,
Much pleasure; then from thee much more must flow,
And soonest our best men with thee do go,
Rest of their bones, and soul's delivery.

Thou art slave to fate, chance, kings, and desperate men,
And dost with poison, war, and sickness dwell,
And poppy or charms can make us sleep as well
And better than thy stroke; why swell'st thou then?
One short sleep past, we wake eternally
And death shall be no more;
Death, thou shalt die.

74. Who wrote this poem, titled "Death, be not Proud?"

A. John Donne

B. William Shakespeare

C. Emily Dickinson

D. Edgar Allen Poe

E. William Wordsworth

The correct answer is A.

John Donne is the author of this poem.

75. What type of poem is this?

A. Ballad

B. Epic

C. Haiku

D. Prose

E. Sonnet

The correct answer is E.

This poem is a sonnet. All sonnets have iambic pentameter. The Haiku is made up of a short poem with specific syllables per line. Prose is told in story form and does not always rhyme. The ballad is free verse, often set to music.

76. What is the rhyme scheme in the first stanza?

A. ABBAABBA

B. AABBABBA

C. ABCABCBC

D. AABBCCAA

E. ABBBAAAB

The correct answer is A.

By looking over the words that rhyme in the first stanza, it's easy to determine the rhyme scheme as ABBAABBA.

77. What is the author implying in the following line?
"Die not, poor Death, nor yet canst thou kill me."

A. He/She is invincible.

B. His/Her soul will go to heaven; therefore, death does not end life.

C. Death does not decide when he/she will die.

D. Poor people do not decide when they will die.

E. He/she will defend themselves against a murderer.

The correct answer is C.

The author implies that although death may be the end of their body on earth, their soul will live on in heaven. Therefore, B is the best option.

78. What does the following line represent?
"One short sleep past, we wake eternally"

A. Being buried

B. A coma

C. Fighting off disease

D. A dream

E. Resurrection

The correct answer is E.

This is a straightforward question: the words "wake" and "eternally" are direct connections to resurrection.

79. The last line of the poem tries to explain ________.

A. That heaven/the afterlife defeats death.

B. that death dies when the human body dies.

C. that death can be defeated with death.

D. that death is only a threat to those that are alive.

E. None of the above.

The correct answer is A.

Because we know the poem views death as inferior to the afterlife, and the author believes heaven is a place their soul will live eternally, A is the best answer.

80. Why are poison, war, and sickness mentioned?

A. To give examples of cowardly death scenarios.

B. To show that you can be killed by others or in a passive way.

C. To provoke memories from the reader.

D. To personify death as a bully.

E. None of the above.

The correct answer is B.

Poison, war, and sickness are all practical ways to die and mentioning them displays death as something that can happen to anyone. Each of these scenarios are nearly impossible to avoid and can be related to by the reader, regardless of their stature.

81. **The author speaks about death as if it's a/an ______.**

A. theory

B. legacy

C. person

D. threat

E. imaginary concept

The correct answer is C.

This poem uses personification to describe death. It's viewed as something that tries to take away from others. Therefore, C is the best answer.

Questions 82-89. Read the following passage carefully before you decide on your answers to the questions.

"You boys know what tropism is, it's what makes a plant grow toward the light. Everything aspires to the light. You don't have to chase down a fly to get rid of it —you just darken the room, leave a crack of light in a window, and out he goes. Works every time. We all have that instinct, that aspiration. Science can't — what was your word? *Dim?* — science can't dim that. All science can do is turn out the false lights so the true light can get us home."

—*Old School*

82. **Who is the author of the novel *Old School*?**

A. Ernest Hemingway

B. Tobias Wolff

C. Geoffrey Chaucer

D. William Blake

E. William Wordsworth

The correct answer is B.

The novel *Old School* was written by Tobias Wolff.

83. Which point of view is this written in?

A. First-person

B. Second-person

C. Third-person

D. Third-person plural

E. None of the above

The correct answer is B.

Throughout the poem, the author uses the word "you," which is a direct indicator of second-person point of view.

84. Tropism is ____.

A. photosynthesis

B. always caused by light

C. the moving of an organism in response to a stimulus

D. an imaginary concept

E. survival of the fittest

The correct answer is C.

Context clues are needed to determine this answer, as tropism is not a common vocabulary word. Using the first and second sentences, you can determine that C is the best answer.

85. Why would the author mention tropism as an instinct or aspiration?

A. All organisms are instinctive when they are hunting.

B. All organisms use strategies like this to attract prey.

C. It represents being able to flee.

D. Everyone wants to be attractive.

E. It represents moving towards a goal.

The correct answer is E.

Again, context clues are critical for zeroing in on the correct answer. Similar to moving in response to a stimulus, the author mentions tropism as an instinct or aspiration because a goal can be viewed as the stimulus.

86. **The word *dim* is significant because ____.**

A. Light is necessary for tropism to occur.

B. Bad influences

C. Dim lights

D. Lights that prompt tropism

E. Parents

The correct answer is B.

Symbolism is important for narrowing in on the answer for this particular question. D has no connection and can easily be eliminated. A and C are literal interpretations, whereas B connects the representation of the dimming of faith.

87. **What do the false lights mentioned in the last line represent?**

A. Bad influences

B. Dim lights

C. Lights that prompt tropism

D. Parents

E. All great persons wear silk.

The correct answer is A.

The best connection to the false lights in the last line is bad influences.

88. **What does this passage imply about the main character?**

A. He questions scientific theories.

B. He doesn't believe science has all the answers.

C. He is highly intelligent.

D. Science is his favorite subject.

E. All of the above.

The correct answer is B.

The author is very skeptical of science and its abilities. While A, C, and D, may all be possible, B is the most apparent.

89. **The literal interpretation of this passage is science. The symbolic interpretation is:**

A. Religion

B. Motivation

C. Instinct

D. Aspiration

E. Economics

The correct answer is A.

The best symbolic interpretation for this passage is religion.

Questions 90-94. Read the following passage carefully before you decide on your answers to the questions.

"Then you must tell 'em dat love ain't somethin' lak uh grindstone dat's de same thing everywhere and do de same thing tuh everything it touch. Love is lak de sea. It's uh movin' thing, but still and all, it takes its shape from de shore it meets, and it's different with every shore."

—*Their Eyes Were Watching God*

90. **In what form is this written?**

A. Phonetic

B. Informal

C. With an accent

D. Vernacular

E. Stream of consciousness

The correct answer is D.

Vernacular is a type of dialect that is commonly only used within communities. While it may seem this person has an accent, they are actually speaking in the vernacular. This makes D the best answer.

91. **______ is used to describe the sea.**

A. Imagery

B. Alliteration

C. Action

D. Personification

E. All of the above

The correct answer is D.

Personification is used to describe the sea when the author said it was a moving thing.

92. How does the author portray love?

A. It's different for each relationship.

B. It's unobtainable.

C. It causes waves in your life.

D. It comes and goes like the tide.

E. None of the above.

The correct answer is C.

This is an easy answer- love is portrayed as a different experience for everyone, which makes A the best answer.

93. What is a grindstone?

A. A stone made of sand

B. A workday

C. A square stone used to grind sediment

D. A round stone used to sharpen tools

E. A plantation

The correct answer is D.

A grindstone is a round stone used to sharpen tools, making D the best answer.

94. What best describes love in this passage?

A. Grindstone

B. Uh movin' thing

C. Still

D. Same thing

E. Everyone

The correct answer is B.

Again, the author portrays love as fluid, moving thing. It's explained as a different experience for everyone, making B the best answer.

Questions 95-100. Read the following passage carefully before you decide on your answers to the questions.

"Oh, Jake," Brett said, "we could have had such a damned good time together."

Ahead was a mounted policeman in khaki directing traffic. He raised his baton. The car slowed suddenly pressing Brett against me.

"Yes," I said. "Isn't it pretty to think so?"

—*The Sun Also Rises*

95. What is the significance of the policeman waiting his baton?

A. It symbolizes that it's time to move along

B. Their love will never be legal

C. If they get caught they will go to jail

D. It shows their love stuck, as if in traffic

E. All of the above

The correct answer is A.

Using the phrase "could have" shows that the characters are thinking their time is finished and their relationship will never be. The policeman raising his baton symbolizes moving along in a literal sense, which draws a strong (and deliberate from the author) connection to the situation Brett and Jake are in.

96. Which is true about Brett?

A. She has always been in love with Jake.

B. She refuses to go anywhere without Jake.

C. She sees Jake in her future.

D. She regrets the past.

E. All of the above.

The correct answer is D.

As mentioned in the previous question, this particular passage sets a scene of looking backwards. It's implied that if she really did love Jake, she would have fought harder for him instead of simply letting him go. D is the best answer for this question because it's most obvious that she has regrets.

97. Which is true about Jake?

A. He sees Brett in his future.

B. He wants to marry Brett.

C. He doesn't think their relationship would ever work out.

D. He loves Brett as a friend.

E. He thinks Brett is pretty.

The correct answer is C.

While Brett is thinking of the "what if" in their relationship, Jake has already come to terms with the fact that it will never work out. He may have loved her in the past, but he has accepted their relationship not moving forward. Because of this, C is the best answer.

98. Which is the best description of this dialogue and its placement in the story?

A. Introduction

B. Cliffhanger

C. Frame story

D. Backstory

E. Setting

The correct answer is B.

There is obvious action in this piece, and the author is trying to provoke emotion in the reader by making them think of the possible outcomes for Brett and Jake's relationship. Because of the rising action, B is the best answer.

99. Why did the car slow down?

A. There was traffic.

B. The policeman waved his baton.

C. The driver needed directions.

D. The driver was picking up another passenger.

E. It was time to get out.

The correct answer is A.

Just like Brett and Jake's relationship, their cab ride has come to an end. The literal interpretation of their cab ride ending ties in with the symbolism of their decision to end all thoughts of being together in the future. Knowing the context of this story, E is the correct answer.

100. Which literatry device would be most appropriate after this dialogue?

A. Flashforward

B. Foreshadowing

C. Backflash

D. Metaphor

E. Flashback

The correct answer is A.

It would be most appropriate to see where the two of them ended up following this conversation. A flashforward could be one, five, even fifty years later. Therefore, the best answer was A.

CPSIA information can be obtained
at www.ICGtesting.com
Printed in the USA
BVHW01s1735110518
516000BV00015B/302/P